T0092245

Exam Ref AZ-500
Microsoft Azure Security
Technologies

Second Edition

Yuri Diogenes
Orin Thomas

Exam Ref AZ-500 Microsoft Azure Security Technologies, Second Edition

Published with the authorization of Microsoft Corporation by:
Pearson Education, Inc.

ISBN-13: 978-0-13-783446-4
ISBN-10: 0-13-783446-2

Library of Congress Control Number: 2022933261

1 2022

TRADEMARKS

Microsoft and the trademarks listed at http://www.microsoft.com on the "Trademarks" webpage are trademarks of the Microsoft group of companies. All other marks are property of their respective owners.

WARNING AND DISCLAIMER

SPECIAL SALES

For information about buying this title in bulk quantities, or for special sales opportunities (which may include electronic versions; custom cover designs; and content particular to your business, training goals, marketing focus, or branding interests), please contact our corporate sales department at corpsales@pearsoned.com or (800) 382-3419.

For government sales inquiries, please contact governmentsales@pearsoned.com.

For questions about sales outside the U.S., please contact intlcs@pearson.com.

EDITOR-IN-CHIEF
Brett Bartow

EXECUTIVE EDITOR
Loretta Yates

SPONSORING EDITOR
Charvi Arora

DEVELOPMENT EDITOR
Rick Kughen

MANAGING EDITOR
Sandra Schroeder

SENIOR PROJECT EDITOR
Tracey Croom

COPY EDITOR
Rick Kughen

INDEXER
Tim Wright

PROOFREADER
Donna Mulder

TECHNICAL EDITOR
Mike Martin

EDITORIAL ASSISTANT
Cindy Teeters

COVER DESIGNER
Twist Creative, Seattle

COMPOSITOR
codeMantra

GRAPHICS
codeMantra

Contents at a glance

Contents

Chapter 3   Manage security operations   181

Chapter 4   Secure data and applications   233

Acknowledgments

The authors would like to thank Loretta Yates and the entire Microsoft Press/Pearson team for their support in this project. We would also like to thank Mike Martin (Microsoft MVP) for reviewing this book and Rick Kughen for the editorial review.

Yuri would also like to thank: My wife and daughters for their endless support; my great God for giving me strength and guiding my path each step of the way; my friend and co-author Orin Thomas for the great partnership on this project; my manager Rebecca Halla for always encouraging me to go above and beyond. Last but not least, thanks to my parents for working hard to give me an education, which is the foundation I use every day to keep moving forward in my career.

About the authors

YURI DIOGENES, MSC Yuri holds a Master of Science in cybersecurity intelligence and forensics investigation (UTICA College) and is the principal PM manager for the Microsoft CxE Microsoft Defender for Cloud Team, where he manages a team of PMs who are responsible for improving the product and helping customers deploy it. Yuri has been working for Microsoft since 2006 in different positions, including five years as a senior support escalation engineer for the CSS Forefront Edge Team. From 2011 to 2017, he was a member of Microsoft's content development team, where he also helped create the Azure Security Center content experience since its launch in 2016. Yuri has published 26 books, mostly about information security and Microsoft technologies. Yuri also holds an MBA and many IT/Security industry certifications, such as CISSP, E|CND, E|CEH, E|CSA, E|CHFI, CompTIA Security+, CySA+, Cloud Essentials Certified, Mobility+, Network+, CASP, CyberSec First Responder, MCSE, and MCTS. You can follow Yuri on Twitter at @yuridiogenes.

ORIN THOMAS Orin Thomas is a principal cloud operations advocate at Microsoft and has written more than three dozen books for Microsoft Press covering topics including Windows Server, Windows Client, Azure, Microsoft 365, Office 365, System Center, Exchange Server, Security, and SQL Server. He has authored Azure Architecture courses at Pluralsight, has authored multiple Microsoft Official Curriculum and EdX courses on a variety of IT Pro topics, and is completing a Doctor of Information Technology on cloud computing security and compliance at Charles Sturt University. You can follow him on Twitter at @orinthomas.

Introduction

The AZ-500 exam deals with advanced topics that require candidates to have an excellent working knowledge of Azure security technologies. Portions of the exam cover topics that even experienced Azure security administrators rarely encounter unless they regularly work with all aspects of Azure. To be successful when taking this exam, candidates need to understand how to manage Azure identity and access. They also need to understand how to implement Azure platform protection, manage Azure security operations, and secure Azure data and applications. They also need to be able to keep up to date with new developments in Azure security technologies, including expanded features and changes to the interface.

Candidates for this exam should have subject matter expertise implementing security controls and threat protection, managing identity and access, and protecting data, applications, and networks in cloud and hybrid environments as part of an end-to-end infrastructure.

Responsibilities for an Azure Security Engineer include maintaining the security posture, identifying and remediating vulnerabilities by using a variety of security tools, implementing threat protection, and responding to security incident escalations. Azure Security Engineers often serve as part of a larger team dedicated to cloud-based management and security or hybrid environments as part of an end-to-end infrastructure.

A candidate for this exam should be familiar with scripting and automation and should have a deep understanding of networking and virtualization. A candidate should also have a strong familiarity with cloud capabilities, Azure products and services, and other Microsoft products and services. To pass, candidates require a thorough theoretical understanding and meaningful, practical experience implementing the involved technologies.

This book's second edition covers the AZ-500 exam objectives beginning in 2022. As Azure's security functionality evolves, so do the AZ-500 exam objectives. Therefore, you should check carefully to determine whether any changes have occurred since this edition of the book was authored and study accordingly.

This book covers every major topic area found on the exam, but it does not cover every exam question. Only the Microsoft exam team has access to the exam questions, and Microsoft regularly adds new questions to the exam, making it impossible to cover specific questions. You should consider this book to be a supplement to your relevant real-world experience and other study materials. If you encounter a topic in this book that you do not feel completely comfortable with, use the "More Info?" links you'll find in the text to find more information and take the time to research and study the topic. Great information is available on *docs. microsoft.com*, MS Learn, and in blogs and forums.

Organization of this book

This book is organized by the "Skills measured" list published for the exam. The "Skills measured" list is available for each exam on the Microsoft Learn website: *http://microsoft.com/ learn*. Each chapter in this book corresponds to a major topic area in the list, and the technical tasks in each topic area determine a chapter's organization. For example, if an exam covers six major topic areas, the book will contain six chapters.

Preparing for the exam

Microsoft certification exams are a great way to build your resume and let the world know about your level of expertise. Certification exams validate your on-the-job experience and product knowledge. Although there is no substitute for on-the-job experience, preparation through study and hands-on practice can help you prepare for the exam. This book is *not* designed to teach you new skills.

We recommend that you augment your exam preparation plan by using a combination of available study materials and courses. For example, you might use the Exam Ref and another study guide for your "at home" preparation and take a Microsoft Official Curriculum course for the classroom experience. Choose the combination that you think works best for you. Learn more about available classroom training and find free online courses and live events at *http://microsoft.com/learn*. Microsoft Official Practice Tests are available for many exams at *http://aka.ms/practicetests*.

Note that this Exam Ref is based on publicly available information about the exam and the author's experience. To safeguard the integrity of the exam, authors do not have access to the live exam.

Microsoft certifications

Microsoft certifications distinguish you by proving your command of a broad set of skills and experience with current Microsoft products and technologies. The exams and corresponding certifications are developed to validate your mastery of critical competencies as you design, develop, implement, and support solutions with Microsoft products and technologies, both on-premises and in the cloud. Certification brings a variety of benefits to the individual, employers, and organizations.

> **MORE INFO** **ALL MICROSOFT CERTIFICATIONS**
>
> For information about Microsoft certifications, including a full list of available certifications, go to *http://www.microsoft.com/learn*.

Check back often to see what is new!

Quick access to online references

Throughout this book, you will find web page addresses that the author has recommended you visit for more information. Some of these addresses (also known as URLs) can be painstaking to type into a web browser, so we've compiled them into a single list that readers of the print edition can refer to while they read.

MicrosoftPressStore.com/ExamRefAZ5002e/downloads

The URLs are organized by chapter and heading. Every time you come across a URL in the book, find the hyperlink in the list to go directly to the webpage.

Errata, updates & book support

We've made every effort to ensure the accuracy of this book and its companion content. You can access updates to this book—in the form of a list of submitted errata and their related corrections—at:

MicrosoftPressStore.com/ExamRefAZ5002e/errata

If you discover an error that is not already listed, please submit it to us at the same page.

For additional book support and information, please visit

MicrosoftPressStore.com/Support.

Please note that product support for Microsoft software and hardware is not offered through the previous addresses. For help with Microsoft software or hardware, go to *http://support.microsoft.com*.

Stay in touch

Let's keep the conversation going! We're on Twitter: *http://twitter.com/MicrosoftPress*.

CHAPTER 1

Manage identity and access

An important step when securing workloads is determining what traffic you'll allow and what traffic you'll block. In the past, you might use the network location and traffic type to make this determination. For example, you might allow traffic that came from a particular IP address and on a particular port and deny that traffic if it didn't meet those specific conditions. Over time, clever attackers have learned to spoof IP address information, allowing them to bypass these traditional barriers. Today, you will hear security practitioners utter the aphorism, "identity is the new control plane." This means when the network location or traffic properties are not a great signifier of whether a host or traffic is trustworthy, the identity that is used to interact with the resource you are trying to protect might be a better guide. This is especially true if those identities are hardened with technologies such as multifactor authentication. In this chapter, you'll learn about managing identities in the cloud, securing access to resources and applications in the cloud, and managing access control to cloud administrative tools.

Skills in this chapter:

- Skill 1.1: Manage Azure Active Directory identities
- Skill 1.2: Manage secure access by using Azure AD
- Skill 1.3: Manage application access
- Skill 1.4: Manage access control

Skill 1.1: Manage Azure Active Directory identities

This objective deals with identities within Azure Active Directory. In Azure Active Directory, identities are represented as users, service principals, managed identities, or groups. Azure Active Directory allows you to use a variety of authentication methods to secure these identities, including one-time passwords and multifactor authentication.

Create and manage a managed identity for Azure resources

You configure security for a service principal when you want to control what access an application has to resources within Azure. When you register an Azure Active Directory application, the following objects will be created in your Azure Active Directory tenancy:

- **An application object**   Application objects are stored within the Azure AD instance and define the application. The schema for an application object's properties is defined by the Microsoft Graph application entity resource type. Application objects are a global representation of an application across all Azure AD tenancies. The application object functions as a template from which common and default properties are determined when Azure AD creates the corresponding service principal object. Application objects have a one-to-one relationship with the software application and a one-to-many relationship with corresponding service principal objects.

- **A service principal object**   A user principal in Azure AD is an object that represents a user. A service principal is an Azure AD object that represents an application. The ServicePrincipal object allows you to specify the access policy and permissions for the application and the user of that application within your organization's Azure AD tenant. A service principal is required for each tenancy where the application is used. A single-tenant application will only have one service principal, and a multitenant application will have a service principal for each tenancy where a user from that tenancy has consented to the application's use. The Microsoft Graph service principal entity defines the schema used for a ServicePrincipal object's properties. The service principal is the representation of the application in a specific Azure AD tenancy.

Registering an application with Azure AD allows you to leverage the Microsoft identity platform's secure sign-in and authorization features for use with that application. Registering an application with Azure AD requires that you provide information, including the URL where the application can be accessed, the URL to forward replies after authentication occurs, and the URI that identifies your application. You will learn more about registering applications with Azure AD later in this chapter.

> **MORE INFO**   **APPLICATION AND SERVICE PRINCIPAL OBJECTS**
>
> You can learn more about application and service principal objects at *https://docs.microsoft. com/en-us/azure/active-directory/develop/app-objects-and-service-principals*.

Service principals are analogous to an on-premises Active Directory service account in that both allow an application to have an identity and security context. Service principals in Azure AD can include the following:

- A reference to an application object through the application ID property
- Local user and group application-role assignment properties
- Local user and admin application permissions
- Local policy data, including information about conditional access policies

- Data about alternate local application settings, including
  - Claims transformation rules
  - Attribute mappings (user provisioning)
  - Directory-specific app roles (when the application supports custom roles)
  - Directory-specific name or logo

Creating a service principal

As you have already learned, Azure AD will create a service principal when you register an application with an Azure AD instance. This is the way most Azure AD service principals will be created. It is possible to create a service principal with the `New-AzADServicePrincipal` cmdlet from an Azure PowerShell session. The simplest way to run Azure PowerShell is through a Cloud Shell session. For example, to create a new service principal named `ExampleService-Principal`, run the following command from an Azure PowerShell session.

```
$servicePrincipal = New-AzADServicePrincipal -DisplayName "ExampleServiceprincipal"
```

Service principals can use two different types of authentication: password-based authentication and certificate-based authentication. If you don't specify a type of sign-in authentication when creating a service principal, password-based authentication will be used, and a random password will be assigned to the service principal account.

To view a list of service principals associated with an Azure AD instance, run the following command from an Azure PowerShell session:

```
Get-AzAdServicePrincipal | format-table
```

> **MORE INFO** **CREATE SERVICE PRINCIPAL**
>
> You can learn more about creating service principals at *https://docs.microsoft.com/en-us/powershell/azure/create-azure-service-principal-azureps*.

Assigning permissions to service principals through roles

To provide access within a subscription to an application, you assign a set of permissions to the service principal associated with the application. The most straightforward way to accomplish this goal is to assign a particular role to the application. For example, if you want to give an application read access to resources within a particular resource group, you could assign the Reader role to the service principal associated with the application.

To assign a role to an application that is already registered with an Azure AD instance, perform the following steps:

1. In the Azure portal, select the subscription that the application is associated with, and then from the **Subscriptions** page, select the **Access Control (IAM)** node, as shown in Figure 1-1.

FIGURE 1-1 Access control (IAM) for a subscription

2. On the **Access Control (IAM)** page, select **Add A Role Assignment**, choose the role that you want to assign to the application, and choose **Azure AD User, Group, Or Service Principal** from the **Assign Access To** drop-down menu, as shown in Figure 1-2, and then in the **Select** text box, specify the name of the application.

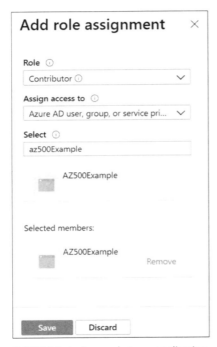

FIGURE 1-2 Assign a role to an application

3. Click **Save** to assign the role to the service principal.

> **MORE INFO   AZURE ROLES**
>
> You can learn more about the roles that you can assign to service principals at *https://docs.microsoft.com/en-us/azure/role-based-access-control/built-in-roles*.

Just as you can assign permissions through a role through the Access Control (IAM) node at the subscription level, you can use the Access Control (IAM) node at the resource group or the resource level to assign a role to a service principal. When assigning permissions to a service principal, you should assign those permissions in the most restrictive way possible. This means that you should only assign roles at the appropriate scope level and only assign the role needed by the application. If the application only requires Reader access to a resource group, don't assign the Contributor role at the subscription level to the application's service principal.

You can use the `New-AzRoleAssignment` PowerShell cmdlet to assign a role to a service principal. For example, to create a new service principal and assign reader permissions at the subscription level to the service principal, enact the following PowerShell commands:

```
$servicePrincipal = New-AzADServicePrincipal -DisplayName "ExampleServiceprincipal"
New-AzRoleAssignment -RoleDefinitionName "Reader" -ApplicationId $servicePrincipal.
ApplicationId
```

Working with service principals in command-line environments requires you to use application IDs rather than the display name of the service principal. This is why the `ApplicationId` is specified in the second command in the previous example, which assigns the role to the service principal created in the first command.

You can determine what roles have been assigned to a service principal at the subscription, resource group, or resource levels by performing the following steps:

1. In the Azure portal, select the subscription, resource group, or resource to which the application is associated, and then from the **Subscriptions** page, select the **Access Control (IAM)** node.

2. Select the **Role Assignments** section. This page lists all roles assigned to this scope. In the **Type** column, service principals are listed with the **App** type, as shown in Figure 1-3.

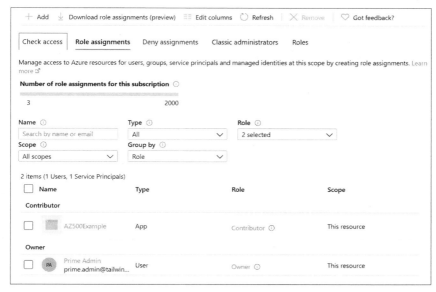

FIGURE 1-3 Checking Role assignments for service principals

Manage Azure AD groups

Groups allow you to group users and then assign them privileges and access to workloads or services. Rather than directly assigning privileges and access to workloads or services to users, you can assign these rights to a group and then indirectly assign them to users by adding the user accounts to the appropriate group. Using groups allows you to assign access and rights by adding and removing users from a group. While it's possible to assign access and rights on a per-user basis, this is administratively cumbersome and makes it challenging to determine which users have a specific right. Determining rights can be much easier to do if rights are only delegated to groups. If you only assign rights to groups or if you need to determine rights, you just have to check the group membership.

You can use the Azure AD administrative console in the Azure portal to manage groups. You can access the Azure Active Directory admin center at *https://aad.portal.azure.com* or through the Azure portal Azure AD blade. Azure AD supports two group types: security groups and Microsoft 365 groups. Figure 1-4 shows how to select the group type when creating the group. Microsoft 365 groups are used for collaboration between users where organizations use services such as Microsoft 365 or Office 365. Users in groups can be internal or external to the organization.

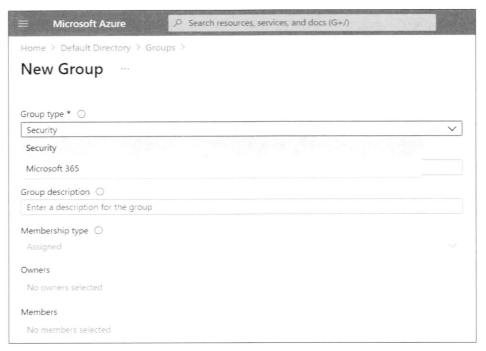

FIGURE 1-4 Create Azure AD Group

Microsoft 365 group types can be configured as assigned or dynamic. When the dynamic option is selected, group membership is determined based on the results of a query against user or device attributes. For example, with Microsoft 365 groups, you can have group membership determined by user attributes such as location or manager.

You can use the following PowerShell commands from the Azure AD PowerShell module to manage Azure AD Groups:

- **Get-AzureADGroup**   Provides information about Azure AD Groups.
- **New-AzureADGroup**   Creates a new Azure AD Group.
- **Set-AzureADGroup**   Configures the properties of an Azure AD Group.
- **Remove-AzureADGroup**   Removes an Azure AD Group.
- **Add-AzureADGroupMember**   Adds a user to an Azure AD Group.
- **Remove-AzureADGroupMember**   Removes a user from an Azure AD Group.
- **Add-AzureADGroupOwner**   Adds a user as an owner of an Azure AD Group. Gives the user limited group management privileges.
- **Remove-AzureADGroupOwner**   Removes a user as the owner of an Azure AD Group.

> **MORE INFO   AZURE AD GROUPS**
>
> You can learn more about Azure AD Groups at *https://docs.microsoft.com/en-us/azure/ active-directory/fundamentals/active-directory-groups-view-azure-portal*.

Creating groups

To create an Azure AD group, perform the following steps:

1. In the Azure portal, select the **Azure Active Directory** menu blade.
2. Under **Manage** in the **Azure Active Directory** menu blade, select **Groups**, as shown in Figure 1-5.

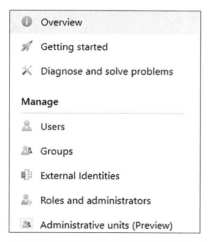

FIGURE 1-5 Azure Active Directory menu blade

3. On the **Groups** page control bar, click **New Group**.

4. On the **New Group** page shown in Figure 1-6, provide the following information and select **Create**:

- **Group Type**   Choose between **Security** and **Office 365**.

- **Group Name**   Provide a name for the group. It is often a good idea to come up with a system for naming groups, rather than naming the group based on whatever comes to mind when filling out the form. Use this system for all groups in the subscription. One strategy is to name groups in a way that indicates how they collect accounts, such as Research Users for user accounts related to research. Group names need to be unique within an Azure Active Directory instance.

- **Group Description**   Provide a meaningful description for the group. This description should be meaningful enough that if you won the lottery and retired to Tahiti, the person who replaced you could understand the purpose of the group.

- **Membership Type**   If you choose a **Security** group, group members must be added manually. If you choose the **Office 365** group type, you will have the following options:

  - **Owners**   Users designated as group owners can modify the membership of the group.

  - **Members**   Allows you to specify group membership. Can include users, groups, service principals, and managed identities.

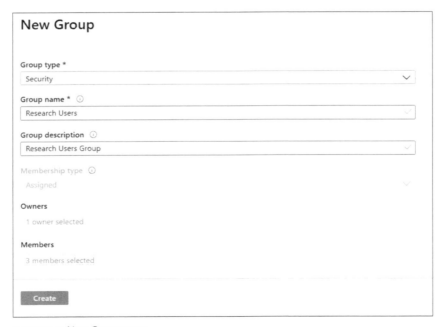

FIGURE 1-6 New Group page

You can create Azure Groups from a Cloud Shell session using the `az ad group create` command. For example, to create a group named `Accounting Users`, use the following command:

```
Az ad group create --display-name "Accounting Users" --mail-nickname "accounting.users"
```

> **MORE INFO   CREATING GROUPS**
>
> You can learn more about this topic at *https://docs.microsoft.com/en-us/azure/active-directory/fundamentals/active-directory-manage-groups*.

Adding and removing group members

You can add members to an Azure AD group from a Cloud Shell session using the `az ad group member add` command. The challenge when using this command is that you must specify the member using the object ID of the member rather than the member name. For example, to add the user with the object ID `ac5ebbfb-22c7-4381-b91d-12aeb3093413` to the group `Accounting Users`, use the following command from an Azure PowerShell session:

```
az ad group member add --group "Accounting Users" --member-id ac5ebbfb-22c7-
4381-b91d-12aeb3093413
```

You can determine the object ID of a user by using the `az ad user show` command and specifying the user's user principal name with the <DS>ID</DS> parameter. For example, to determine the object ID of the user `delta.user@tailwindtraders.net`, run the following command in Cloud Shell:

```
az ad user show --id delta.user@tailwindtraders.net
```

Nested groups

Azure AD allows you to add a security group as a member of another security group, which is known as a nested group. When you do this, the member group will inherit the attributes and properties of the parent group. Nesting groups allows you to further simplify the management of large amounts of users. For example, you might have groups for the managers in Melbourne, Sydney, and Adelaide. You could add these three groups to an Australian Managers group and then assign top-level group rights and permissions to Australian Managers, rather than assigning those rights to each city-level Managers group. This also provides you with flexibility should you add additional city-level managers groups, such as Brisbane and Perth, at some point in the future because you'd just add these groups to the Australian Managers group to assign the same permissions.

At the time of writing, Azure AD does not support the following nesting scenarios:

- Adding an Azure AD group to a group synchronized from on-premises Active Directory
- Adding Azure AD security groups to Office 365 groups
- Adding Office 365 to groups other than other Office 365 groups
- Assigning apps to nested groups

- Assigning licenses to nested groups
- Nesting distribution groups

To nest groups using the Azure portal, perform the following steps:

1. On the **Groups – All Groups** page of the Azure Active Directory blade of the Azure portal, click the group you want to nest. This will open the group's properties, as shown in Figure 1-7. In this example, the `Melbourne` group will be added to the `Australia` group.

FIGURE 1-7 List of Azure AD groups

2. Click the **Group Memberships** item in the **Manage** section of the group's properties, as shown in Figure 1-8.

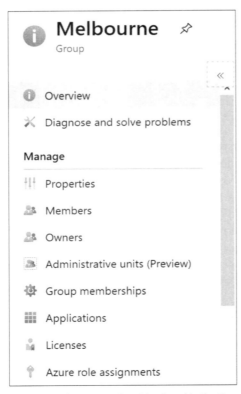

FIGURE 1-8 Group memberships listed in the Groups menu

3. On the Group Memberships page, click **Add Memberships**.

4. On the **Select Groups** page, select the group you want to nest the group within. In this case, we will select the Australia group, as shown in Figure 1-9. Click **Select** to nest the group. A group can be nested within multiple groups.

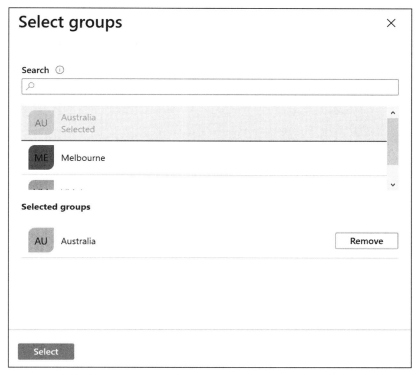

FIGURE 1-9 Selecting group to nest

To remove a group from another group, open the parent group's group membership page and then remove the nested group by selecting that group and clicking **Remove Memberships**.

MORE INFO **NESTING GROUPS**

You can learn more about this topic at *https://docs.microsoft.com/en-us/azure/active-directory/fundamentals/active-directory-groups-membership-azure-portal*.

Manage Azure AD users

You can use the Azure AD Admin Center in the Azure portal, Azure PowerShell, or the Microsoft 365 admin center to manage Azure AD user accounts. The Azure AD admin center gives you a better set of options for managing the properties of user accounts than does the Microsoft 365 admin center because you can edit extended user properties, as shown in Figure 1-10.

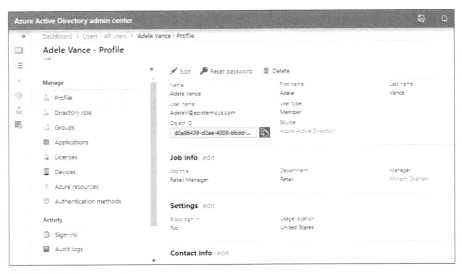

FIGURE 1-10 User properties page

To create a new Azure AD User, perform the following steps:

1. In the Azure AD console, select **Users–All Users** and then click **New User**.

2. On the **New User** blade shown in Figure 1-11, provide the following information:

   - **Name**   The user's actual name.

   - **User Name**   The user's sign-in name in UPN format.

   - **Profile**   The user's first name, last name, job title, and department.

   - **Properties**   This specifies the source of authority for the user. By default, if you are creating the user using the Azure AD admin center or the Microsoft 365 admin center, the source of authority will be Azure Active Directory.

   - **Groups**   This defines which groups the user should be a member of.

   - **Directory Role**   Choose whether the account has a User, Global Administrator, or a Limited Administrator role.

   - **Password**   This is the automatically generated password. With the **Show Password** option, you can transmit the password to the user through a secure channel.

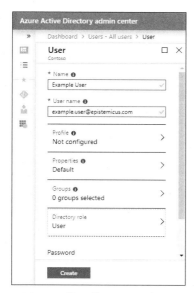

FIGURE 1-11 New User properties page

You can also use the Azure AD admin center to perform the following user administration tasks:

- Update profile information
- Assign directory roles
- Manage group membership
- Manage licenses
- Manage devices
- Manage access to Azure resources
- Manage authentication methods

When you delete a user from Azure AD, the account remains in the Azure Active Directory Recycle Bin for 30 days. This means that you can recover the account online should it be necessary to do so. If you delete a user from your on-premises Active Directory environment but have enabled the on-premises Active Directory Recycle Bin, recovering the user from the on-premises Active Directory Recycle Bin will recover the user account in Microsoft 365. If you don't have the Active Directory Recycle Bin enabled, you will need to create another account with a new GUID.

MORE INFO CREATING AZURE AD USERS

You can learn more about Azure AD PowerShell cmdlets for managing users at *https://docs. microsoft.com/en-us/powershell/azure/active-directory/new-user-sample.*

Manage external identities by using Azure AD

This objective deals with creating B2B and guest accounts, as well as ways to allow external access to resources hosted in a Microsoft 365 tenancy. You perform these actions when you want to enable people in a partner organization or external users such as temporary contractors to interact with resources hosted in Microsoft 365 services such as SharePoint Online. To master this objective, you'll need to understand how to create B2B accounts, how to create guest accounts, and the factors you will need to consider when designing a solution to allow external users to access Microsoft 365 resources.

Create B2B accounts

Business-to-business (B2B) accounts are a special type of guest user account that resides within Azure Active Directory to which you can assign privileges. B2B accounts are generally used when you want to allow one or more users from a partner organization to access resources hosted within your organization's Microsoft 365 tenancy. For example, if users in Contoso's partner organization, Tailwind Traders, need to interact with and publish content to a Contoso SharePoint Online site, one method of providing the necessary access is to create a set of B2B accounts.

B2B accounts have the following properties:

- They are stored in a separate Azure AD tenancy from your organization, but they are represented as a guest user in your organization's tenancy. The B2B user signs in using their organization's Azure AD account to access resources in your organization's tenancy.
- They are stored in your organization's on-premises Active Directory and then synced using Azure AD Connect and a guest user type. This is different from the usual type of synchronization, where user accounts are synced from an on-premises directory, but the Azure AD accounts are traditional Azure AD accounts and are not assigned the guest user type.

Azure Active Directory accounts use the user type to display information about the account's relationship to the organization's tenancy. The two following values are supported:

- **Member** If the user type is Member, the user is considered to belong to the host organization. This is appropriate for full-time employees, some types of contractors, or anyone else on the organizational payroll or within the organizational structure. Figure 1-12 shows a user account with the user type set to member.
- **Guest** The Guest user type indicates that the user is not directly associated with the organization. The guest user type applies to B2B and more generally to guest accounts. It is used when the account is based in another organization's directory or associated with another identity provider, such as a social network identity.

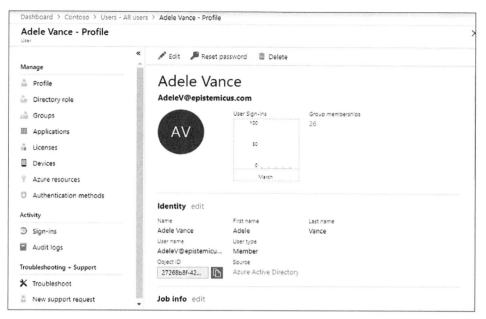

FIGURE 1-12 Account with the user type set to member

The account's user type does not determine how the user signs in; it is merely an indication of the user's relationship to the organization that controls the Azure AD tenancy. It can also be used to implement policies that depend on the value of this attribute. It is the source attribute property that indicates how the user authenticates. This property can have the following values:

- **Invited user**   A guest or B2B user who has been invited but has yet to accept their invitation.

- **External Active Directory**   An account that resides in a directory managed by a partner organization. When the user authenticates, they do so against the partner organization's Azure AD instance.

- **Microsoft account**   A guest account that authenticates using a Microsoft account, such as an Outlook.com or Hotmail.com account.

- **Windows Server Active Directory**   A user who is signed in from an on-premises instance of Active Directory that is managed by the same organization that controls the tenancy. This usually involves the deployment of Azure AD Connect. In the case of a B2B user, though, the user type attribute is set to guest.

- **Azure Active Directory**   A user who is signed in using an Azure AD account that is managed by the organization. In the case of a B2B user, the user type attribute is set to guest.

When you create the first type of B2B account, an invitation is sent to the user to whom you want to grant B2B access. The process of creating and sending this invitation also creates an account within your organization's Azure AD directory. This account will not have any credentials associated with it because authentication will be performed by the B2B user's identity provider. Figure 1-13 shows the screen used to send an invitation to a user.

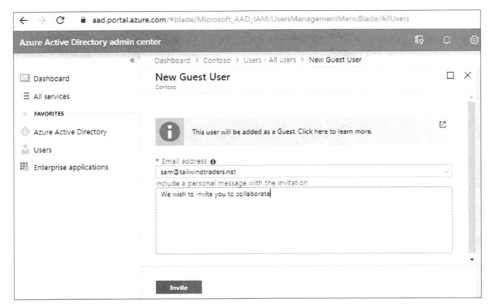

FIGURE 1-13 Creating a guest B2B user in the Azure AD Admin Center

Until the invitation is accepted, the source property of an invited B2B guest user account will be set to Invited User, as shown in Figure 1-14. You can also resend the invitation if the target user does not receive or respond to it.

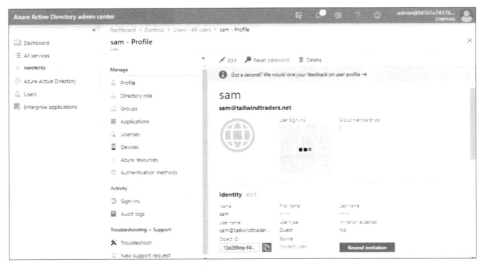

FIGURE 1-14 Source attribute set to Invited User

When the user accepts the invitation, the source attribute will be updated to external Azure Active Directory, as shown in Figure 1-15. If the user's account is synchronized from an on-premises Active Directory instance, but the user type is set to Guest, the source property will be listed as Windows Server Active Directory.

FIGURE 1-15 Source attribute set to External Azure Active Directory

---

> **MORE INFO** **AZURE AD B2B COLLABORATION**
>
> You can learn more about Azure AD B2B collaboration users at *https://docs.microsoft.com/en-us/azure/active-directory/external-identities/user-properties*.

Create guest accounts

A B2B account is a Guest account. Although the exam objectives suggest a substantial difference exists between these two types of accounts, it is perhaps more accurate to say that a Guest account might be considered a type of B2B account where the account is a Microsoft account or a social account. For example, a Guest account might have an *@outlook.com* email address, or it might be a social media account such as a Facebook account. The main difference between the two is that, in general, a B2B account implies a business-to-business relationship, whereas a Guest account implies a business-to-individual relationship.

You create a guest account in exactly the same way as a B2B account, as outlined in the preceding section. You send an invitation, an account is created, the user accepts the invitation, and then the individual uses the account to access Microsoft 365 resources to which they have been granted permissions.

You can view a list of all users in an Azure AD instance that have guest accounts by selecting **Guest Users Only** from the **Show** drop-down list on the **All Users** page, as shown in Figure 1-16.

FIGURE 1-16 Viewing guest accounts

Guest users are blocked from performing certain tasks, including enumerating users, groups, and other Azure AD resources. You can remove the guest user default limitations by performing the following steps:

1. On the **Azure Active Directory** blade, under **Manage**, select **User settings**.
2. On the **User settings** blade, select **Manage External Collaboration Settings**.
3. On the **External collaboration settings** page, select **No** under **Guest users Permissions Are Limited**, as shown in Figure 1-17.

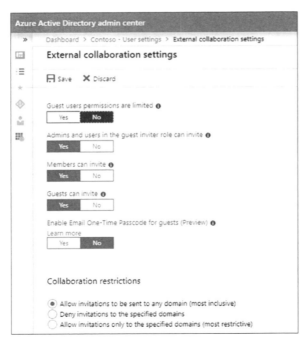

FIGURE 1-17 External collaboration settings

MORE INFO **ADDING GUEST USERS**

You can learn more about this topic at *https://docs.microsoft.com/en-us/azure/active-directory/external-identities/b2b-quickstart-add-guest-users-portal*.

Design solutions for external access

When designing a solution to enable external access to Microsoft 365 resources, you should understand that Microsoft 365 external sharing and Azure AD B2B collaboration are almost the same thing. Except for OneDrive and SharePoint Online, all external sharing uses the Azure AD B2B collaboration invitation APIs.

OneDrive and SharePoint Online have a separate invitation manager, and their functionality differs slightly from Microsoft 365 external sharing and Azure AD B2B collaboration. For example, unlike Azure AD B2B, OneDrive and SharePoint Online will only add a user to the Azure AD instance after the user has redeemed their invitation. In contrast, Azure AD B2B adds the user to the directory during invitation creation. This means you can perform actions such as granting access to an Azure AD B2B guest user before they have accepted their invitation because they will be present in the directory—something that is not possible with invitations sent through OneDrive and SharePoint Online.

You manage external sharing for SharePoint Online using the Sharing page of the SharePoint Admin Center. To configure SharePoint so that only Azure AD B2B sharing is enabled, select **Allow Sharing Only With The External Users That Already Exist In Your Organization's Directory**, as shown in Figure 1-18.

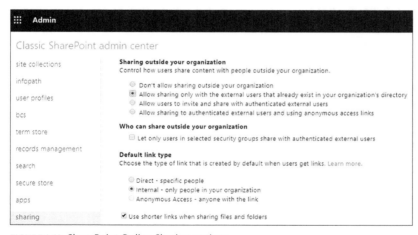

FIGURE 1-18 SharePoint Online Sharing options

MORE INFO **B2B AND MICROSOFT 365 EXTERNAL SHARING**

You can learn more about external sharing and Azure AD B2B collaboration at *https://docs.microsoft.com/en-us/azure/active-directory/external-identities/o365-external-user*.

You can use the External Collaboration Settings page (see Figure 1-19), accessible from the Azure AD User Settings blade, to configure the following collaboration settings:

- **Guest Users Permissions Are Limited** Enabled by default, this option enables you to configure guest users so that they have the same permissions as standard users.

- **Admins And Users In The Guest Inviter Role Can Invite** Invitations can be sent from users who hold the administrator and guest inviter roles.

- **Members Can Invite** Invitations can be sent by users who are not administrators and who have not been assigned the guest inviter roles.

- **Guests Can Invite** Users with guest status can invite other users as B2B users or guests.

- **Enable Email One-Time Passcode For Guests** This is a one-time passcode for guests who do not have an Azure AD or Microsoft account and for which Google Federation has not been configured. Guests who use one-time passcodes remain authenticated for 24 hours.

- **Allow Invitations To Be Sent To Any Domain** The is the default setting, which enables guest and B2B invitations to be sent to any domain.

- **Deny Invitations To Specified Domains** This enables you to create a block list of domains to which guest and B2B invitations cannot be sent.

- **Allow Invitations Only To The Specified Domains** Use this option to allow guest and B2B invitations only to specific domains. Invitations to domains not on the allowed list are blocked.

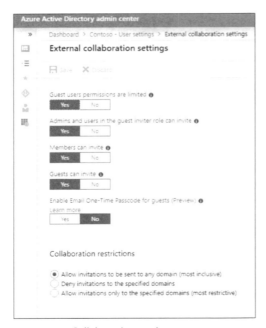

FIGURE 1-19 Collaboration settings

EXAM TIP

You can configure an allow list of specific domains to which invitations can be sent, and you can configure a block list where you only block invitations to specific domains.

Manage administrative units

Azure AD administrative units are containers for Azure AD users and groups that you can use to limit administrative permissions. For example, if you want to limit administrative rights to a specific set of users and groups, you could place those users and groups in an administrative unit and assign permissions using the administrative unit as the permission scope. All the user and group objects located within that administrative unit will be subject to the permissions assigned at the administrative unit level.

The administrative unit structure will be dependent on the needs of each organization. Some organizations might create an administrative unit structure based on geographical boundaries; other organizations might create an administrative unit structure based on their company divisions. Administrative units in Azure AD are analogous to Organizational Units in Active Directory Domain Services. Users with the Global Administrator or Privileged Role Administrators can do the following:

- Create administrative units
- Add users and groups to administrative units
- Delegate administrative roles to administrative units

To add an administrative unit through the Azure portal, perform the following steps:

1. In the Azure AD Admin Center or Azure portal, select the **Azure Active Directory** node and then select **Administrative Units**.
2. In the **Administrative Units** blade, select **Add**. You will be asked to provide a name for the administrative unit in the Name box and have the option of providing a description for the administrative unit.
3. Click **Add** to complete the process of adding the administrative unit.

You can use the New-AzureADMSAdministrativeUnit PowerShell cmdlet when connected to Azure AD to create a new administrative unit. For example, to create a new administrative unit named Tasmania with the description Tasmania Users, run the following command:

```
New-AzureADMSAdministrativeUnit -Description "Tasmania Users" -DisplayName "Tasmania"
```

Once you have created the administrative unit, you can add users, groups, and assign roles and administrators. To add a user using the Azure portal, open the **Administrative Unit** and select **Users**, as shown in Figure 1-20, and then click **Add Member**.

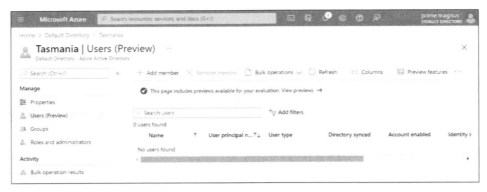

FIGURE 1-20 Administrative units

To add a group using the Azure portal, open the **Administrative Unit**, select **Groups**, and click **Add**. To add roles and administrators for the Administrative Unit, you will need an Azure AD P1 or P2 license. By default, the following administrative roles are assigned permissions to the Administrative Unit, as shown in Figure 1-21:

- Authentication Administrator
- Groups Administrator
- Helpdesk Administrator
- License Administrator
- Password Administrator
- User Administrator

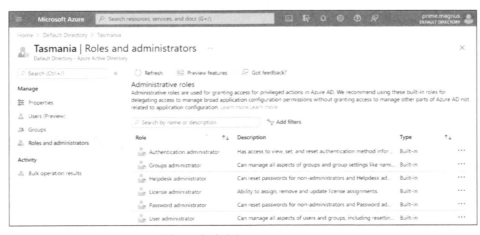

FIGURE 1-21 Administrative unit Roles and administrators

Perform the following steps to add a user or group to one of the existing roles scoped only with permissions to objects within the Administrative Unit:

1. Open the **Administrative Unit** in the Azure portal and select **Roles And Administrators**.

2. Select the role that you want to assign over the objects contained within the administrative unit and then select **Add Assignments**.

3. On the **Add Assignments** pane, select the users or groups that you want to assign to the role.

The best practice when using role-based access control technologies is to assign roles to specially created groups and then add users to that group. Removing a user's privileges is a matter of removing their account from specific groups. This is a simpler process than removing privileges for a specific user on a resource-by-resource basis.

> **MORE INFO**   **AZURE AD ADMINISTRATIVE UNITS**
>
> You can learn more about Azure AD administrative units at *https://docs.microsoft.com/en-us/azure/active-directory/roles/administrative-units*.

EXAM TIP

Remember that you can assign rights to an application by associating the application's service principal with specific Azure AD roles.

Skill 1.2: Manage secure access by using Azure AD

This objective deals with the steps that can be taken to secure access to Azure resources by using Azure Active Directory. This objective deals with configuring privileged identity management, conditional access policies, implementing Azure AD Identity protection, managing passwordless authentication, and performing access reviews. This section covers the following topics:

Configure Azure AD Privileged Identity Management (PIM)

Azure AD Privileged Identity Management (PIM) allows you to make role assignments temporary and contingent on approval, rather than making them permanent, as is the case when you manually add a member to the role. PIM requires Azure AD P2, which must be enabled before it can be configured. To configure an Azure AD administrative role for use with PIM, perform the following steps:

1. In the Azure AD admin center, select **Roles And Administrators**.

2. Select the role to which you want to add a user. This will open the role's properties page.

3. On the **Role Properties** page, click **Manage In PIM**. The role will open, and any members assigned permanently to the role will be listed with the status of **Permanent**, as shown in Figure 1-22.

FIGURE 1-22 Members of the Password Administrators role

4. Select the user you want to convert from **Permanent** to **Eligible**. An eligible user can request access to the role, but that user will not have its associated rights and privileges until that access is granted. On the user's properties page, click **Make Eligible**.

   You can edit the conditions under which an eligible user can be granted access by performing the following steps:

   1. On the **Privileged Identity Management** blade, click **Azure AD Roles**.

   2. Under **Manage**, as shown in Figure 1-23, click **Settings**.

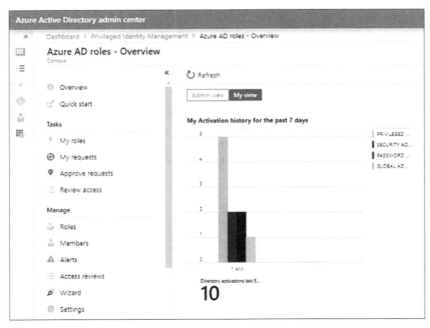

FIGURE 1-23 Manage PIM

3. Click **Roles** and then select the role that you want to configure. Figure 1-24 shows the PIM settings for the **Security Administrator** role, where role activation can occur for an hour at most but where MFA and an approval are not required.

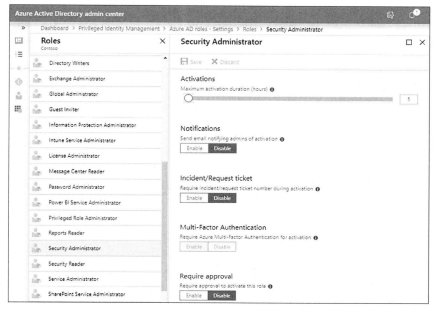

FIGURE 1-24 Manage PIM

Users can activate roles that they are eligible for from the **Privileged Identity Management** area of the Azure AD Administrative console. Administrators with the appropriate permissions can also use the **Privileged Identity Management** area of the Azure AD Administrative console to approve requests that require approval and review role activations.

MORE INFO   **PRIVILEGED IDENTITY MANAGEMENT**

You can learn more about PIM at *https://docs.microsoft.com/en-us/azure/active-directory/privileged-identity-management/pim-configure*.

PIM requires that you configure Azure AD users with appropriate licenses. PIM requires one of the following license categories to be assigned to users who will perform PIM-related tasks:

- Azure AD Premium P2
- Enterprise Mobility + Security (EMS) E5
- Microsoft 365 M5

The PIM-related tasks that require a license are as follows:

- Any user who is eligible for an Azure AD role that is managed using PIM
- Any user who can approve or reject PIM activation requests

- Users assigned to Azure resource roles with just-in-time or time-based assignments
- Any user who can perform an access review
- Any user who is assigned to an access review

> **MORE INFO**   **PIM LICENSE REQUIREMENTS**
>
> You can learn more about PIM license requirements at *https://docs.microsoft.com/en-us/ azure/active-directory/privileged-identity-management/subscription-requirements*.

You cannot use PIM to manage the following classic subscription administrator roles:

- Account Administrator
- Service Administrator
- Co-Administrator

The first person to activate PIM will be assigned the Security Administrator and Privileged Administrator roles for the tenancy.

> **MORE INFO**   **ACTIVATING PRIVILEGED IDENTITY MANAGEMENT**
>
> You can learn more about activating PIM at *https://docs.microsoft.com/en-us/azure/active- directory/privileged-identity-management/pim-security-wizard*.

Implement conditional access policies, including multifactor authentication

Conditional Access policies allow you to require additional steps to be taken when a certain set of circumstances occur. For example, you could configure a conditional access policy to require MFA to occur if a user attempts to access a specific resource in Azure or if a user is accessing Azure from an unusual location. Conditional access policies can also be used to completely block access to Azure resources when certain conditions are met, such as when someone attempts to access an application from a region from which IP address ranges have been blocked.

Conditional access policies

Conditional access policies will only be enforced after the first-factor authentication has been completed. Conditional access policies require an Azure AD P2 or equivalent subscription. Commonly used conditional access policies include:

- Require MFA for all users with administrative roles
- Require MFA prior to performing Azure management tasks
- Block sign-ins for legacy authentication protocols
- Require trusted location when registering for Azure MFA

- Block access from specific locations
- Require organization-managed devices for certain applications

Conditional access policies can be applied based on user circumstances that include (but are not limited to) the following:

- **IP address location**   An administrator can designate certain IP address ranges as trusted, such as the public IP addresses associated with the organization's Internet gateway devices. Administrators can also specify regional IP address ranges as being blocked from access, such as those belonging to people trying to access resources from Tasmania.
- **Device**   Whether the user is attempting to access Azure AD resources from a trusted device or from a new untrusted device.
- **Application**   Whether the user is attempting to access a specific Azure AD application.
- **Group membership**   Whether the user is a member of a specific group.

In addition to the simple option to block access, conditional access policies can be configured to

- Require multifactor authentication
- Require a device to be marked as compliant
- Require the device to be Hybrid Azure AD–joined
- Require an approved client app
- Require an app protection policy

To create a conditional access policy, perform the following steps:

1. In the Azure Active Directory area of the Azure portal, select **Security** and then select **Conditional Access**, as shown in Figure 1-25.

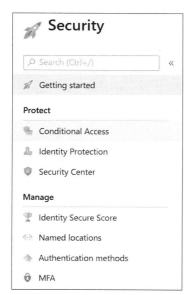

FIGURE 1-25 Security page with Conditional Access highlighted

2. On the **Conditional Access | Policies** page shown in Figure 1-26, select **New Policy**.

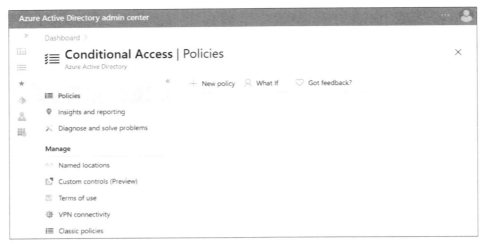

FIGURE 1-26 Conditional Access policies

3. On the **New Conditional Access Policy** page shown in Figure 1-27, provide the following information:

- **Name**   A name for the conditional access policy.
- **Users And Groups**   Users and groups that the policy applies to.
- **Cloud Apps Or Actions**   Which cloud apps or user actions the policy applies to. Policies can apply to some or all cloud apps. You can also specify specific user actions that will trigger the conditional access policy, such as attempting to access a specific Azure resource (such as a virtual machine).
- **Conditions**   The conditions associated with the policy. These include **User Risk**, **Sign-In Risk**, **Device Platforms**, **Locations**, **Client Apps**, and **Device State**.
- **Access Controls**   Select which additional controls are required to grant access. This gives you the option of requiring MFA, a compliant device, a Hybrid Azure AD–joined device, an approved client app, an app protection policy, or that the user performs a password change.
- **Session**   Allows you to specify the behavior of specific cloud applications. Options include **Conditional Access App Control**, **Sign-In Frequency**, and **Persistent Browser Session**.
- **Enable Policy**   Can be set to **Report Only**, which you should use to determine how the policy will function prior to enforcing, enabling, or disabling it.

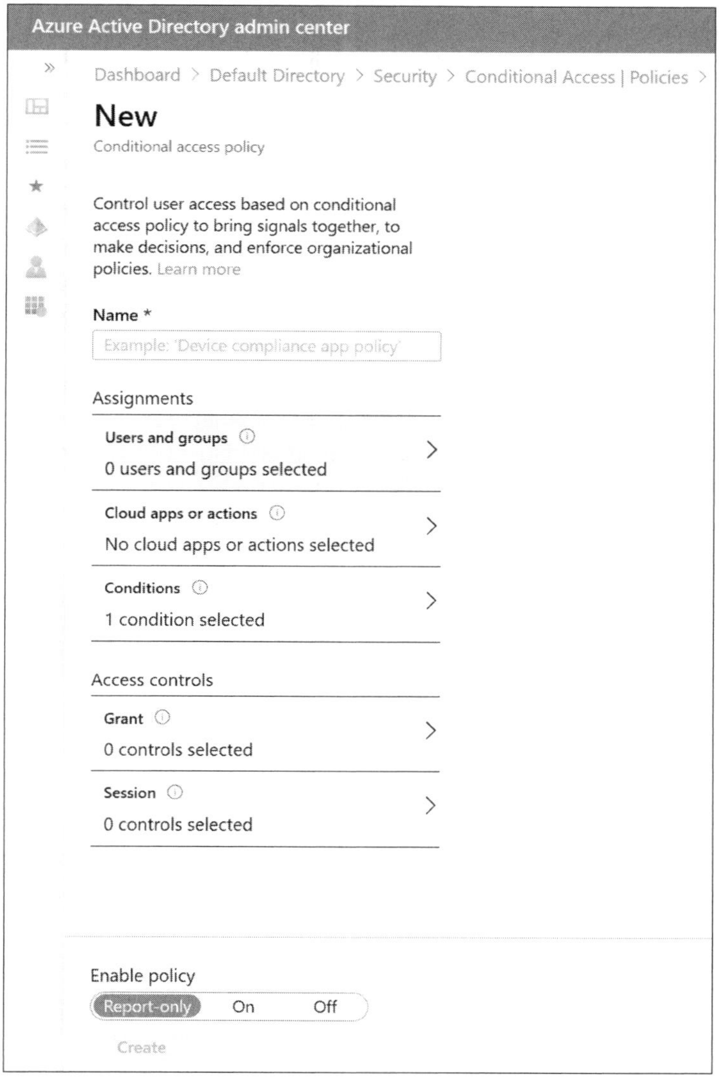

FIGURE 1-27 New Conditional Access policy

4. Click **Create** to create the policy.

MORE INFO **CONDITIONAL ACCESS POLICIES**

You can learn more about Conditional access policies at *https://docs.microsoft.com/en-us/ azure/active-directory/conditional-access/overview*.

Implementing MFA

When implementing MFA, you need to decide which MFA capabilities will be available to the users associated with your organization's Azure AD tenancy. MFA requires that more than one authentication method be used when signing in to a resource. Usually, this involves the user providing their username and password credentials and then providing one of the following:

- **A code generated by an authenticator app**   This can be the Microsoft Authenticator app or a third-party authenticator app, such as the Google authenticator app.

- **A response provided to the Microsoft Authenticator app**   When this method is used, Azure AD provides an on-screen code to the user authenticating the app; this code also must be selected on an application that is registered with Azure AD.

- **A phone call to a number registered with Azure AD**   The user needs to provide a preconfigured PIN that they will be instructed to enter by the automated service that performs the phone call. Microsoft provides a default greeting during authentication phone calls, so you don't have to record one for your organization.

- **An SMS message sent to a mobile phone number registered with Azure AD**   The user provides the code sent in the message as a second factor during authentication.

When designing your solution, you'll need to ensure that users have access to the appropriate MFA technology. This might require you to come up with a method of ensuring that all users in your organization already have the Microsoft Authenticator app installed on their mobile devices before you enable MFA on their accounts.

> **MORE INFO**   **PLAN FOR MULTIFACTOR AUTHENTICATION**
>
> You can learn more about designing a multifactor authentication solution for Office 365 deployments at *https://docs.microsoft.com/en-us/office365/admin/security-and-compliance/multi-factor-authentication-plan*.

MFA is not enabled by default on Azure AD tenancies. Before you can configure accounts to use MFA, you'll need to enable MFA on the tenancy. To enable MFA on an Azure AD tenancy and configure MFA for specific users, perform the following steps:

1. In Azure Active Directory admin center, navigate to **Users** and then click **All Users**.

2. Click **More**, and then click **Multifactor Authentication**, as shown in Figure 1-28.

FIGURE 1-28 Set up Azure MFA

3. After selecting this option, MFA will be enabled for the tenancy, and you'll be provided with a list of users that is similar to that shown in Figure 1-29.

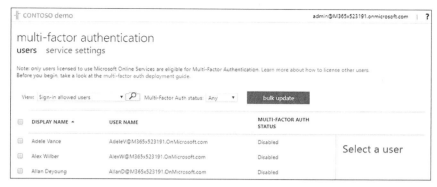

FIGURE 1-29 Set up users for Azure MFA

4. Select the users you want to set up for MFA, as shown in Figure 1-30, and then click **Enable**.

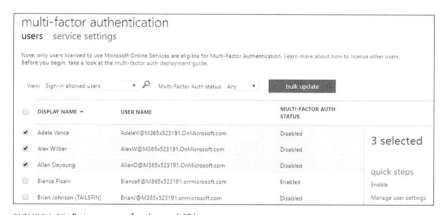

FIGURE 1-30 Set up users for Azure MFA

5. On the **About Enabling Multi-Factor Auth** dialog box shown in Figure 1-31, click **Enable Multi-Factor Auth**.

FIGURE 1-31 Enabling multifactor authorization

6. The next time that users sign in, they will be prompted to enroll in multifactor authentication and will be presented with a dialog box similar to that shown in Figure 1-32, asking them to provide additional information.

FIGURE 1-32 More information required

7. Choose between providing a mobile or office phone number or configuring a **Mobile App** using the **How Should We Contact You?** drop-down menu shown in Figure 1-33.

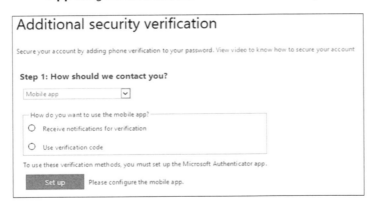

FIGURE 1-33 Contact preferences

8. When you specify one of these options, you are presented with a QR code. Within the app, you can add a new account by scanning the QR code. Once you have configured the application, you will be required to confirm that configuration has completed successfully by approving a sign-in through the app, as shown in Figure 1-34.

FIGURE 1-34 Verify on the app

9. Once this is done, you'll be prompted to provide additional security information in the form of a phone number, as shown in Figure 1-35.

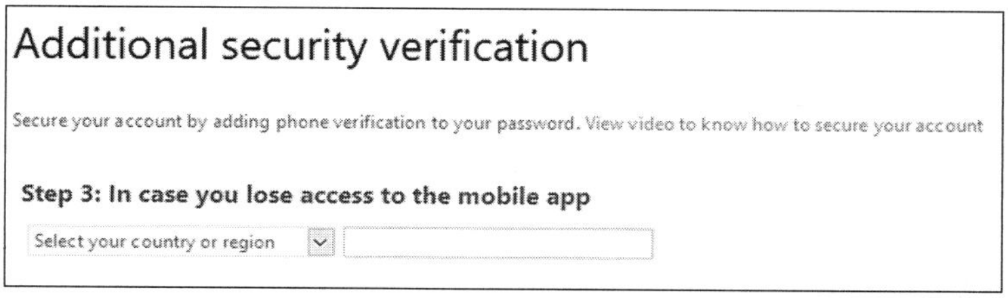

FIGURE 1-35 Verify on the app

You can configure the following multifactor authentication service settings, as shown in Figure 1-36.

- **App Passwords**   Allow or disallow users from using app passwords for non-browser apps that do not support multifactor authentication.
- **Trusted IP Addresses**   Configure a list of trusted IP addresses where MFA will be skipped when federation is configured between the on-premises environment and the Microsoft 365 Azure AD tenancy.
- **Verification Options**   Specify which verification options are available to users, including phone call, text message, app-based verification, or hardware token.
- **Remember Multi-Factor Authentication**   Decide whether to allow users to have MFA authentication remembered for a specific period of time on a device so that MFA does not need to be performed each time the user signs in. The default is 14 days.

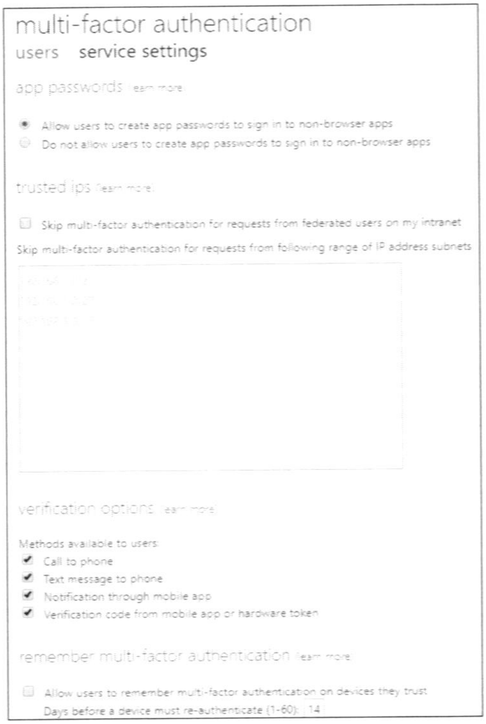

FIGURE 1-36 MFA service settings

> **MORE INFO** SET UP MULTIFACTOR AUTHENTICATION
>
> You can learn more about multifactor authentication at *https://docs.microsoft.com/en-us/ azure/active-directory/authentication/concept-mfa-howitworks*.

Administer MFA users

Once MFA is configured for users, there might be certain times when you want to force users to provide updated contact methods, you might want to revoke all app passwords, or you might want to restore MFA on all remembered devices. You can do this by performing the following steps:

1. With an account that has been assigned the Global Admin role, open the Azure AD admin center and select the **All Users** node, as shown in Figure 1-37. Select the user to manage MFA.

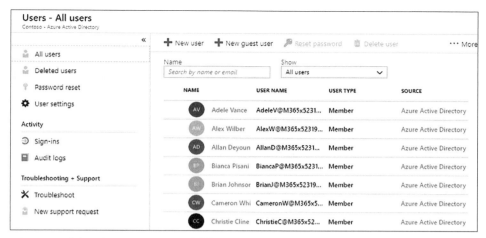

FIGURE 1-37 Select the user to manage MFA

2. On the user's properties page, select **Authentication Methods**.

3. On the **Authentication Methods** page shown in Figure 1-38, select which action to perform.

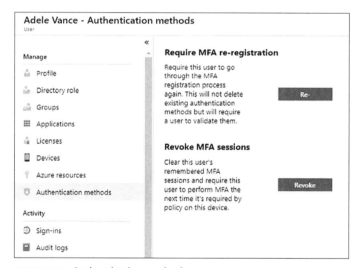

FIGURE 1-38 Authentication methods

If you want to perform a bulk reset for multiple users, use the following steps:

1. From the **All users** page shown in Figure 1-39, click **Multi-Factor Authentication.**

FIGURE 1-39 List of users

2. On the **Users** tab of the **Multi-factor Authentication** page shown in Figure 1-40, select the users for whom you want to reset MFA settings and click **Manage User Settings**.

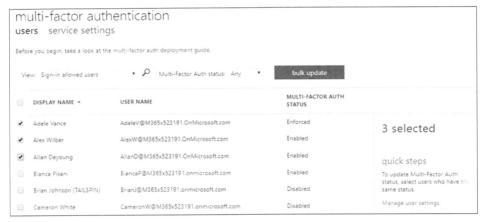

FIGURE 1-40 List of users

3. On the **Manage User Settings** page shown in Figure 1-41, select which tasks you want to perform, such as requiring users to provide contact methods again, deleting all existing app passwords, and restoring MFA on remembered devices. After making the selection, click **Save**.

FIGURE 1-41 Managing user settings

Account lockout

Account Lockout settings for MFA, shown in Figure 1-42, allow you to configure the conditions under which MFA lockout will occur. On this page, you can configure the number of MFA denials that will trigger the account lockout process, how long before the account lockout counter is reset, and the number of minutes until the account will be unblocked. For example, if the account lockout counter is reset after 10 minutes, and the number of MFA denials to trigger account lockout is set to 5, then 5 denials in 10 minutes will trigger a lockout. However, 5 denials over a course of 30 minutes would not trigger a lockout because the account lockout counter would reset during that period.

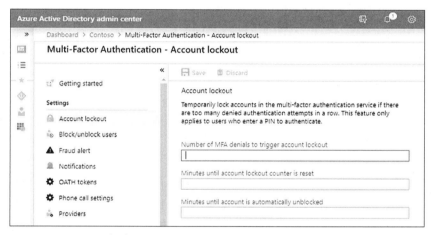

FIGURE 1-42   Account lockout settings

Block/unblock users

The **Block/Unblock Users** setting shown in Figure 1-43 allows you to block specific users of an on-premises MFA server from being able to receive an MFA request. Any requests sent to a user on the blocked users list will automatically be denied. Users on this list remain blocked for 90 days, after which they are removed from the blocked users list. To unblock a blocked user, click **Unblock**.

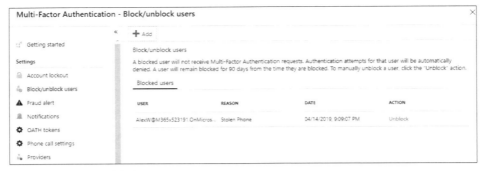

FIGURE 1-43 Block/Unblock Users

Fraud alert settings

Figure 1-44 shows the **Fraud Alert** settings, which allow you to configure whether users can report fraudulent verification requests. A fraudulent verification request might occur when an attacker has access to a user's password but does not have access to an alternative MFA method. A user becomes aware of this by receiving an MFA prompt, either through their app, an SMS, or a phone call when they haven't attempted to authenticate against a Microsoft 365 workload. When a user reports fraud, you can choose an option to have their account automatically blocked for 90 days, which indicates that the password is likely to be compromised.

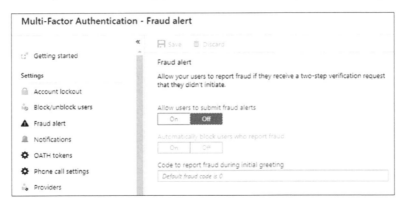

FIGURE 1-44 Fraud alert

OATH tokens

The OATH tokens page shown in Figure 1-45 allows you to upload a specially formatted CSV file containing the details and keys of the OATH tokens you want to use for multifactor authentication. The specially formatted CSV file should include a formatted header row, as shown here with the UPN (user principal name), serial number, secret key, time interval, manufacturer, and model. Each file is associated with a specific user. If a user has multiple OATH tokens, these should be included in the file associated with their account.

FIGURE 1-45 OATH tokens

Phone call settings

Phone call settings allow you to configure the caller ID number that is displayed when the user is contacted for MFA authentication. This number must be a United States number. You can also use the phone call settings page shown in Figure 1-46 to configure custom voice messages. The voice messages must be in `.wav` or `.mp3` format, must be no larger than 5 MB, and should be shorter than 20 seconds.

FIGURE 1-46 Phone Call Settings

> **MORE INFO   MANAGING MFA SETTINGS**
>
> You can learn more about managing MFA settings at *https://docs.microsoft.com/en-us/azure/ active-directory/authentication/howto-mfa-mfasettings*.

Report MFA utilization

Azure MFA provides a number of reports that you can use to understand how MFA is being used in your organization, including:

- **Blocked User History**   Provides a history of requests to block or unblock users.
- **Usage And Fraud Alerts**   Provides information on a history of fraud alerts submitted by users. Also, this report provides information on the overall MFA usage.
- **Usage For On-Premises Components**   Provides information on the utilization of MFA through the Network Policy Server extension, Active Directory Federation Services, and on-premises MFA server.
- **Bypassed User History**   Provides information on a specific user's requests to bypass MFA.
- **Server Status**   Provides status data of MFA servers associated with your organization's Azure AD tenancy.

> **MORE INFO**   **AZURE MULTIFACTOR AUTHENTICATION REPORTS**
>
> You can learn more about Azure multifactor authentication reports at *https://docs.microsoft. com/en-us/azure/active-directory/authentication/howto-mfa-reporting*.

EXAM TIP

Remember the steps you can take to automatically lock out users who incorrectly answer MFA prompts.

Implement Azure AD Identity Protection

Azure AD Identity Protection allows you to automate the detection and remediation of identity-based risks, including the following:

- **Atypical travel**   When a user's account sign-in indicates they have performed unusual shifts in location. This could include a user signing in from Sydney and then Los Angeles in a two-hour period when the flight between the two cities takes about seven times that amount of time.
- **Anonymous IP address**   When a user signs in from an anonymous IP address. While a user might be using an anonymizing VPN to access organizational resources, attackers also use tools such as TOR nodes when launching compromise attempts.
- **Unfamiliar sign-in properties**   When a user's sign-in properties differ substantially from those that have been observed in the past.
- **Malware-linked IP address**   When the IP address the user is signing in from is known to be part of a malware botnet or has exhibited other malicious network activity in the past.

- **Leaked credentials** When the user's credentials have been discovered in a data breach, such as those recorded on *havelbeenpwned.com*.
- **Azure AD threat intelligence** When the sign-in behavior correlates with known attack patterns identified by Microsoft's internal or external threat intelligence sources.

Enabling Azure AD Identity protection requires an Azure AD P2 license.

Azure AD Identity Protection allows you to configure two types of risk policy: a sign-in risk policy and a user-risk policy:

- **Sign-in risk** These policies analyze signals from each sign-in and determine how likely it is that the sign-in was not performed by the person associated with the user account. If a sign-in is determined to be risky, administrators can specify whether to block access or allow access but require multifactor authentication.
- **User-risk** These policies are based on identifying deviations from the user's normal behavior. For example, the user signs in from an unusual location at a time that substantially differs from when they usually sign in. User risk policies allow administrators to block access, allow access, or allow access but require a password change when the policy is triggered.

To enable user risk and sign-in risk policies, perform the following steps:

1. In the Azure Active Directory admin center, select **Security** in the **Manage** area and then select **Identity Protection**.

2. In the **Protect** section of the **Identity Protection** blade, which is shown in Figure 1-47, select **User Risk Policy**.

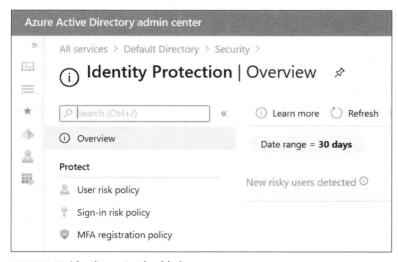

FIGURE 1-47 Identity protection blade

3. Click **User Risk Policy**. On the **User Risk Policy** blade, which is shown in Figure 1-48, configure the following settings.

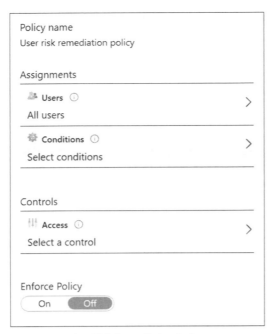

FIGURE 1-48 User Risk Remediation Policy

- **Assignments: Users** Determine which users the user risk remediation policy applies to.
- **Assignments: Conditions** Allows you to determine at which risk level the policy applies. You can choose between **Low And Above**, **Medium And Above**, or **High**.
- **Controls: Access** For a user risk policy, you can choose between **Block**, **Allow**, and **Allow And Require Password Change**.
- **Enforce policy** The policy can be switched **On** or **Off**.

4. Click **Sign-In Risk Policy**. On the **Sign-In Risk Remediation Policy** blade, which is shown in Figure 1-49, configure the following settings and click **Save**:

- **Assignments: Users** Determine which users the user risk remediation policy applies to.
- **Assignments: Conditions** Allows you to determine at which risk level the policy applies. You can choose between **Low And Above**, **Medium And Above**, or **High**.
- **Controls: Access** For a user risk policy, you can choose between **Block**, **Allow**, and **Allow And Require Multi-Factor Authentication**.
- **Enforce policy** The policy can be switched **On** or **Off**.

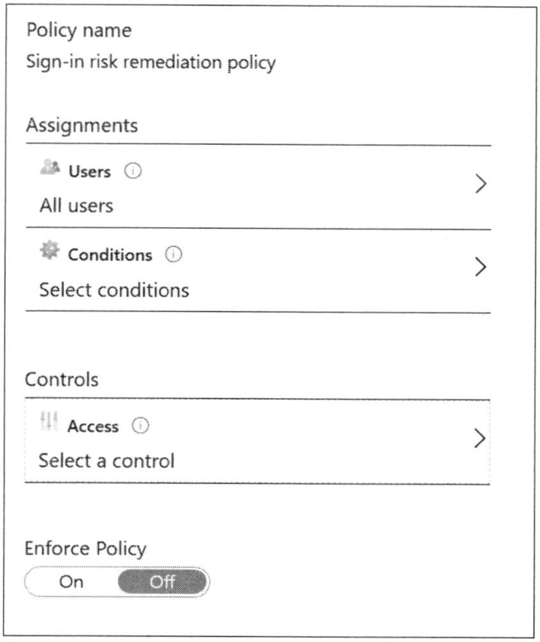

FIGURE 1-49 Sign-In Risk Remediation Policy

> **MORE INFO**   **AZURE AD IDENTITY PROTECTION**
>
> You can learn more about Azure AD identity protection at *https://docs.microsoft.com/en-us/azure/active-directory/identity-protection/overview-identity-protection*.

Implement passwordless authentication

Passwordless authentication allows you to replace authentication using a password with authentication requiring something you have and something you know. An example of this might be a biometric, such as your face or fingerprint combined with a code generated by an authenticator device.

Microsoft currently offers three passwordless authentication options. These are

- **Windows Hello for Business**   This method uses biometric authentication technologies included with Windows computers, such as Windows Hello compatible cameras for facial recognition or Windows Hello compatible fingerprint readers. Most appropriate for users who are the only people who regularly interact with a specific Windows computer.

- **Security key sign-in**   Allows access via FIDO2 Security keys. This method is appropriate for users who sign in to shared machines, such as those in a call center. Because it requires the physical FIDO2 security key, this is also an excellent method of protecting privileged identities because this key can, in turn, be secured in a safe that another person has the access code for.

- **Phone sign-in through Microsoft Authenticator App**   The Microsoft Authenticator App runs on iOS and Android phones and supports identity verification via biometrics or PIN-based authentication. When using this method, a user will be prompted on the screen to select a specific number displayed amongst a list of options on the Microsoft Authenticator App and perform identity verification via biometrics or a PIN.

Deploying passwordless authentication requires the following administrative roles:

- **Global administrator**   This role allows the implementation of the combined registration experience in the directory.

- **Authentication administrator**   This role can implement and manage authentication methods for individual user accounts.

- **User**   Although not an administrative role, this account is necessary to be able to configure an authenticator app on a device or enroll a security device for their specific accounts once passwordless authentication is enabled for their accounts.

To enable passwordless phone sign-in authentication, perform the following steps:

1.   In the Azure Active Directory admin portal, click **Security**.

2.   On the **Security** page shown in Figure 1-50, click **Authentication Methods**.

FIGURE 1-50 Authentication Methods section of the Security page

3. On the **Authentication Methods** page shown in Figure 1-51, select the authentication method that you want to enable, toggle the slider to **On**, and then choose whether you want to enable the authentication method for some or all Azure AD users by choosing **All Users** or **Select Users**.

FIGURE 1-51 Enable passwordless authentication method

> **MORE INFO** **PASSWORDLESS AZURE AD AUTHENTICATION**
>
> You can learn more about passwordless authentication at *https://docs.microsoft.com/en-us/azure/active-directory/authentication/concept-authentication-passwordless*.

Configure access reviews

Many security incidents have occurred because an attacker has gained access through a forgotten account with administrative privileges. Access reviews allow you to determine whether existing PIM role assignments are still relevant and which role assignments can be removed because they are no longer being actively used.

Access Review of the Azure resource PIM role

There are two types of access review: access reviews of Azure resource PIM roles and access reviews of Azure AD PIM roles. To perform an access review of an Azure resource PIM role, perform the following steps:

1. In the Azure AD admin center blade of the Azure portal, select **Identity Governance** in the **Manage** area and then select **Privileged Identity Management**.

2. On the **Privileged Identity Management** blade, click **Azure Resources**, as shown in Figure 1-52.

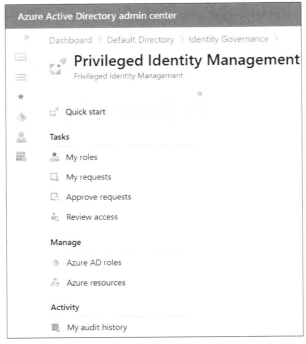

FIGURE 1-52 Azure resources

3. Existing access reviews will be displayed on the report shown in Figure 1-53.

FIGURE 1-53 Azure Resource access review report

4. Click **New** to create a new access review. Provide the following information:

- **Access Review Name** A name for the access review.
- **Start Date** Date when the review is scheduled to start.
- **Frequency** How often the review should occur. You can choose a one-time frequency, or you can select **Weekly**, **Monthly**, **Quarterly**, **Annually**, or **Semiannually**.
- **Duration** Specify the number of days over which the access review will occur. A longer duration will give you a better idea of how often privileged roles are used.
- **End** Specify how to end recurring access reviews. You can specify an end date or configure the review to end after a specific number of cycles.

- **Users** Specify the roles that you are reviewing the membership of.
- **Reviewers** Specify which people will review all the users.
- **Upon Completion** As shown in Figure 1-54, configure how you want the results of the access review implemented. If you want to automatically remove access for users, set **Auto Apply Results To Resources** to **Enable**. If you want to manually apply results once the review is complete, set this to **Disable**.

FIGURE 1-54 Upon Completion Settings

- **Should Reviewer Not Respond** In this drop-down menu, you have the following options:
  - **No Change** This will ensure that no changes are made to current PIM settings.
  - **Remove Access** This will remove access of users where access is no longer found to be necessary.
  - **Approve Access** This will approve user access.
  - **Take Recommendations** Use the system's recommendation when it comes to removing or approving continued access.

The steps for configuring an access review of an Azure AD PIM role are similar to those that you perform when configuring a review to Azure resources, except that you select **Azure AD Roles** instead of **Azure Resources** on the **Manage** menu of the **Privileged Identity Management** blade of the Azure AD admin center.

> **MORE INFO** **REVIEW ACCESS TO AZURE AD ROLES**
>
> You can learn more about reviewing access to Azure AD roles at *https://docs.microsoft.com/en-us/azure/active-directory/privileged-identity-management/pim-how-to-perform-security-review*.

Monitor privileged access for Azure AD Privileged Identity Management (PIM)

Privileged Identity Management (PIM) allows you to implement time-based and approval-based activation of administrative roles. For example, you could configure PIM so that a help desk employee only has the right to change a user's password for a maximum of 60 minutes once the request for that right has been approved by a specific authorized user. PIM differs from earlier administrative models where the help desk might always be able to change Azure AD user passwords. PIM allows you to do the following:

- Configure just-in-time privileged access to Azure AD and Azure resources. Just-in-time access is access limited to an amount of time, rather than providing permanent access to those resources.

- Assign time-bound access to resources using start and end dates.

- Require approval from another user when activating privileged roles.

- Require multifactor authentication to occur before role activation.

- Require users to provide recorded written justification of why they need to perform activation. This allows auditors at a later stage to correlate the administrative activity that occurs with the stated reason for providing privileged access.

- Provide notifications, such as email alerts sent to a distribution list, when privileged roles are activated.

- Perform access reviews to determine how often privileges are used and whether specific users still require roles.

- Export an audit history that can be examined by internal or external auditors.

To view all activity associated with Azure AD roles, you need to view the resource audit history. To view resource audit history, perform the following steps:

1. In the Azure AD admin center blade of the Azure portal, select **Identity Governance** in the **Manage** area, as shown in Figure 1-55.

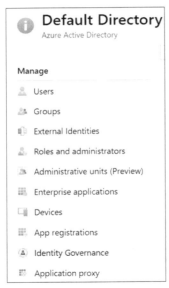

FIGURE 1-55 Identity Governance

2. On the **Identity Governance** blade, select **Azure AD Roles** under **Privileged Identity Management**.

3. Click **Resource Audit** and then use the filters to view the appropriate information, as shown in Figure 1-56.

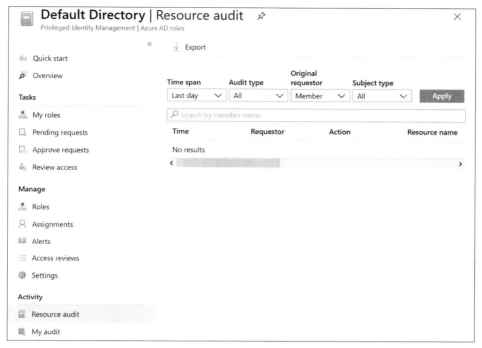

FIGURE 1-56 Resource Audit

MORE INFO   **VIEW AUDIT HISTORY**

You can learn more about reviewing PIM audit logs at *https://docs.microsoft.com/en-us/azure/active-directory/privileged-identity-management/pim-how-to-use-audit-log*.

EXAM TIP

Remember the requirements for enabling MFA on an Azure AD tenancy.

Skill 1.3: Manage application access

This objective deals with the steps that can be taken to configure and manage application access. This includes understanding how to integrate single sign-in providers, create app registrations and configure permission scopes, manage app registration permission consent, manage API permissions, and service principal authentication methods.

Integrate single sign-on (SSO) and identity providers for authentication

Azure Active Directory supports a variety of identity providers for authentication, including on-premises Active Directory Domain Services and certificate-based authentication. You learned about using external identity providers in Skill 1.1.

Install and configure Azure AD Connect

Azure AD Connect allows you to connect your on-premises Active Directory accounts with an Azure AD instance. This is useful not only for applications running in Azure, but it allows you to implement single sign-on if your organization is using Microsoft 365 or Office 365. Single sign-on allows you to use one identity to access on-premises and cloud resources. In many scenarios, the user won't even be required to re-authenticate.

Azure AD Connect is software that you install on a computer that manages the process of synchronizing objects between the on-premises Active Directory and the Azure Active Directory instance. You can install Azure AD Connect on computers running the Windows Server 2012 or later operating systems:

Azure AD Connect has the following requirements:

- It must be installed on a Windows Server instance that has the GUI version of the operating system installed. You cannot install Azure AD connect on a computer running the Server Core operating system.
- You can deploy Azure AD Connect on a computer that is either a domain controller or a member server. A server can be used if you use the custom options.
- The server hosting Azure AD Connect requires .NET Framework 4.5.1 or later.
- The server hosting Azure AD Connect requires Microsoft PowerShell 3.0 or later.
- The Azure AD Connect server must not have PowerShell Transcription enabled through Group Policy.
- If you are deploying Azure AD Connect with Active Directory Federation Services, you must use Windows Server 2012 R2 or later for the Web Application Proxy. Also, Windows remote management must be enabled on the servers that will host AD FS roles.
- If global administrators will have multifactor authentication enabled (MFA), then this URL must be configured as a trusted site: *https://secure.aadcdn.microsoftonline-p.com*.

CONNECTIVITY REQUIREMENTS

The computer with Azure AD Connect installed must be a member of a domain in the forest that you want to synchronize, and it must have connectivity to a writable domain controller in each domain of the forest you want to synchronize on the following ports:

- **DNS**   TCP/UDP Port 53
- **Kerberos**   TCP/UDP Port 88
- **RPC**   TCP Port 135

- **LDAP** TCP/UDP Port 389
- **TLS/SSL** TCP Port 443
- **SMB** TCP 445

The computer with Azure AD Connect installed must be able to establish communication with the Microsoft Azure servers on the Internet over TCP port 443. The computer with Azure AD Connect installed can be located on an internal network as long as it can initiate communication on TCP port 443. The computer hosting Azure AD Connect does not need a publicly routable IP address. The computer hosting Azure AD Connect always initiates synchronization communication to Microsoft Azure. Microsoft Azure Active Directory does not initiate synchronization communication to the computer hosting Azure AD Connect on the on-premises network.

Because the Azure AD Connect instance requires access to the Internet, you should not install Azure AD Connect on a domain controller. If you are going to be replicating more than 50,000 objects, Microsoft recommends that you deploy SQL Server on a computer that is separate from the computer that will host Azure AD Connect. If you plan to host the SQL Server instance on a separate computer, ensure that communication is possible between the computer hosting Azure AD Connect and the computer hosting the SQL Instance on TCP port 1433.

If you are going to use a separate SQL Server instance, ensure that the account used to install and configure Azure AD Connect has systems administrator rights on the SQL instance and that the service account used for Azure AD Connect has public permissions in the Azure AD Connect database.

SQL SERVER REQUIREMENTS

When you deploy Azure AD connect, you can have Azure AD Connect install an SQL Server Express instance, or you can choose to have Azure AD Connect leverage a full instance of SQL Server. SQL Server Express is limited to a maximum database size of 10 GB. In terms of Azure AD Connect, this means that Azure AD Connect can only manage 100,000 objects. This is likely to be adequate for all but the largest environments.

For environments that require Azure AD Connect to manage more than 100,000 objects, you'll need to have Azure AD Connect leverage a full instance of SQL Server. Azure AD Connect can use all versions of Microsoft SQL Server, from Microsoft SQL Server 2012 with the most recent service pack to SQL Server 2019. It is important to note that SQL Azure is not supported as a database for Azure AD Connect. If you are deploying a full instance of SQL Server to support Azure AD Connect, ensure that the following prerequisites are met:

- **Use a case-insensitive SQL collation** Case-insensitive collations have the _CI_ identifier included in their names. Case-sensitive collations (those that use the _CS_ designation) are not supported for use with Azure AD Connect.
- **You can only use one sync engine per SQL instance** If you have an additional Azure AD Connect sync engine or use Microsoft Identity Manager in your environment, each sync engine requires its own separate SQL instance.

REQUIREMENTS FOR DEPLOYMENT ACCOUNTS

You use two accounts when configuring Azure AD Connect. One account must have specific Azure AD permissions; the other account must have specific on-premises Active Directory permissions. The accounts that you use to install and configure Azure AD Connect have the following requirements:

- The account used to configure Azure AD Connect must have Global Administrator privileges in the Azure AD tenancy. You should create a separate account for this task and configure the account with a complex password that does not expire. This account is used to synchronize between on-premises AD and Azure AD.

- The account used to install and configure Azure AD Connect must have Enterprise Administrator permissions within the on-premises Active Directory forest if you will be using Express installation settings. This account is only required during installation and configuration. Once Azure AD Connect is installed and configured, this account no longer needs Enterprise Administrator permissions. The best practice is to create a separate account for Azure AD Connect installation and configuration and to temporarily add this account to the Enterprise Admins group during the installation and configuration process. Once Azure AD Connect is installed and configured, this account can be removed from the Enterprise Admins group. You should not attempt to change the account used after Azure AD Connect is set up and configured because Azure AD Connect always attempts to run using the original account.

- The account used to install and configure Azure AD Connect must be a member of the local Administrators group on the computer on which Azure AD Connect is installed.

INSTALLING AZURE AD CONNECT

Installing Azure AD Connect with Express settings is appropriate if your organization has a single Active Directory forest and you want to use password synchronization for authentication. The Azure AD Connect Express settings are appropriate for most organizations. You can download the Azure AD Connect installation files from Microsoft's download center website.

To install Azure AD Connect with Express settings, perform the following steps:

1. Double click the `AzureADConnect.msi` file that you've downloaded from the Microsoft download center. You will be prompted with a security warning. After clicking **Run**, Azure AD Connect will be installed on your computer. When the installation is complete, you will be presented with a splash screen detailing the license terms and displaying a privacy notice. You'll need to agree to these terms before clicking **Continue**.

2. If your organization has an internal non-routable domain, it will be necessary for you to use custom settings. The best practice is to use domain synchronization when your on-premises Active Directory instance and your Azure Active Directory instance use the same routable domain name. Click **Continue**.

3. On the **Install Required Components** page, shown in Figure 1-57, choose between the following options:

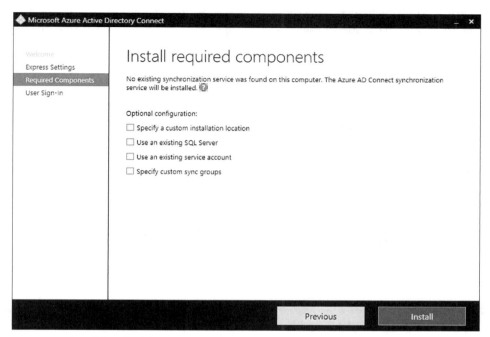

FIGURE 1-57 Install Required Components page

- **Specify A Custom Installation Location** Choose this option if you want to install Azure AD Connect in a separate location, such as on another volume.

- **Specify An Existing SQL Server** Choose this option if you want to specify an alternate SQL server instance. By default, Azure AD Connect will install an SQL Server Express instance.

- **Use An Existing Service Account** You can configure Azure AD Connect to use an existing service account. By default, Azure AD Connect will create a service account. You can configure Azure AD Connect to use a Group Managed Service account. You'll need to use an existing service account if you are using Azure AD Connect with a remote SQL Server instance or if communication with Azure will occur through a proxy server that requires authentication.

- **Specify Custom Sync Groups** When you deploy Azure AD Connect, it will create four local groups on the server that hosts the Azure AD Connect Instance. These groups are the Administrators group, Operators group, Password Reset group, and the Browse group. If you want to use your own set of groups, you can specify them here. These groups must be local to the host server and not a member of the domain.

4. Once you have specified which custom options you require—and you aren't required to choose any—click **Install**.

5. On the **User Sign-In** page shown in Figure 1-58, specify what type of sign-in you want to allow. You can choose between the following options, the details of which were covered earlier in this chapter:

   - Password Synchronization
   - Pass-Through Authentication
   - Federation With AD FS
   - Federation With PingFederate
   - Do Not Configure
   - Enable Single Sign-On

Most organizations will choose **Password Synchronization** because this is the most straightforward option.

FIGURE 1-58 User Sign-In options page

6. On the **Connect To Azure AD** page, provide the credentials of an account with Global Administrator privileges in Azure AD. Microsoft recommends you use an account in the default onmicrosoft.com domain associated with the Azure AD instance to which you will be connecting. If you choose the **Federation With AD FS** option, ensure that you do not sign in using an account in a domain that you will enable for federation. Figure 1-59 shows a sign-in with a **Password Synchronization** scenario.

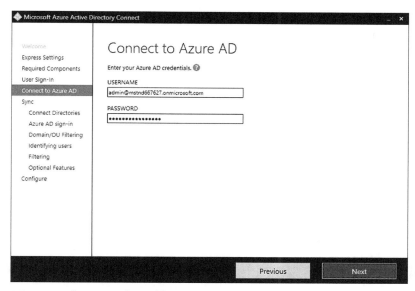

FIGURE 1-59 Connect to Azure AD page

7. Once Azure AD Connect has connected to Azure AD, you will be able to specify the directory type to synchronize, as well as the forest. Click **Add Directory** to add a specific forest. When you add a forest by clicking **Add Directory**, you will need to specify the credentials of an account that will perform periodic synchronization. Unless you are certain that you have applied the minimum necessary privileges to an account, you should provide Enterprise Administrator credentials and allow Azure AD Connect to create the account, as shown in Figure 1-60. This will ensure that the account is only assigned the privileges necessary to perform synchronization tasks.

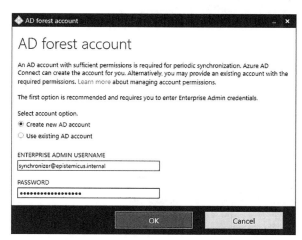

FIGURE 1-60 AD Forest Account page

8. Once the credentials have been verified, as shown in Figure 1-61, click **Next**.

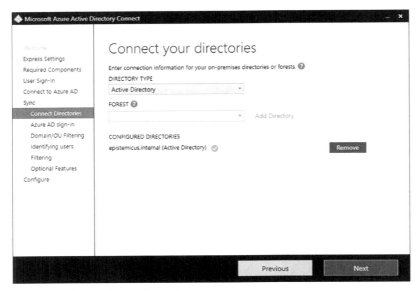

FIGURE 1-61 Connect Your Directories page

9. On the **Azure AD Sign-In Configuration** page, shown in Figure 1-62, review the UPN suffix and then inspect the on-premises attribute that will be used as the Azure AD username. You'll need to ensure that accounts use a routable Azure AD username.

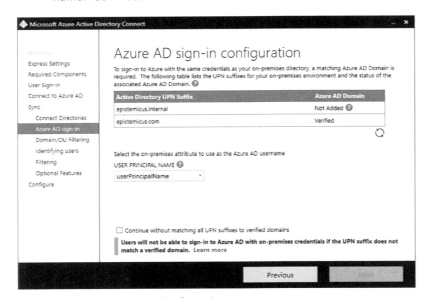

FIGURE 1-62 Azure AD Sign-In Configuration page

10. On the **Domain And OU Filtering** page, select whether you want to sync all objects or just objects in specific domains and OUs.

11. On the **Uniquely Identifying Users** page shown in Figure 1-63, specify how users are to be identified. By default, users should only have one representation across all directories. If users exist in multiple directories, you can have matches identified by a specific active directory attribute, with the default being the **Mail Attribute**.

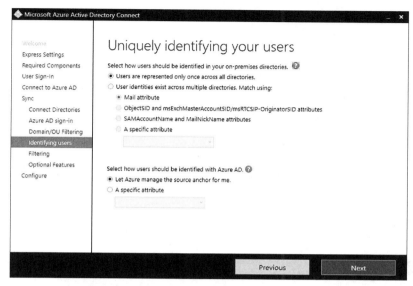

FIGURE 1-63 Uniquely Identifying Your Users

12. On the **Filter Users And Devices** page, specify whether you want to synchronize all users and devices or only members of a specific group. Figure 1-64 shows members of the M365-Pilot-Users group being configured so that their accounts will be synchronized with Azure.

FIGURE 1-64 Filter Users And Devices page

13. On the **Optional Features** page shown in Figure 1-65, select any optional features that you want to configure. These features include the following:

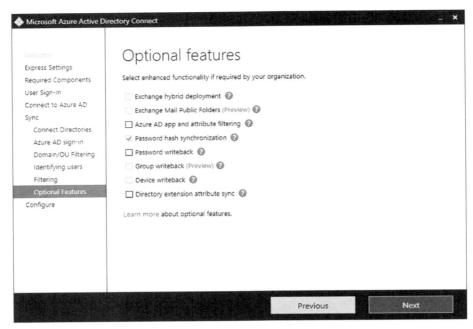

FIGURE 1-65 Optional Features

- **Exchange Hybrid Deployment** This option is suitable for organizations that have an Office 365 deployment and where there are mailboxes hosted both on-premises and in the cloud.
- **Exchange Mail Public Folders** This feature allows organizations to synchronize mail-enabled public folder objects from an on-premises Active Directory environment to Microsoft 365.
- **Azure AD App And Attribute Filtering** Selecting this option allows you to be more selective about which attributes are synchronized between the on-premises environment and Azure AD.
- **Password Synchronization** Synchronizes a hash of the user's on-premises password Azure AD. When the user authenticates to Azure AD, the submitted password is hashed using the same process, and if the hashes match, the user is authenticated. Each time a user updates their password on-premises, the updated password hash synchronizes to Azure AD.
- **Password Writeback** Password writeback allows users to change their passwords in the cloud and have the changed password written back to the on-premises Active Directory instance.
- **Group Writeback** Changes made to groups in Azure AD are written back to the on-premises AD instance.

- **Device Writeback** Information about devices registered by the user in Azure AD is written back to the on-premises AD instance.
- **Directory Extension Attribute Sync** Allows you to extend Azure AD schema based on extensions made to your organization's on-premises Active Directory instance.

14. On the **Ready To Configure** page, you can choose to start synchronization or to enable staging mode. Azure AD Connect will prepare the synchronization process when you configure staging mode, but it will not synchronize any data with Azure AD.

Using UPN suffixes and non-routable domains

Before performing a synchronization between an on-premises Active Directory environment and an Azure Active Directory instance, you must ensure that all user account objects in the on-premises Active Directory environment are configured with a value for the UPN suffix that can function for both the on-premises environment and any application that you want to use it with in the cloud. This is not a problem when an organization's internal Active Directory domain suffix is a publicly routable domain. For example, a domain name, such as `contoso.com` or `adatum.com`, which is resolvable by public DNS servers, will suffice. Things become more complicated when the organization's internal Active Directory domain suffix is not publicly routable.

If a domain is non-routable, the default Azure AD instance domain, such as `adatum2020.onmicrosoft.com`, should be used for the UPN suffix. This requires modifying the UPN suffix of accounts stored in the on-premises Active Directory instance. Modification of UPN after initial synchronization has occurred is not supported. So, you need to ensure that on-premises Active Directory UPNs are properly configured before performing initial synchronization using Azure AD Connect. Perform the following steps to add a UPN suffix to the on-premises Active Directory if the Active Directory domain uses a non-routable namespace:

1. Open the **Active Directory Domains And Trust** console and select **Active Directory Domains And Trusts**.
2. On the **Action** menu, click **Properties**.
3. On the **UPN Suffixes** tab, enter the UPN suffix to be used with Azure Active Directory. Figure 1-66 shows the UPN suffix of `epistemicus.com`.

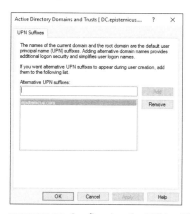

FIGURE 1-66 Configuring the UPN suffix for a routable domain

4. Once the UPN suffix has been added in the **Active Directory Domains And Trusts** dialog box, you can assign the UPN suffix to user accounts. You can do this manually, as shown in Figure 1-67, by using the **Account** tab of the user's **Properties** dialog box.

FIGURE 1-67 Configure UPN

5. You can also use Microsoft PowerShell scripts to reset the UPNs of multiple user accounts. For example, the following script resets UPN suffixes of all user accounts in the `epistemicus.internal` domain to `epistemicus.onmicrosoft.com`.

```
Get-ADUser -Filter {UserPrincipalName -like "*@epistemicus.internal"} -SearchBase
"DC=epistemicus,DC=internal" |
ForEach-Object {
$UPN =
$_.UserPrincipalName.Replace("epistemicus.internal","epistemicus.onmicrosoft.com")
Set-ADUser $_ -UserPrincipalName $UPN
}
```

SIGN-IN OPTIONS

Azure AD Connect supports a variety of sign-in options. You configure which one you want to use when setting up Azure AD Connect. The default method, Password Synchronization, is appropriate for most organizations that will use Azure AD Connect to synchronize identities to the cloud.

PASSWORD SYNCHRONIZATION

Hashes of on-premises Active Directory user passwords synchronize to Azure AD. Changed passwords immediately synchronize to Azure AD. Actual passwords are never sent to Azure AD and are not stored in Azure AD. This allows for a seamless single sign-on for users of computers that are joined to an Active Directory domain that synchronizes to Azure AD. Also, password synchronization allows you to enable password write-back for self-service password reset functionality through Azure AD.

PASS-THROUGH AUTHENTICATION

The user's password is validated against an on-premises Active Directory domain controller when authenticating to Azure AD. Passwords and password hashes are not present in Azure AD. Pass-through authentication allows for on-premises password policies to apply. Pass-through authentication requires that Azure AD Connect have an agent on a computer joined to the domain that hosts the Active Directory instance that contains the relevant user accounts. Pass-through authentication also allows seamless single sign-on for users of domain-joined machines.

With pass-through authentication, the user's password is validated against the on-premises Active Directory controller. The password doesn't need to be present in Azure AD in any form. This allows for on-premises policies, such as sign-in hour restrictions, to be evaluated during authentication to cloud services.

Pass-through authentication uses a simple agent on a Windows Server 2012 R2, Windows Server 2016, or Windows Server 2019 domain-joined machine in the on-premises environment. This agent listens for password validation requests. It doesn't require any inbound ports to be open to the Internet.

In addition, you can also enable single sign-on for users on domain-joined machines that are on the corporate network. With single sign-on, enabled users only need to enter a user-name to help them securely access cloud resources.

ACTIVE DIRECTORY FEDERATION

This allows users to authenticate to Azure AD resources using on-premises credentials. When you choose the Federation with AD FS option, Active Directory Federation Services is installed and configured. Also, a Web Application Proxy server is installed to facilitate communication between the on-premises AD FS deployment and Microsoft Azure Active Directory. This is the most complicated identity synchronization configuration, and it is only likely to be implemented in environments with complicated identity configurations.

> **MORE INFO   AZURE AD CONNECT SIGN-IN OPTIONS**
>
> You can learn more about sign-in options by consulting the following article: *https://docs.microsoft.com/en-us/azure/active-directory/connect/active-directory-aadconnect-user-signin*.

Implement and manage Azure AD self-service password reset

A self-service password reset is challenging to deploy in an on-premises environment, but it is relatively straightforward to deploy in an environment that uses Azure AD as a source of identity authority. A self-service password reset allows users to reset their own passwords when they forget them, rather than having a member of the IT staff do it for them. To enable self-service password reset, perform the following steps:

1. Open the Azure Active Directory portal at *https://aad.portal.azure.com* with an account that has tenant administrator permissions.

2. In the Azure Active Directory admin center, click the **Users** node, which will open the **Users** blade, as shown in Figure 1-68.

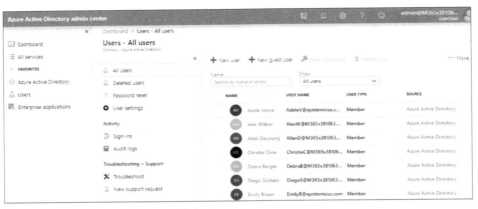

FIGURE 1-68 Azure Active Directory Admin Center

3. On the **Users** blade of the Azure Active Directory admin center, click **Password Reset**.

4. On the **Password Reset – Properties** page, click **All**, as shown in Figure 1-69, to enable the self-service password reset for all Microsoft 365 users.

FIGURE 1-69 Enable Self Service Password Reset

Once enabled, users will be prompted for additional information the next time that they sign-in. This information will be used to verify their identities if they use the self-service password reset tool. Users can reset their passwords by navigating to the website *https://passwordreset.microsoftonline.com* shown in Figure 1-70 and completing the form.

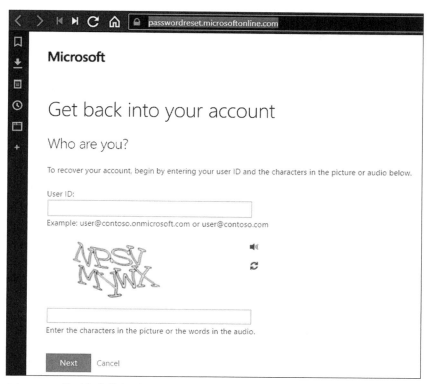

FIGURE 1-70 Enable Self-Service Password Reset

> **MORE INFO   SELF-SERVICE PASSWORD RESET**
>
> You can learn more about configuring a self-service password at *https://docs.microsoft.com/ en-us/azure/active-directory/authentication/concept-sspr-howitworks*.

Configure authentication methods including password hash and pass-through authentication (PTA) and OATH

Another authentication design aspect is deciding which authentication methods will be supported for accounts in your organization's Azure AD instance. For example, you must decide whether you want to support self-service password reset or Azure multifactor authentication, as shown in Figure 1-71.

FIGURE 1-71 Multiple methods of verifying identity during authentication

You can use the authentication methods listed in Table 1-1 with accounts hosted in Azure Active Directory.

TABLE 1-1 Authentication methods and usage

Authentication method	Where it can be used
Password	Multifactor authentication and self-service password reset
Security questions	Self-service password reset only
Email address	Self-service password reset only
Microsoft Authenticator app	Multifactor authentication and self-service password reset
OATH Hardware Token	Multifactor authentication and self-service password reset
SMS	Multifactor authentication and self-service password reset
Voice Call	Multifactor authentication and self-service password reset
App passwords	Multifactor authentication in some cases

These authentication methods have the following properties:

- **Password** The password assigned to an Azure AD account is an authentication method. While you can perform password-less authentication, you cannot disable the password as an authentication method.

- **Security Questions** These are only available to Azure AD Self-Service Password Reset and can only be used with accounts that have not been assigned administrative roles. Questions are stored on the user object within Azure AD and cannot be read or modified by an administrator. They should be used in conjunction with another method. Azure AD includes the following predefined questions, and it is possible to create custom questions:

  - In what city did you meet your first spouse/partner?
  - In what city did your parents meet?
  - In what city does your nearest sibling live?
  - In what city was your father born?
  - In what city was your first job?
  - In what city was your mother born?
  - What city were you in on New Year's 2000?
  - What is the last name of your favorite teacher in high school?
  - What is the name of a college you applied to but didn't attend?
  - What is the name of the place in which you held your first wedding reception?
  - What is your father's middle name?
  - What is your favorite food?
  - What is your maternal grandmother's first and last name?
  - What is your mother's middle name?
  - What is your oldest sibling's birthday month and year? (for example, November 1985)
  - What is your oldest sibling's middle name?
  - What is your paternal grandfather's first and last name?
  - What is your youngest sibling's middle name?
  - What school did you attend for sixth grade?
  - What was the first and last name of your childhood best friend?
  - What was the first and last name of your first significant other?
  - What was the last name of your favorite grade school teacher?
  - What was the make and model of your first car or motorcycle?
  - What was the name of the first school you attended?
  - What was the name of the hospital in which you were born?
  - What was the name of the street of your first childhood home?
  - What was the name of your childhood hero?
  - What was the name of your favorite stuffed animal?
  - What was the name of your first pet?
  - What was your childhood nickname?

- What was your favorite sport in high school?
- What was your first job?
- What were the last four digits of your childhood telephone number?
- When you were young, what did you want to be when you grew up?
- Who is the most famous person you have ever met?

- **Email address**   This is only used for Azure AD self-service password resets and should be separate from the user's Microsoft 365 Exchange Online email address.
- **Microsoft Authenticator app**   Is available for Android and iOS. Either involves the user being notified through the mobile app and being asked to select the same number on the mobile app as is displayed on the log-in prompt, or it involves the user entering a set of periodically changing numbers displayed on the mobile app.
- **OATH hardware tokens**   Azure AD supports the use of OATH-TOTP SHA-1 tokens of both the 30- and 60-second variety. Secret keys can have a maximum of 128 characters. Once a token is acquired, it must be uploaded in comma-separated format, including UPN, serial number, secret key, time interval, manufacturer, and model. Note that OATH is different from OAuth. OATH is a reference architecture for authentication; OAuth is a standard related to authorization.
- **Mobile Phone**   Can be used either to send a code through text message that must be entered into a dialog box to complete authentication or where a phone call is made to the user who then needs to provide a personal authentication PIN. Phone numbers must include the country code.
- **App Passwords**   A number of non-browser apps do not support multifactor authentication. An app password allows these users to continue to authenticate using these apps when multifactor authentication is not supported. An app password can be generated for each app, allowing each app password to be individually revoked.

> ***MORE INFO***   **AUTHENTICATION METHODS**
>
> You can learn more about authentication methods at *https://docs.microsoft.com/en-us/azure/active-directory/authentication/concept-authentication-methods*.

Certificate-based authentication

Certificate-based authentication allows you to eliminate the need for a username and password combination. Certificate-based authentication is supported on Windows, Android, and iOS devices and has the following requirements:

- It is only supported for Federated environments for browser applications or where native clients use modern authentication through the Active Directory Authentication Library (ADAL). Exchange Active Sync (EAS) for Exchange Online (EXO) is exempt from the federation requirement and can be used with both federated and managed accounts.

- The organization's root certificate authority (CA) and any intermediate CAs must be integrated with Azure AD.

- Each organizational CA must publish a Certificate Revocation List (CRL) in a location that is accessible to the Internet.

- The Windows, Android, or iOS device must have access to an organizational CA that is configured to issue client certificates.

- The Windows, Android, or iOS device must have a valid certificate installed.

- Exchange ActiveSync clients require that the client certificate have the user's routable email address included in the Subject Alternative Name field.

To add an organizational CA that is trusted by Azure Active Directory, you need to ensure that the CA is configured with a CRL publication location that is accessible on the Internet and to then export the CA certificate. Once you have the CA certificate exported, which will include the Internet-accessible location where the CRL is published, use the New-AzureADTrustedCertificateAuthority PowerShell cmdlet to add the organizational CA's certificate to Azure Active Directory. You can view a list of trusted CAs for your organization's Azure AD instance using the Get-AzureADTrustedCertificateAuthority cmdlet.

> **MORE INFO** **CERTIFICATE BASED AZURE AD AUTHENTICATION**
>
> You can learn more about certificate-based Azure AD authentication at *https://docs.microsoft.com/en-us/azure/active-directory/authentication/active-directory-certificate-based-authentication-get-started*.

Configure password writeback

Password writeback occurs when a user uses self-service password (SSPR) functionality to update his or her password in Azure, and that updated password is then written to an on-premises Active Directory Domain Services instance. Azure AD also supports SSPR on Azure AD native accounts where no writeback to an on-premises instance is necessary. To implement SSPR for organizations with on-premises Active Directory Domain Services, first, you need to install Azure AD Connect to synchronize on-premises identities to Azure.

> **MORE INFO** **PASSWORD WRITEBACK**
>
> You can learn more about Password writeback at *https://docs.microsoft.com/en-us/azure/active-directory/authentication/tutorial-enable-sspr-writeback*.

Create an app registration

Registering an application with Azure Active Directory allows you to use Azure Active Directory's functionality, such as user identity and permissions, with the application. To register an application with Azure Active Directory using the Azure portal, perform the following steps:

1. In the Azure portal, open the **Azure Active Directory** blade.

2. In the **Manage** section shown in Figure 1-72, click **App Registrations**.

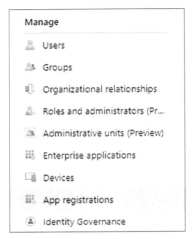

Manage

- 👤 Users
- 👥 Groups
- 🎛 Organizational relationships
- 👥 Roles and administrators (Pr...
- 🏛 Administrative units (Preview)
- ▦ Enterprise applications
- ⬚ Devices
- ▦ App registrations
- Ⓐ Identity Governance

FIGURE 1-72 App Registrations section of the Azure Active Directory blade

3. On the **App Registrations** blade of the **Azure Active Directory** section of the Azure portal, click **New Registration**. Figure 1-73 shows the New Registration item.

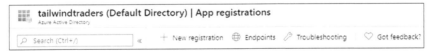

▦ **tailwindtraders (Default Directory) | App registrations**
Azure Active Directory

🔍 Search (Ctrl+/)   «   ＋ New registration 🌐 Endpoints ✎ Troubleshooting   ♡ Got feedback?

FIGURE 1-73 App Registrations blade with the New Registration option

4. On the **Register An Application** page, shown in Figure 1-74, choose which users can use this application or access this API. You can choose from the following options:

   - **Accounts In This Organizational Directory Only**   Appropriate for single-tenant scenarios where the only people who will use the application have accounts that reside within the Azure AD instance. You can switch to the multi-tenant option and back to the single-tenant option after registration is complete using the **Authentication** page in the Azure portal.

   - **Accounts In Any Organizational Directory**   Choose this option when you want to make the application available to users in your own and other Azure AD tenancies. This is also known as the multi-tenant option. You can switch between this option and the single-tenant option using the **Authentication** page in the Azure portal.

- **Accounts In Any Organizational Directory And Personal Microsoft Accounts** This option allows users who have accounts in Azure AD tenancies and personal Microsoft accounts, such as *Hotmail.com* and *outlook.com* accounts, can use the application. Currently, you can't switch from this mode to multi-tenant or single-tenant in the Azure portal, but you can make this change if you use the application manifest editor.

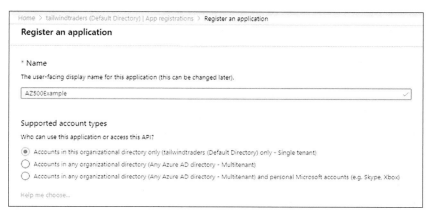

FIGURE 1-74 Supported account types for app registration

5. The **Redirect URI (Optional)** section, shown in Figure 1-75, allows you to specify the type of app that is being registered, with the options being **Web** or **Public Client (Mobile & Desktop)**. If you are registering a web app, you need to specify the base URL of the app (for example, *https://newapp.tailwindtraders.net:31544*). If you choose the **Public Client** option, you instead need to provide the Uniform Resource Identifier (URI) that Azure AD will use to return token responses that are specific to the application that you are registering.

FIGURE 1-75 Redirect URI

6. After providing this information, click **Register**.
7. Once the app registration process is complete, the app will be assigned a unique application or client ID, and it will be listed on the **App Registrations** page in the Azure portal, as shown in Figure 1-76.

FIGURE 1-76 App Registrations

> **MORE INFO** **REGISTERING AN APPLICATION**
>
> You can learn more about registering an application at *https://docs.microsoft.com/en-us/azure/active-directory/develop/quickstart-register-app*.

Managing access to apps

How you assign access to applications depends on the edition of Azure AD that your organization has licensed. If your organization only has a free edition of Azure AD, you'll only be able to assign access to applications on a per-user basis. If your organization licenses a paid edition of Azure AD, then you'll be able to perform a group-based assignment. When you perform a group-based assignment, whether a user can access an application will depend on whether the user is a member of the group at the time they attempt to access the application.

Any form of Azure AD group can be used to assign access to applications, including attribute-based dynamic groups, on-premises Active Directory groups, or self-service managed groups. Currently, nested group memberships are not supported when it comes to assigning access to applications through Azure AD.

> **MORE INFO** **MANAGING ACCESS TO APPS**
>
> You can learn more about managing access to apps at *https://docs.microsoft.com/en-us/azure/active-directory/manage-apps/what-is-access-management*.

Assigning users access to an application

To assign access to an application to a user or group, perform the following steps:

1. In the Azure AD admin center, select **Azure Active Directory**, and in the **Manage** section, click **Enterprise Applications**, as shown in Figure 1-77.

FIGURE 1-77 Azure AD Manage section

2. On the **Enterprise Applications** blade, ensure that **All Applications** is selected, as shown in Figure 1-78, and then select the application to which you want to enable user access.

FIGURE 1-78 All Applications

3. Once the application opens, click **Users And Groups** from the application's navigation pane, which is shown in Figure 1-79.

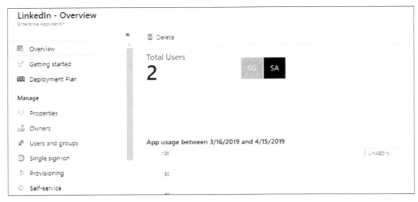

FIGURE 1-79 Application overview

4. On the application's **Users And Groups** page, shown in Figure 1-80, click **Add User**. Note that you use the **Add User** button to add a group assignment if Azure AD is licensed at the appropriate level.

FIGURE 1-80 Users And Groups

5. On the **Add Assignment** page shown in Figure 1-81, search for the user or group to which you want to grant application access.

FIGURE 1-81 Add Assignment for Users And Groups

6.   Select a user or group and then click **Select**, as shown in Figure 1-82.

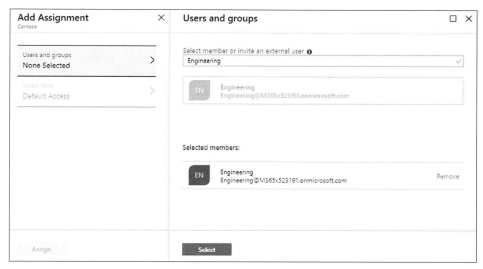

FIGURE 1-82 Selecting the group assignment

7.   Once the user or group is selected, click **Assign**. Verify that the assignment has occurred by reviewing the newly updated list of users and groups, as shown in Figure 1-83.

FIGURE 1-83 Users And Groups

> **MORE INFO**   **ASSIGN USERS AND GROUPS ACCESS**
>
> You can learn more about assigning access to users and groups at *https://docs.microsoft.com/ en-us/azure/active-directory/manage-apps/methods-for-assigning-users-and-groups*.

Configure app registration permission scopes

Configuring application registration permission scopes controls what information an application has access to. The Microsoft identity platform's way of implementing OpenID Connect uses several scopes that correspond to the Microsoft Graph. When configuring app registration, you can use the following permission scopes to determine what information the application can access:

- **OpenID**   Use this scope if an application performs a sign-in using OpenID Connect. This permission grants an app a unique identifier for the user in the form of a subclaim and also gives the app access to the UserInfo endpoint. This scope is used when inter-acting with the Microsoft identity platform to acquire ID tokens, which can then be used by the application for authentication.

- **Email**   The email scope gives the app access to a user's email address in the form of an email address associated with a user account.

- **Profile**   The profile scope can be used to provide the application with information about the user. This may include a user's given name, surname, preferred username, and object ID.

- **Offline_access**   The offline_access scope will provide an app with access to resources on behalf of the user for an extended period. If a user consents to the offline_access scope, the app can receive a long-lived refresh token, which can be updated as older tokens expire.

> **MORE INFO   PERMISSIONS AND CONSENT**
>
> You can learn more about permissions and consent in a Microsoft identity platform endpoint at *https://docs.microsoft.com/en-us/azure/active-directory/develop/v2-permissions-and-consent*.

Manage app registration permission consent

App registration permission consent allows users and administrators to control how and what data can be accessed by applications. The Microsoft identity platform supports the following types of permissions:

- **Delegated permissions**   These permissions are used by apps that are leveraged by a signed-in user. The user or an administrator consents to the permissions required by the app. The app then uses a delegated permission to function as the signed-in user when attempting to access the target resource.

- **Application permissions**   These permissions are used by apps that execute without a signed-in user. These might be long-running background applications. Application permissions can only be consented to by an administrator.

Effective permissions are the least-privileged set of permissions calculated when compar-ing the permissions that the application has been granted directly and the permissions of the signed-in user. To configure a list of statically requested permissions for an application, perform the following steps:

1. On the **App Registrations** blade of the Azure Active Directory console, select the regis-tered application for which you want to configure static permissions.

2. Under **Manage**, click **API Permissions**, as shown in Figure 1-84.

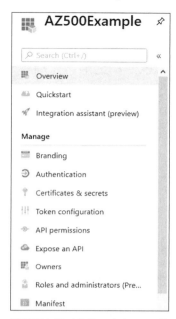

FIGURE 1-84 API Permissions on the Manage menu of a registered app

3. On the **API Permissions** blade shown in Figure 1-85, configure which permissions you would like the application to have. You can use this page to add permissions or to grant admin consent. Admin consent allows you to grant the application permissions to a specific Azure AD tenancy.

FIGURE 1-85 Manage API Permissions

MORE INFO   **APP REGISTRATION PERMISSION AND CONSENT**

You can learn more about app registration permission and consent at *https://docs.microsoft.com/en-us/azure/active-directory/develop/v2-permissions-and-consent*.

Manage API permissions to Azure subscriptions and resources

API management policies allow you to control the behavior of an API. An API management policy is a collection of statements that apply sequentially to requests to or to responses from the API. For example, these policies include format conversion from XML to JSON or call rate limiting. Call rate limiting can be a useful way of ensuring that an API hosted in Azure doesn't get flooded by requests, which can lead to unusually high subscription charges. API management policies are XML documents that are divided into inbound, outbound, back end, and on-error sections.

API management policies are evaluated depending on the scope at which they apply. Policy scopes are evaluated in the following order:

1. Global scope
2. Product scope
3. API scope
4. Operation scope

You can view all policies that apply in the current scope by clicking **Recalculate Effective Policy For Selected Scope** in the API management policy editor.

To set or edit an Azure API management policy, perform the following steps:

1. In the Azure portal, select the APIM instance. On the **APIs** tab, select the imported API.
2. On the **Design** tab, select the operation against which you want to apply the policy. You also have the option of applying the policy to all operations.
3. Click the **</>** (code editor) icon in the **Inbound Processing** or **Outbound Processing** sections.
4. Enter the desired policy code into the appropriate section of code.

> **MORE INFO**   **API MANAGEMENT ACCESS RESTRICTION POLICIES**
>
> You can learn more about API management access restriction policies at *https://docs.microsoft. com/en-us/azure/api-management/api-management-policies*.

Configure an authentication method for a service principal

You can use two different forms of authentication for service principals—password-based authentication or certificate-based authentication. By default, service principals will use password-based authentication. If you don't configure a password during service principal creation, a random password is created for the service principal. If you choose to create a password for the service principal, the password must meet the restrictions for Azure AD passwords. Microsoft recommends using the randomly generated password.

You can create a service principal with a randomly generated password and then extract the value of that password using the following Azure PowerShell commands (where ServicePrincipalName is the name you want to use for the service principal):

```
$sp = New-AzADServicePrincipal -DisplayName ServicePrincipalName
$BSTR = [System.Runtime.InteropServices.Marshal]::SecureStringToBSTR($sp.Secret)
$UnsecureSecret = [System.Runtime.InteropServices.Marshal]::PtrToStringAuto($BSTR)
```

Service principals that use certificate-based authentication can use PEM files, text-encoded CRT, or CER files as a way of associating a base64-encoded public certificate ASCII string. You can't use a binary encoding of a public certificate with a service principal when configuring certificate-based authentication.

You can create a service principal that uses certificate-based authentication using the following Azure PowerShell commands (where ServicePrincipalName is the name you want to use for the service principal):

```
$cert = <public certificate as base64-encoded string>
$sp = New-AzADServicePrincipal -DisplayName ServicePrincipalName -CertValue $cert
```

> **MORE INFO**   **SERVICE PRINCIPAL AUTHENTICATION**
>
> You can learn more about service principal authentication at *https://docs.microsoft.com/ en-us/powershell/azure/create-azure-service-principal-azureps*.

Skill 1.4: Manage access control

Access control is another term for assigning permissions to resources. In this section, you'll learn how to configure Azure role permissions for management groups, subscriptions, resource groups, and resources. Also, you'll learn about existing role and resource permissions, assigning existing Azure AD roles, and creating and assigning custom roles.

Configure Azure role permissions for management groups, subscriptions, resource groups, and resources

Azure Role Based Access Control (RBAC) allows you to configure fine-grained access management to Azure resources. Using RBAC, you can control what a security principal can do and where the security principal can do it. You do this with a combination of security principals, roles, and scopes.

As you recall from earlier in the chapter, security principals are Azure objects that represent individuals, collections of individuals, applications, or services. Security principals include:

- **Individual people**   These are represented as Azure AD users or user objects that are referenced within Azure AD from other tenancies.
- **Collections of individuals**   These are represented as Azure AD groups.

- **Applications and services**   These are represented as service principals or managed identities.

An RBAC role is a collection of permissions. Permissions can be thought of as a set of operations—such as read, write, and delete—that can be performed against the Azure object to which the role is assigned.

The scope is the boundary to which the permissions defined in the role apply to. You can configure the scope for a role assignment to occur at the management group, subscription, resource group, or individual Azure resource level. Scope assignments function in a parent-child relationship, which means the assignment of permissions that occurs at the parent scope level is inherited at the child scope level. For example, if you configure the scope for a role assignment to be at the resource group level, all the resources within that group will have that role assignment. If you configure a role scoped at the management group level, all the subscriptions within that management group, the resource groups within those subscriptions, and the resources within those resource groups will inherit the scoping done at the topmost layer.

Assigning permissions to Azure subscriptions and resources requires combining security principals that represent who you want to assign the permission to, the role definition that defines the permissions, and the scope that defines where the permissions are assigned.

MORE INFO   **UNDERSTANDING RBAC**

You can learn more about understanding RBAC at *https://docs.microsoft.com/en-us/azure/role-based-access-control/overview*.

Configure RBAC within Azure AD

Azure RBAC (Role Based Access Control) allows you to configure fine-grained access control to Azure resources, such as virtual machines and storage accounts. When you configure RBAC, you assign a role and a scope, with the scope being the resource you want to have managed. Azure RBAC includes more than 70 roles. Providing the details of all 70 is beyond the scope of this text, but there are 4 fundamental roles that people who are responsible for managing Microsoft 365 should be aware of. These roles can be assigned to specific Azure subscriptions, resource groups, or resources:

- **Owner**   Users who hold this role have full access to all resources within the scope of the assignment and can delegate access to others.
- **Contributor**   Users who hold this role can create and manage resources within the scope of the assignment but cannot grant access to others.
- **Reader**   Users who hold this role can view resources within the scope of the assignment but can't perform other tasks and cannot grant access to others.
- **User Access Administrator**   Users who hold this role can manage user access to Azure resources within the scope of the assignment.

Delegate admin rights

To view which users are assigned a specific role, perform the following steps:

1. In the Azure AD admin center, select **Roles And Administrators**, as shown in Figure 1-86.

FIGURE 1-86 Roles And Administrators

2. To see the membership information of a role, click the role you want. Figure 1-87 shows members of the Password Administrators role.

FIGURE 1-87 Members of the Password Administrators role

You can use the following Azure PowerShell cmdlets to view roles and role membership:

- **Get-AzureADDirectoryRole**   View a list of Azure AD Directory roles
- **Get-AzureADDirectoryRoleMember**   View the users assigned membership in an Azure AD Directory role

Configure resource group permissions

Any permission assigned at the resource group level will apply to all resources stored within
that resource group. For example, if you assign the virtual machine administrator role at the
resource group level to a group of users, those users will have that role for all virtual machines
stored within the resource group. To assign permissions at the resource group level, assign
a specific role to a user, group, service principal, or managed identity. To assign a role at the
resource group level, perform the following steps:

1.   On the **Resource Groups** blade in the Azure portal, select the resource group for which
     you want to configure the permission, as shown in Figure 1-88.

FIGURE 1-88 Assigning roles at the resource group level

2.   On the **Resource Groups** blade, click **Access Control (IAM)**.
3.   On the **Access control (IAM)** page, choose **Add** > **Role Assignment**.
4.   On the **Add Role Assignment** page, which is shown in Figure 1-89, select the role that
     you want to assign, specify which user, group, service principal, or system managed iden-
     tity you want the role to apply to, and then specify the identity of that security principal.

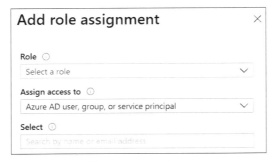

FIGURE 1-89 Add Role Assignment

Interpret role and resource permissions

There are a large number of preexisting roles available within Azure, and it is likely that an existing role will meet your needs, so you likely will not need to configure a custom role. First, you should specify exactly what actions a security principal should and should not be able to perform. Once you have generated this list, you should review the existing roles and determine if one of the existing roles meets your needs or if you need to create a custom role.

When configuring Azure RBAC, make sure that you follow the principal of least privilege. This means that you should only grant the access required to perform specific tasks. Doing so reduces the chance of unauthorized or accidental actions being performed. For example, if a group only requires the ability to view the configuration of an Azure resource, you only need to assign a role that has the Read permission to that resource. If a group only requires Azure portal access to one virtual machine in a resource group (even if the resource group hosts multiple virtual machines), set the scope of the role assignment to the virtual machine rather than the resource group when assigning the role to that group.

Interpret permissions

The key to understanding what can be done with permissions is that there are permissions related to management operations and permissions related to data operations. For management plane operations, the permissions determine actions that can be taken against objects in the Azure management plane, including the Azure portal, Azure CLI, Azure PowerShell, and Azure REST API. These are defined as `Actions` and `NotActions`. At the data operations level, there are actions that can be taken against data, such as data stored within a storage account. These are defined as `DataActions` and `NotData Actions`. To list the permissions within a role, use the `Get-AzRoleDefinition` PowerShell cmdlet. For example, to view the permissions associated with the Contributor role, run the following command:

```
Get-AzRoleDefinition "Contributor" | FL Actions, NotActions
```

Permissions are cumulative. If a user is granted `Actions` or `DataActions` across multiple roles and scopes, all permissions will apply. When multiple roles apply to a security principal, any `NotActions` or `NotData` actions that apply will override any `Actions` or `DataActions` that apply.

> **MORE INFO**   **MANAGEMENT AND DATA OPERATIONS**
>
> You can learn more about management and data operations at *https://docs.microsoft.com/ en-us/azure/role-based-access-control/role-definitions#management-and-data-operations*.

Check access

To view the access that a user has to a specific resource, perform the following steps:

1. In the Azure portal, select the specific resource for which you want to check access.

2. Select **Access control (IAM)** to open the Access Control (IAM) blade.

3. Click the **Check Access** tab.

4. In the **Check Access** section, use the **Find** drop-down menu to select the Azure AD user, group, or service principal option and type the name of the user whose access you want to check, as shown in Figure 1-90. Select the user.

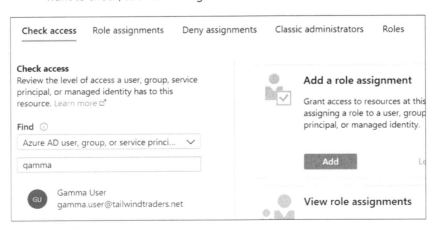

FIGURE 1-90 The Check Access tab

5. On the **Assignments** tab shown in Figure 1-91, review the user's role assignments and deny assignments to the resource.

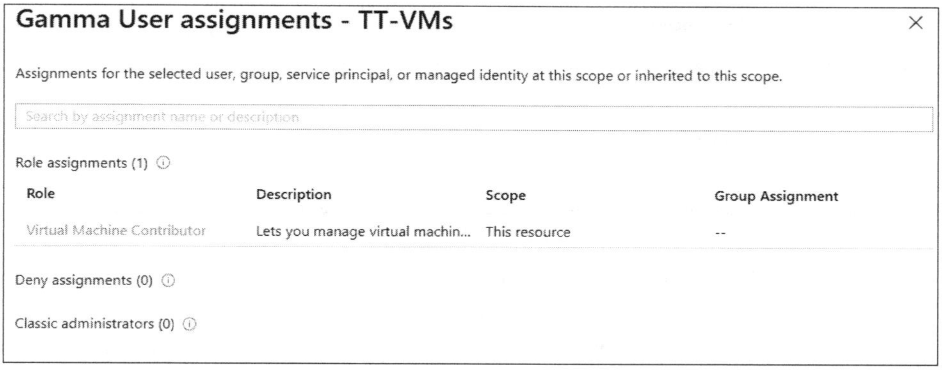

FIGURE 1-91 The Role assignments tab

> **MORE INFO**   **VIEW USER ACCESS TO RESOURCES**
>
> You can learn more about View user access to resources at *https://docs.microsoft.com/en-us/azure/role-based-access-control/check-access*.

Assign built-in Azure AD roles

Azure Active Directory includes many roles that provide a variety of permissions to different aspects of Azure AD and Microsoft 365 workloads. These roles and the permissions they grant are listed in Table 1-2:

TABLE 1-2 Azure AD Roles

Role	Description
Application Administrator	Can administer enterprise applications, application registrations, and application proxy settings.
Application Developer	Can create application registrations.
Authentication Administrator	Can view current authentication method settings. Can set or reset non-password credentials. Can force MFA on the next sign-in.
Billing Administrator	Can purchase and manage subscriptions. Can manage support tickets and monitor service health.
Cloud Application Administrator	Can manage all aspects of enterprise applications and registrations but cannot manage the application proxy.
Cloud Device Administrator	Can enable, disable, and remove devices in Azure AD. Can view Windows 10 BitLocker Drive Encryption Keys through the Azure portal.
Compliance Administrator	Manage features in the Microsoft 365 compliance center, Microsoft 365 admin center, Azure, and Microsoft 365 Security and Compliance Center.

Role	Description
Conditional Access Administrator	Administrative rights over Azure AD conditional access configuration.
Customer Lockbox access approver	Manages Customer Lockbox requests. Can also enable and disable the Customer Lockbox feature.
Device Administrators	Users assigned this role will become local administrators on all computers running Windows 10 that are joined to Azure AD.
Directory Readers	Role for applications that do not support the consent framework. Should not be assigned to users.
Directory Synchronization Accounts	Assigned to the Azure AD Connect service and not used for user accounts.
Directory Writers	A legacy role assigned to applications that do not support the consent framework. Should only be assigned to applications, not user accounts.
Dynamics 365 Administrator / CRM Administrator	Administrative access to Dynamics 365 Online.
Exchange Administrator	Administrative access to Exchange Online.
Global Administrator / Company Administrator	Administrative access to all Azure AD features. This includes administrative access to services that use Azure AD Identities, including Microsoft 365 security center, Microsoft 365 compliance center, Exchange Online, SharePoint Online, and Skype for Business Online. The account used to sign up for the tenancy becomes the global administrator. Global administrators can reset the passwords of any user, including other global administrators.
Guest Inviter	Can manage Azure AD B2B guest user invitations.
Information Protection Administrator	Can manage all aspects of Azure Information Protection, including configuring labels, managing protection templates, and activating protection.
Intune Administrator	Has full administrative rights to Microsoft Intune.
License Administrator	Can manage license assignments on users and groups. Cannot purchase or manage subscriptions.
Message Center Reader	Can monitor notification and Microsoft advisories in the Microsoft 365 Message Center.
Password Administrator / Helpdesk Administrator	Can perform the following tasks for all users except those who have administrative roles: ■ Change passwords ■ Invalidate refresh tokens ■ Manage service requests ■ Monitor service health
Power BI Administrator	Has administrator permissions over Power BI.

Role	Description
Privileged Role Administrator	Can manage all aspects of Azure AD Privileged Identity Management. Can manage role assignments in Azure AD.
Reports Reader	Can view reporting data in the Microsoft 365 reports dashboard.
Security Administrator	Has administrator-level access to manage security features in the Microsoft 365 security center, Azure AD Identity Protection, Azure Information Protection, and Microsoft 365 Security and Compliance Center.
Security Reader	Has read-only access to security Microsoft 365–related security features.
Service Support Administrator	Can open and view support requests with Microsoft for Microsoft 365–related services.
SharePoint Administrator	Has global administrator permissions for SharePoint Online workloads.
Skype for Business / Lync Administrator	Has global administrator permissions for Skype for Business workloads.
Teams Administrator	Can administer all elements of Microsoft Teams.
Teams Communications Administrator	Can manage Microsoft Teams workloads related to voice and telephony, including telephone number assignment and voice and meeting policies.
Teams Communications Support Engineer	Can troubleshoot communication issues within Teams and Skype for Business. Can view details of call records for all participants in a conversation.
Teams Communications Support Specialist	Can troubleshoot communication issues within Teams and Skype for Business. Can only view user details in the call for a specific user.
User Account Administrator	Can create and manage user accounts. Can create and manage groups. Can manage user views and support tickets and can monitor service health.

> **MORE INFO**   **AZURE AD ADMINISTRATOR ROLES**
>
> You can learn more about Azure AD Administrator roles at *https://docs.microsoft.com/en-us/azure/active-directory/users-groups-roles/directory-assign-admin-roles.*

To assign a user to a specific role within Azure AD, perform the following steps:

1. In the Azure AD admin center, select **Roles And Administrators**.
2. Select the role to which you want to add a user. This will open the role's properties page.
3. On the **Role Properties** page, click **Add Member**. Figure 1-92 shows adding the user Adele Vance to the Security Administrator role.

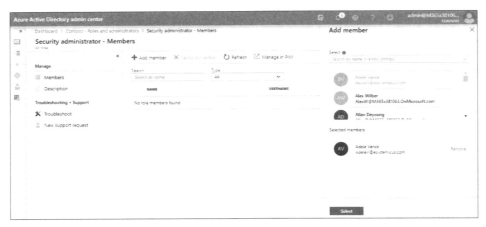

FIGURE 1-92 Members of the Security Administrators role

You can use the following Azure PowerShell cmdlets to manage role memberships:

- **Add-AzureADDirectoryRoleMember** Adds a user to an Azure AD Directory role
- **Remove-AzureADDirectoryRoleMember** Removes a user from an Azure AD Directory role

> **MORE INFO** **VIEW AND ASSIGN AZURE AD ADMINISTRATOR ROLES**
>
> You can learn more about viewing and assigning administrator roles at *https://docs.microsoft. com/en-us/azure/active-directory/users-groups-roles/directory-manage-roles-portal*.

Create and assign custom roles, including Azure roles and Azure AD roles

If one of the many existing RBAC roles doesn't meet your organization's requirements, you can create a custom RBAC role. For example, there are three RBAC roles related to virtual machines: Virtual Machine Administrator Login, Virtual Machine Contributor, and Virtual Machine Users Login. If you want to allow a user to restart a VM (but not log in to the VM or delete the VM), you could create a custom RBAC role that allows that specific permission. As with existing Azure RBAC roles, you can assign custom roles to users, groups, service principals, and managed identities at the management group, subscription, resource group, and individual resource levels.

You can create a custom role through the Azure portal, Azure PowerShell, Azure CLI, or Azure REST API, or you can create an ARM Template. In general, creating a custom role involves following these basic steps:

1. Determine which method you will use to create the custom role. Determine what permissions the role requires. You can learn what operations are available to define your permission by viewing the Azure Resource Manager resource provider operations. For management operations, these will be `Actions` or `NotActions`. For data operations, these will be `DataActions` or `NotDataActions`.

2. Create the role. You can do this by cloning an existing role and then making modifications or by creating a new role from scratch. The most straightforward method of doing this is through the Azure portal.

3. Test the custom role. Make sure that you test the role thoroughly to determine that it only allows what you want it to allow and doesn't have some unexpected permissions, such as allowing Wally the VM operator to type something in Cloud Shell that locks out every other user in the Azure AD tenancy.

When creating a custom RBAC role, remember to only add the fewest necessary privileges to the role. When you create a custom role, it will appear in the Azure portal with an orange—rather than blue—resource icon. Custom RBAC roles are available between subscriptions that are associated with the same Azure AD tenancy. Each Azure AD tenancy supports up to 5,000 custom roles.

To clone and then modify a role in the Azure portal, perform the following steps:

1. In the Azure portal, open the **Access Control (IAM)** blade at the subscription level or resource group level where you want the custom role to be assignable.

2. Select the **Roles** tab to see the list of all available built-in and custom roles.

3. Select the role that you want to clone and modify. Figure 1-93 shows the **Virtual Machine Contributor** role being selected for cloning.

FIGURE 1-93 Select a role to clone

4. On the **Basics** tab of the **Create A Custom Role** page shown in Figure 1-94, provide a **Custom Role Name**.

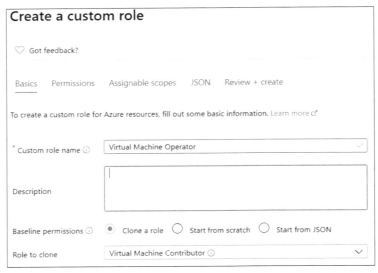

FIGURE 1-94 Create A Custom Role wizard with the Basics tab selected

5. On the **Permissions** tab shown in Figure 1-95, you can delete existing permissions or add new permissions.

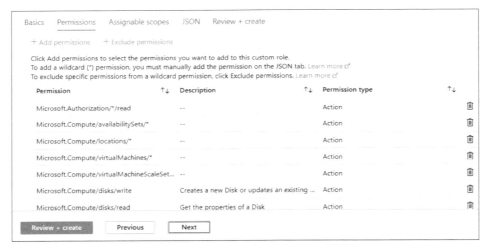

FIGURE 1-95 Create A Custom Role wizard with the Permissions tab selected

6. On the **Assignable Scopes** tab, you can specify where the role can be assigned. You can select subscriptions associated with the Azure AD tenancy, as well as resource groups that are contained within those subscriptions.

7. On the **JSON** tab, you can view the custom role formatted in JSON. This tab gives you the opportunity to edit the role in JSON. If you want to add a wildcard permission, you do so on this tab because this is not possible at other points during the creation of a custom role.

8. Once you have reviewed the JSON code, click **Review And Create** to create the custom role.

MORE INFO **AZURE CUSTOM ROLES**

You can learn more about Azure custom roles at *https://docs.microsoft.com/en-us/azure/role-based-access-control/custom-roles*.

EXAM TIP

Remember to always apply the principal of least privilege when attempting to determine which role to assign to a user who needs access to a resource.

Thought experiment

In this thought experiment, demonstrate your skills and knowledge of the topics covered in this chapter. You can find answers to this thought experiment in the next section.

Identity and access at Tailwind Traders

You are one of the Azure administrators for Tailwind Traders, an online general store that specializes in a variety of products used around the home. As a part of your duties for Tailwind Traders, you have registered a new application with your Azure AD instance. Even though the application is registered, you want to limit what actions the application can perform against resources in the Tailwind Traders Azure Subscription by applying a custom RBAC role. Tailwind Traders has been using PIM for some time as a method of improving security to resources within subscriptions owned by the organization. Because the access was configured some time ago, you are aware that several users who were configured as eligible for PIM roles have changed job roles. To improve security, you want to remove PIM eligibility if it is no longer required. Another goal of Tailwind Traders is to allow some users of the new application to access the application from outside the workplace. However, from a security perspective, anyone accessing the application from outside the Tailwind Traders internal network should take extra steps to verify their identity. With this information in mind, answer the following questions:

- How can you assign the custom RBAC role to the new application?
- How can you determine which staff to remove from eligibility for PIM roles?
- How can you ensure that all users perform MFA if they are accessing the new application from a location outside the Tailwind Traders office?

Thought experiment answers

This section contains the solution to the thought experiment. Each answer explains why the answer choice is correct.

1. You can assign roles to the new application by assigning roles to the service principal created when the application was registered. By assigning the custom RBAC role to the service principal, you assign that role to the application.

2. You should configure an access review to determine which users that have been configured as eligible for PIM roles aren't actually using those roles.

3. You can configure a conditional access policy to force users to perform MFA when they are in an untrusted location, such as any network location outside the trusted networks identified as belonging to Tailwind Traders.

Chapter summary

- Security principals are created automatically when you register an application with Azure AD.
- You can assign RBAC roles to security principals as a way of assigning permissions to applications.
- Azure AD groups allow you to collect Azure security principals, including users, service principals, and other groups.
- Azure AD users represent individuals within Azure AD. They can be cloud only accounts, or they can be replicated from an on-premises Active Directory Domain Services environment.
- Password writeback allows passwords changed within Azure AD to be written back to an Active Directory Domain Services environment.
- Privileged Identity Management allows just-in-time administration and just-in-time access to Azure resources.
- Conditional Access Policies allow you to implement more stringent authentication requirements if certain conditions are met.
- Application registration permission scopes allow you to control what resources and data an application can access.
- Custom RBAC roles can be configured if an existing RBAC role does not have permissions that are appropriate to your organization's needs.

CHAPTER 2

Implement platform protection

One of the main aspects of cloud computing is the shared responsibility model, where the cloud solution provider (CSP) and the customer share different levels of responsibilities, depending on the cloud service category. When it comes to platform security, Infrastructure as a Service (IaaS), customers will have a long list of responsibilities. However, in a Platform as a Service (PaaS) scenario, there are still some platform security responsibilities; they are not as extensive as when using IaaS workloads.

Azure has native platform security capabilities and services that should be leveraged to provide the necessary level of security for your IaaS and PaaS workloads while maintaining a secure management layer.

Skills in this chapter:

- Skill 2.1: Implement advanced network security
- Skill 2.2: Configure advanced security for compute

Skill 2.1: Implement advanced network security

To implement an Azure network infrastructure, you need to understand the different connectivity options available in Azure. These options will enable you to implement a variety of scenarios with different requirements. This section of the chapter covers the skills necessary to implement advanced network security.

Overview of Azure network components

Azure networking provides built-in capabilities to enable connectivity between Azure resources, connectivity from on-premises networks to Azure resources, and branch office to branch office connectivity in Azure.

While those skills are not directly called out in the AZ-500 exam outline, it is important for you to understand these concepts. If you're already comfortable with your skill level, you can skip to "Secure the connectivity of virtual networks," later in this chapter.

To better understand the different components of an Azure network, let's review Contoso's architecture diagram shown in Figure 2-1.

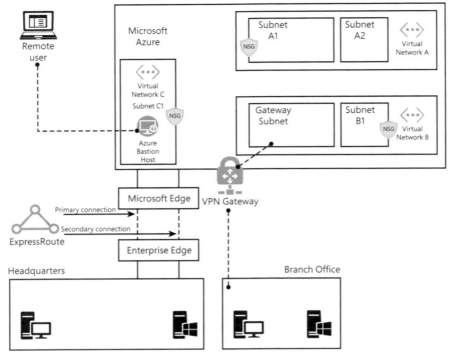

FIGURE 2-1 Contoso network diagram

In Figure 2-1, you can see Azure infrastructure (on top), with three virtual networks. Contoso needs to segment its Azure network in different virtual networks (VNets) to provide better isolation and security. Having VNets in its Azure infrastructure allows Contoso to connect Azure Virtual Machines (VMs) to securely communicate with each other, the Internet, and Contoso's on-premises networks.

A VNet is much like a traditional physical, on-premises network where you operate in your own data center. However, a VNet offers some additional benefits, including scalability, availability, and isolation. When you create a VNet, you must specify a custom private IP address that will be used by the resources that belong to this VNet. For example, if you deploy a VM in a VNet with an address space of 10.0.0.0/24, the VM will be assigned a private IP, such as 10.0.0.10/24.

> **IMPORTANT** **MULTIPLE VNETS AND VIRTUAL NETWORK PEERING**
>
> An Azure VNet is scoped to a single region/location. If you need to connect multiple virtual networks from different regions, you can use Virtual Network Peering.

Notice in Figure 2-1 that there are subnets in each VNet in Contoso's network. Contoso needs to segment the virtual network into one or more subnetworks and allocate a portion of the virtual network's address space to each subnet. With this setup, Contoso can deploy

Azure resources in a specific subnet, just like it used to do in its on-premises network. From an organizational and structure perspective, subnets have allowed Contoso to segment its VNet address space into smaller segments that are appropriate for its internal network. By using subnets, Contoso also was able to improve address allocation efficiency.

Another important trio of components is shown in Figure 2-1: subnets A1, B1, and C1. Each of these subnets has a network security group (NSG) bound to it, which provides an extra layer of security based on rules that allow or deny inbound or outbound network traffic.

NSG security rules are evaluated by their priority, and each is identified with a number between 100 and 4096, where the lowest numbers are processed first. The security rules use 5-tuple information (source address, source port, destination address, destination port, and protocol) to allow or deny the traffic. When the traffic is evaluated, a flow record is created for existing connections, and the communication is allowed or denied based on the connection state of the flow record. You can compare this type of configuration to the old VLAN segmentation that was often implemented with on-premises networks.

> **IMPORTANT TRAFFIC INTERRUPTIONS MIGHT NOT BE INTERRUPTED**
>
> Existing connections might not be interrupted when you remove a security rule that enabled the flow. An interruption of traffic occurs when connections are stopped, and no traffic is flowing in either direction for at least a few minutes.

Contoso is headquartered in Dallas, and it has a branch office in Sydney. Contoso needs to provide secure and seamless RDP/SSH connectivity to its virtual machines directly from the Azure portal over TLS. Contoso doesn't want to use jumpbox VMs and instead wants to allow remote access to back-end subnets through the browser. For this reason, Contoso implemented Azure Bastion, as you can see in the VNet C, subnet C1 in Figure 2-1.

Azure Bastion is a platform-managed PaaS service that can be provisioned in a VNet.

For Contoso's connectivity with Sydney's branch office, it is using a VPN gateway in Azure. A virtual network gateway in Azure is composed of two or more VMs that are deployed to a specific subnet called a gateway subnet. The VMs that are part of the virtual network gateway contain routing tables and run specific gateway services. These VMs are automatically created when you create the virtual network gateway, and you don't have direct access to those VMs to make custom configurations to the operating system.

When planning your VNets, consider that each VNet may only have one virtual network gateway of each type, and the gateway type may only be VPN or ExpressRoute. Use VPN when you need to send encrypted traffic across the public Internet to your on-premises resources.

> **EXAM TIP IP ADDRESS CONFIGURATION**
>
> When taking the exam, pay extra attention to scenarios that include IP addresses for different subnets and potential connectivity issues because of incorrect IP configuration.

For example, let's say that Contoso needs a faster, more reliable, secure, and consistent latency to connect its Azure network to its headquarters in Dallas. Contoso decides to use ExpressRoute, as shown in Figure 2-1. ExpressRoute allows Contoso to extend its on-premises networks into the Microsoft cloud (Azure or Office 365) over a private connection because ExpressRoute does not go over the public Internet.

In Figure 2-1, notice that the ExpressRoute circuit consists of two connections, both of which are Microsoft Enterprise Edge Routers (MSEEs) at an ExpressRoute Location from the connectivity provider or your network edge. While you might choose not to deploy redundant devices or Ethernet circuits at your end, the connectivity providers use redundant devices to ensure that your connections are handed off to Microsoft in a redundant manner. This Layer 3 connectivity redundancy is a requirement for Microsoft SLA to be valid.

Network segmentation is important in many scenarios, and you need to understand the design requirements to suggest the implementation options. Let's say you want to ensure that Internet hosts cannot communicate with hosts on a back-end subnet but can communicate with hosts on the front-end subnet. In this case, you should create two VNets: one for your front-end resources and another for your back-end resources.

When configuring your virtual network, also take into consideration that the resources you deploy within the virtual network will inherit the capability to communicate with each other. You can also enable virtual networks to connect to each other, or you can enable resources in either virtual network to communicate with each other by using virtual network peering. When connecting virtual networks, you can choose to access other VNets that are in the same or different Azure regions. Follow the steps below to configure your virtual network using the Azure portal:

1. Navigate to the Azure portal at *https://portal.azure.com*.

2. In the search bar, type **virtual networks**, and under **Services**, click **Virtual Networks**. The **Virtual Networks** page appears, as shown in Figure 2-2.

FIGURE 2-2 Azure Virtual Networks page

3. Click the **Add** button, and the **Create Virtual Network** page appears, as shown in Figure 2-3.

4. On the **Basics** tab, select the **Subscription** for the VNet and the **Resource Group**.

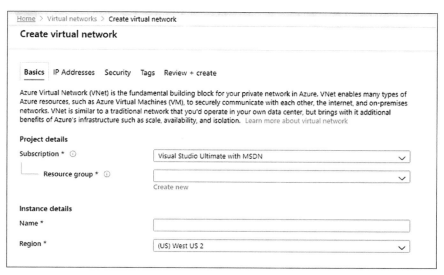

FIGURE 2-3 The Create Virtual Network page allows you to customize your VNet deployment

5. In the **Name** field, type a comprehensive name for the VNet, and in the **Region** field, select the Azure region in which the VNet is going to reside. Finally, click the **IP Addresses** tab.

6. On the **IP Addresses** page, in the **IPv4** field, type the address space in classless inter-domain routing (CIRD) format; for example, you could enter **10.3.0.0/16**.

7. Click the **Add Subnet** button. The **Add Subnet** blade appears, as shown in Figure 2-4.

FIGURE 2-4 Add Subnet blade

8. In the **Subnet Name** field, type a name for this subnet.

9. In the **Subnet Address Range**, type the IP range for this subnet in CIDR format, such as **10.3.0.0/16**. Keep in mind that the smallest supported IPv4 subnet is /29, and the largest is /8.

10. Click the **Add** button; the subnet that you just created appears under the **Subnet Name** section.

11. Leave the default selections for now and click the **Review + Create** button. The validation result appears, which is similar to the one shown in Figure 2-5.

FIGURE 2-5 Summary of the selections with the validation results

12. Click the **Create** button.

13. The **Overview** page appears with the deployment final status. On this page, click the **Go To Resource** button and review these options on the left navigation pane: **Overview**, **Address Space**, and **Subnets**.

Notice that the parameters you configured during the creation of your VNet will be distributed among the different options on the VNet page. As you saw in the previous steps, creating a VNet using the Azure portal is a straightforward process, though in some circumstances, you might need to automate the creation process, and you can use PowerShell to do just that.

When you are creating your virtual network, you can use any IP range that is part of RFC 1918, which includes

- 224.0.0.0/4 (multicast)
- 255.255.255.255/32 (broadcast)
- 127.0.0.0/8 (loopback)
- 169.254.0.0/16 (link-local)
- 168.63.129.16/32 (internal DNS)

Also, consider the following points:

- Azure reserves x.x.x.0 as a network address and x.x.x.1 as a default gateway.
- x.x.x.2 and x.x.x.3 are mapped to the Azure DNS IPs to the VNet space.
- x.x.x.255 is reserved for a network broadcast address.

To automate that, you can either use PowerShell on your client workstation (using Connect-AzAccount to connect to your Azure subscription) or by using Cloud Shell directly from *https://shell.azure.com*. To create a virtual network using PowerShell, you need to use the New-AzVirtualNetwork cmdlet, as shown here:

```
$AZ500Subnet = New-AzVirtualNetworkSubnetConfig -Name AZ500Subnet -AddressPrefix
"10.3.0.0/24"
New-AzVirtualNetwork -Name AZ500VirtualNetwork -ResourceGroupName ContosoCST -Location
centralus -AddressPrefix "10.3.0.0/16" -Subnet $AZ500Subnet
```

In this example, you have the *$AZ500Subnet* variable, which configures a new subnet for this VNet using the New-AzVirtualNetworkSubnetConfig cmdlet. Next, the New-AzVirtualNetwork cmdlet is used to create the new VNet, and it calls the $AZ500Subnet variable at the end of the command line to create the subnet.

After creating your VNet, you can start connecting resources to it. In an IaaS scenario, it is very common to connect your virtual machines (VMs) to the VNet. Assuming you have Virtual Machine Contributor privileges in the subscription, you can quickly deploy a new VM using the New-AzVM PowerShell cmdlet, as shown here:

```
New-AzVm '
    -ResourceGroupName "ContosoCST" '
    -Location "East US" '
    -VirtualNetworkName "AZ500VirtualNetwork" '
    -SubnetName "AZ500Subnet" '
    -Name "AZ500VM" '
```

Routing

In a physical network environment, you usually need to start configuring routes as soon as you expand your network to have multiple subnets. In Azure, the routing table is automatically created for each subnet within an Azure VNet. The default routes created by Azure and assigned to each subnet in a virtual network can't be removed. The default route that is created contains an address prefix and the next hop (where the package should go). When traffic leaves the subnet, it goes to an IP address within the address prefix of a route; the route that contains the prefix is the route used by Azure.

When you create a VNet, Azure creates a route with an address prefix that corresponds to each address range that you defined within the address space of your VNet. If the VNet has multiple address ranges defined, Azure creates an individual route for each address range. You don't need to worry about creating routes between subnets within the same VNet because Azure automatically routes traffic between subnets using the routes created for each address range. Also, differently from your physical network topology and routing mechanism, you don't need to define gateways for Azure to route traffic between subnets. In an Azure routing table, this route appears as:

- **Source** Default
- **Address prefix** Unique to the virtual network
- **Next hop type** Virtual network

If the destination of the traffic is the Internet, Azure leverages the system-default route `0.0.0.0/0` address prefix, which routes traffic for any address not specified by an address range within a virtual network to the Internet. The only exception to this rule is if the destination address is for one of Azure's services. In this case, instead of routing the traffic to the Internet, Azure routes the traffic directly to the service over Azure's backbone network. The other scenarios in which Azure will add routes are as follows:

- **When you create a VNet peering** In this case, a route is added for each address range within the address space of each virtual network peering that you created.
- **When you add a Virtual Network Gateway** In this case, one or more routes with a virtual network gateway listed as the next hop type are added.
- **When a VirtualNetworkServiceEndpoint is added** When you enable a service endpoint to publish an Azure service to the Internet, the public IP addresses of the services are added to the route table by Azure.

You might also see None in the routing table's **Next Hop Type** column. Traffic routed to this hop is automatically dropped. Azure automatically creates default routes for `10.0.0.0/8`, `192.168.0.0/16` (RFC 1918), and `100.64.0.0/10` (RFC 6598).

EXAM TIP

The exam might include scenarios that involve routing-related problems. Make sure to pay close attention to the details about the routing configuration and whether any routing configurations are missing.

At this point, you might ask: "If all these routes are created automatically, in which scenario should I create a custom route?" You should do this only when you need to alter the default routing behavior. For example, if you add an Azure Firewall or any other virtual appliance, you can change the default route (`0.0.0.0/0`) to point to this virtual appliance. This will enable the appliance to inspect the traffic and determine whether to forward or drop the traffic. Another example is when you want to ensure that traffic from hosts doesn't go to the Internet; you can control the routing rules to accomplish that.

To create a custom route that is effective for your needs, you need to create a custom routing table, create a custom route, and associate the routing table to a subnet, as shown in the PowerShell sequence that follows.

1. Create the routing table using New-AzRouteTable cmdlet, as shown here:

```
$routeTableAZ500 = New-AzRouteTable '
  -Name 'AZ500RouteTable' '
  -ResourceGroupName ContosoCST '
  -location EastUS
```

2. Create the custom route using multiple cmdlets. First, you retrieve the route table information using Get-AzRouteTable, and then you create the route using Add-AzRouteConfig. Lastly, you use the Set-AzRouteTable to write the routing configuration to the route table:

```
Get-AzRouteTable '
  -ResourceGroupName "ContosoCST" '
  -Name "AZ500RouteTable" '
  | Add-AzRouteConfig '
  -Name "ToAZ500Subnet" '
  -AddressPrefix 10.0.1.0/24 '
  -NextHopType "MyVirtualAppliance" '
  -NextHopIpAddress 10.0.2.4 '
  | Set-AzRouteTable
```

3. Now that you have the routing table and the custom route, you can associate the route table with the subnet. Notice here that you first write the subnet configuration to the VNet using the Set-AzVirtualNetwork cmd. After that, you use Set-AzVirtualNetworkSubnetConfig to associate the route table to the subnet:

```
$virtualNetwork | Set-AzVirtualNetwork
Set-AzVirtualNetworkSubnetConfig '
  -VirtualNetwork $virtualNetwork '
  -Name 'CustomAZ500Subnet' '
  -AddressPrefix 10.0.0.0/24 '
  -RouteTable $routeTableAZ500 | '
Set-AzVirtualNetwork
```

Virtual network peering

When you have multiple VNets in your Azure infrastructure, you can connect those VNets using VNet peering. You can use VNet peering to connect VNets within the same Azure region or across Azure regions; doing so is called global VNet peering.

When the VNets are in the same region, the network latency between VMs that are communicating through the VNet peering is the same as the latency within a single virtual network. It's also important to mention that the traffic between VMs in peered virtual networks is not through a gateway or over the public Internet; instead, that traffic is routed directly through the Microsoft backbone infrastructure. To create a VNet peering using the Azure portal, follow these steps:

1. Navigate to the Azure portal at *https://portal.azure.com*.
2. In the search bar, type **virtual networks**, and under **Services**, click **Virtual Networks**.
3. Click the VNet that you want to peer, and on the left navigation pane, click **Peerings** (see Figure 2-6).

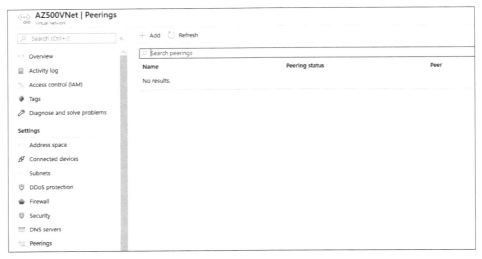

FIGURE 2-6 Configuring VNet peering

4. Click the **Add** button, and the **Add Peering** page appears, as shown in Figure 2-7.
5. In the **Name** field, type a name for this peering.
6. In the **Subscription** field, select the subscription that has the VNet to which you want to connect.
7. In the **Virtual Network** field, click the drop-down menu and select the VNet that you want to peer.
8. In the **Name Of The Peering From Remote Virtual Network** field, type the name that you want to appear for this peering connection on the other VNet.
9. The next two options—**Allow Virtual Network Access From [VNet name] To Remote Virtual Network** and **Allow Virtual Network Access From Remote Virtual To [VNet name]**—are used to control the communication between those VNets. If you want full connectivity from both directions, make sure to leave the **Enabled** option selected (default selection) for both. Enabling communication between virtual networks allows resources connected to either virtual network to communicate with each other with the same bandwidth and latency as if they were connected to the same virtual network.

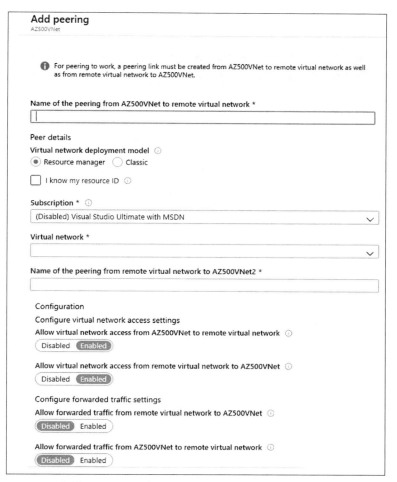

FIGURE 2-7 Adding a new peering

10. The next two options—**Allow Forwarded Traffic From Remote Virtual Network To [VNet name]** and **Allow Forwarded Traffic From [VNet name] To Remote Virtual Network**—are related to allowing forwarded traffic. You should select **Enable** for both settings only when you need to allow traffic that didn't originate from the VNet to be forwarded by a virtual network appliance through a peering. For example, consider three virtual networks named VNetTX, VNetWA, and MainHub. A peering exists between each spoke VNet (VNetTX and VNetWA) and the Hub virtual network, but peerings don't exist between the spoke VNets. A network virtual appliance is deployed in the Hub VNet, and user-defined routes can be applied to each spoke VNet to route the traffic between the subnets through the network virtual appliance. If this option is disabled, there will be no traffic flow between the two spokes through the hub.

11. Click **OK** to finish the configuration.

To configure a VNet peering using PowerShell, you just need to use the `Add-AzVirtual`
`NetworkPeering` cmdlet, as shown here:

```
Add-AzVirtualNetworkPeering -Name 'NameOfTheVNetPeering' -VirtualNetwork SourceVNet
-RemoteVirtualNetworkId RemoteVNet
```

A peered VNet can have its own gateway, and the VNet can use its gateway to connect to an
on-premises network. One common use of VNet peering is when you are building a hub-spoke
network. In this type of topology, the hub is a VNet that acts as a central hub for connectivity
to your on-premises network. The spokes are VNets that are peering with the hub, allowing
them to be isolated, which increases their security boundaries. An example of this topology is
shown in Figure 2-8.

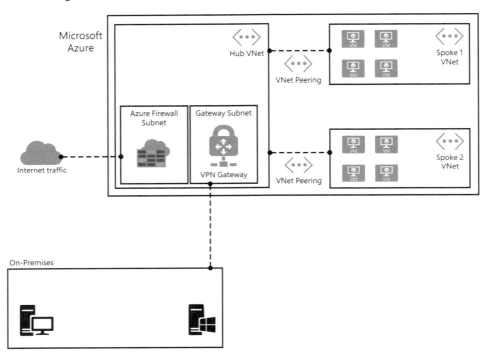

FIGURE 2-8 Hub-spoke network topology using VNet peering

A hybrid network uses the hub-spoke architecture model to route traffic between Azure
VNets and on-premises networks. When there is a site-to-site connection between the Azure
VNet and the on-premises data center, you must define a gateway subnet in the Azure VNet.
All the traffic from the on-premises data center would then flow via the gateway subnet.

Network address translation

Azure has a Virtual Network NAT (network address translation) capability that enables
outbound-only Internet connectivity for virtual networks. This is a common scenario when you

want that outbound connectivity to use a specified static public IP address (static NAT), or you want to use a pool of public IP addresses (Dynamic NAT).

Keep in mind that outbound connectivity is possible without the use of an Azure load balancer or a public IP address directly attached to the VM. Figure 2-9 shows an example of the topology with a NAT Gateway.

You can implement NAT by using a public IP prefix directly, or you can distribute the public IP addresses of the prefix across multiple NAT gateway resources. NAT also changes the network route because it takes precedence over other outbound scenarios, and it will replace the default Internet destination of a subnet. From an availability standpoint (which is critical for security), NAT always has multiple fault domains, which means it can sustain multiple failures without service outage.

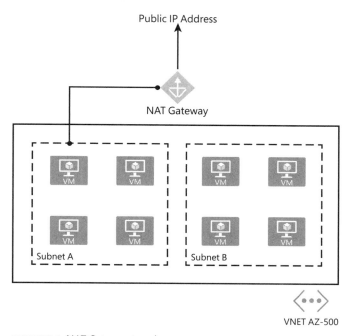

FIGURE 2-9 NAT Gateway topology

IMPORTANT NAT GATEWAY BILLING

A NAT gateway is billed with two separate meters: resource hours and data processed. Consult the Azure NAT pricing page for the latest pricing.

To create a NAT Gateway for your subnet, you first need to create a public IP address and a public IP prefix. Follow the steps below to perform these tasks:

1. Navigate to the Azure portal at *https://portal.azure.com*.

2. In the main dashboard, click the **Create A Resource** button.

3. On the **New** page, type **Public IP** and click the **Public IP Address** option that appears in the list.

4. On the **Public IP Address** page, click the **Create** button; the **Create Public IP Address** page appears, as shown in Figure 2-10.

FIGURE 2-10 Creating a public IP address to be used by NAT Gateway

5. Type the name for this public IP address and select the subscription, resource group, and the Azure location. For this example, you can leave all other options with their default selections. Once you finish, click the **Create** button.

6. Now you should repeat steps 1 and 2. In the third step, type **public IP prefix** and click the **Public IP Prefix** option that appears in the drop-down menu.

7. On the **Create A Public IP Prefix** page, configure the following relevant options:

   ■ Select the appropriate **Subscription**.

   ■ Select the appropriate **Resource Group**.

   ■ Type the **Prefix Name**.

   ■ Select the appropriate **Azure Region**.

   ■ In the **Prefix Size** drop-down menu, select the appropriate size for your deployment.

8. Once you finish configuring these options, click the **Review + Create** button and click **Create** to finish.

9. Now that you have the two requirements fulfilled, you can create the NAT Gateway.

10. Navigate to the Azure portal at *https://portal.azure.com*.

11. In the main dashboard, click the **Create A Resource** button.

12. On the New page, type **NAT Gateway** and click the **NAT Gateway** option in the list.

13. On the **NAT Gateway** page, click **Create**. The **Create Network Address Translation (NAT) Gateway** page appears, as shown in Figure 2-11.

14. On the **Basics** tab, make sure to configure the following options:

    ■ Select the appropriate **Subscription** and **Resource Group**.

    ■ Type the **NAT Gateway Name**.

    ■ Select the appropriate **Azure Region** and **Availability Zone**.

15. Move to the next tab, **Outbound IP**, and select the Public IP Address and Prefix Name that you created previously.

16. Next, on the **Subnet** tab, you will configure which subnets of a VNet should use this NAT gateway.

17. The **Tags** tab is optional, and you should use it only when you need to logically organize your resources in a particular taxonomy to easily identify them later.

18. You can review a summary of the selections in the **Review + Create** tab. Once you finish reviewing it, click the **Create** button.

You can also use the New-AzNatGateway cmdlet to create a NAT Gateway using PowerShell, as shown:

```
New-AzNatGateway -ResourceGroupName "AZ500RG" -Name "nat_gt" -IdleTimeoutInMinutes
4 -Sku "Standard" -Location "eastus2" -PublicIpAddress PublicIPAddressName
```

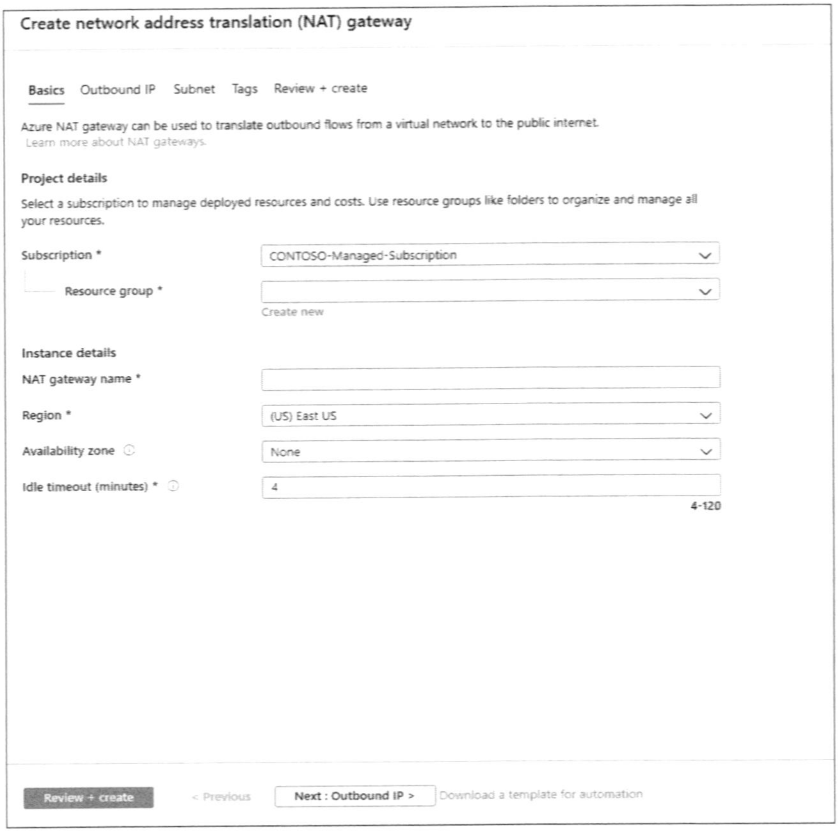

FIGURE 2-11 Creating a NAT Gateway in Azure

Secure the connectivity of hybrid networks

With organizations migrating to the cloud, virtual private networks (VPNs) are constantly used to establish a secure communication link between on-premises and cloud network infrastructure. Many organizations will also keep part of their resources on-premises while taking advantage of cloud computing to host different services, which creates a hybrid environment. While this is one common scenario, there are many other scenarios where a VPN can be used. You can use Azure VPN to connect two different Azure regions or subscriptions.

Azure natively offers a service called VPN gateway, which is a specific type of virtual network gateway that is used to send encrypted traffic between an Azure virtual network and on-premises resources. You can also use a VPN gateway to send encrypted traffic between Azure virtual networks. When planning your VPN Gateway implementation, be aware that each virtual network can have only one VPN gateway, and you can create multiple connections to the same VPN gateway. When deploying a hybrid network that needs to create a cross-premises connection, you can select from different types of VPN connectivity. The available options are:

- **Point-to-Site (P2S) VPN** This type of VPN is used in scenarios where you need to connect to your Azure VNet from a remote location. For example, you would use P2S when you are working remotely (hotel, home, conference, and the like), and you need to access resources in your VNet. This VPN uses SSTP (Secure Socket Tunneling Protocol) or IKE v2 and does not require a VPN device.

- **Site-to-Site (S2S) VPN** This type of VPN is used in scenarios where you need to connect on-premises resources to Azure. The encrypted connection tunnel uses IPsec/IKE (IKEv1 or IKEv2).

- **VNet-to-VNet** As the name states, this VPN is used in scenarios where you need to encrypt connectivity between VNets. This type of connection uses IPsec (IKE v1 and IKE v2).

- **Multi-Site VPN** This type of VPN is used in scenarios where you need to expand your site-to-site configuration to allow multiple on-premises sites to access a virtual network.

ExpressRoute is another option that allows connectivity from your on-premises resources to Azure. This option uses a private connection to Azure from your WAN, instead of a VPN connection over the Internet.

VPN authentication

The Azure VPN connection is authenticated when the tunnel is created. Azure generates a pre-shared key (PSK), which is used for authentication. This pre-shared key is an ASCII string character no longer than 128 characters. This authentication happens for policy-based (static routing) or routing-based VPN (dynamic routing). You can view and update the pre-shared key for a connection with these PowerShell cmdlets:

- **Get-AzVirtualNetworkGatewayConnectionSharedKey** This command is used to show the pre-shared key.

- **Set-AzVirtualNetworkGatewayConnectionSharedKey** This command is used to change the pre-shared key to another value.

For point-to-site (P2S) VPN scenarios, you can use native Azure certificate authentication, RADIUS server, or Azure AD authentication. For native Azure certificate authentication, a client certificate is presented on the device, which is used to authenticate the users who are connecting. The certificate can be one that was issued by an enterprise certificate authority (CA), or it can be a self-signed root certificate. For native Azure AD, you can use the native Azure AD credentials. Keep in mind that native Azure AD is only supported for the OpenVPN protocol and Windows 10 (Windows 10 requires the use of the Azure VPN Client).

If your scenario requires the enforcement of a second factor of authentication before access to the resource is granted, you can use Azure Multi-Factor Authentication (MFA) with conditional access. Even if you don't want to implement MFA across your entire company, you can scope the MFA to be employed only for VPN users using conditional access capability.

MORE INFO   **CONFIGURING MFA FOR VPN ACCESS**

You can see the steps for configuring MFA for VPN access at *http://aka.ms/az500mfa.*

Another option available for P2S is the authentication using RADIUS (which also supports IKEv2 and SSTP VPN). Keep in mind that RADIUS is only supported for VpnGw1, VpnGw2, and VpnGw3 SKUs. For more information about the latest VPN SKUs, visit *http://aka.ms/az500vpnsku.* Figure 2-12 shows an example of the options that appear when you are configuring a P2S VPN, and you need to select the authentication type.

FIGURE 2-12 Authentication options for VPN

The options that appear right under the **Authentication Type** section will vary according to the Authentication Type you select. In Figure 2-12, **Azure Certificate** is chosen, and the page shows options to enter the **Name** and **Public Certification Data** for the **Root Certificates** and the **Name** and **Thumbprint** for the **Revoked Certificates**. If you select **RADIUS authentication**, you will need to specify the **Server IP Address** and the **Server Secret**. Lastly, if you select the **Azure Active Directory** option, you will need to specify the **Tenant's URL**; the **Audience** (which identifies the recipient resource the token is intended for); and the **Issuer** (which identifies the Security Token Service (STS) that issued the token). Lastly, choose the Azure AD tenant.

Your particular scenario will dictate which option to use. For example, Contoso's IT department needs to implement a VPN solution that can integrate with a certificate authentication infrastructure that it already has through RADIUS. In this case, you should use RADIUS certificate authentication. When using the RADIUS certificate authentication, the authentication request is forwarded to a RADIUS server, which handles the certificate validation. If the scenario requires that the Azure VPN gateway perform the certificate authentication, the right option would be to use the Azure native certificate authentication.

ExpressRoute encryption

If your connectivity scenario requires a higher level of reliability, faster speeds, consistent latencies, and higher security than typical connections over the Internet, you should use ExpressRoute, which provides layer 3 connectivity between your on-premises network and the Microsoft Cloud.

ExpressRoute supports two different encryption technologies to ensure the confidentiality and integrity of the data that is traversing from on-premises to Microsoft's network. The options are

- Point-to-point encryption by MACsec
- End-to-end encryption by IPsec

MACsec encrypts the data at the media access control (MAC) level or at network layer 2. When you enable MACsec, all network control traffic is encrypted, which includes the border gateway protocol (BGP) data traffic and your (customer) data traffic. This means that you can't encrypt only some of your ExpressRoute circuits.

If you need to encrypt the physical links between your network devices and Microsoft's network devices when you connect to Microsoft via ExpressRoute Direct, MACsec is preferred. MACsec also allows you to bring your own MACsec key for encryption and store it in Azure Key Vault. If this is the design choice, remember that you will need to decide when to rotate the key.

> **TIP EXPRESSROUTE DIRECT**
>
> Although MACsec is only available on ExpressRoute Direct, it comes disabled by default on ExpressRoute Direct ports.

Keep in mind that when you update the MACsec key, the on-premises resources will temporally lose connectivity to Microsoft over ExpressRoute. This happens because MACsec configuration only supports pre-shared key mode, so you must update the key on both sides. In other words, if there is a mismatch, traffic flow won't occur. Plan the correct maintenance window to reduce the impact on production environments.

The other option is to use end-to-end encryption with IPsec, which encrypts data at the Internet protocol (IP)–level or at the network layer 3. A very common scenario is to use IPsec to encrypt the end-to-end connection between on-premises resources and your Azure VNet. In a scenario where you need to encrypt layers 2 and 3, you can enable MACsec and IPsec.

> **MORE INFO CREATE IPSEC OVER EXPRESSROUTE**
>
> You can learn how to create IPsec over ExpressRoute for Virtual WAN at
> *http://aka.ms/az500vpnexpressroute.*

Point-to-site

To implement a point-to-site (P2S) VPN in Azure, you first need to decide what authentication method you will use based on the options that were presented earlier in this section. The authentication method will dictate how the P2S VPN will be configured. When configuring the P2S VPN, you will see the options available under **Tunnel Type**, as shown in Figure 2-13.

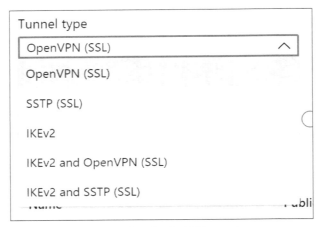

FIGURE 2-13 Different options for the VPN tunnel

- Another important variable to select is the protocol that will be used. Use Table 2-1 to select the most-appropriate protocol based on the advantages and limitations:

TABLE 2-1 Advantages and limitations

Protocol	Advantages	Limitations
OpenVPN Protocol	This is a TLS VPN-based solution that can traverse most firewalls on the market. Can be used to connect from a variety of operating systems, including Android, iOS (versions 11.0 and above), Windows, Linux, and Mac devices (OSX versions 10.13 and above).	Basic SKU is not supported. Not available for the classic deployment model.
Secure Socket Tunneling Protocol (SSTP)	Can traverse most firewalls because it uses TCP port 443.	Only supported on Windows devices. Supports up to 128 concurrent connections, regardless of the gateway SKU.
IKEv2	Standard-based IPsec VPN solution. Can be used to connect to Mac devices (OSX versions 10.11 and above).	Basic SKU is not supported. Not available for the classic deployment model. Uses nonstandard UDP ports, so you need to ensure that these ports are not blocked on the user's firewall. The ports in use are UDP 500 and 4500.

Site-to-site

A site-to-site (S2S) VPN is used in most scenarios to allow the communication from one
location (on-premises) to another (Azure) over the Internet. To configure an S2S, you need the
following prerequisites fulfilled before you start:

- An on-premises VPN device that is compatible with Azure VPN policy–based configuration or route-based configuration. See the full list at *https://aka.ms/az500s2sdevices*.

- Externally facing public IPv4 address.

- IP address range from your on-premises network that will be utilized to allow Azure to
  route to your on-premises location.

> **MORE INFO   CREATING AN S2S VPN**
>
> Once you have those requirements, you can create your S2S VPN. For more information on the
> steps, see *https://aka.ms/az500s2svpn*. If your VPN connection is over IPsec (IKE v1 and IKE v2),
> you need to have a VPN device or an RRAS.

Secure connectivity of virtual networks

Network security groups (NSG) in Azure allow you to filter network traffic by creating rules that
allow or deny inbound network traffic to or outbound network traffic from different types of
resources. You can think of an NSG as a Virtual LAN or VLAN in a physical network infrastructure. For example, you could configure an NSG to block inbound traffic from the Internet to a
specific subnet that only allows traffic from a network virtual appliance (NVA).

Network security groups can be enabled on the subnet or to the network interface in the
VM, as shown in Figure 2-14.

In the diagram shown in Figure 2-14, you have two different uses of NSG. In the first case,
the NSG is assigned to the subnet A. This can be a good way to secure the entire subnet with a
single set of NSG rules. However, there will be scenarios where you might need to control the
NSG on the network interface level, which is the case of the second scenario (subnet B), where
VM 5 and VM 6 have an NSG assigned to the network interface.

When inbound traffic is coming through the VNet, Azure processes the NSG rules that are
associated with the subnet first—if there are any—and then it processes the NSG rules that are
associated with the network interface. When the traffic is leaving the VNet (outbound traffic),
Azure processes the NSG rules associated with the network interface first, followed by the NSG
rules associated with the subnet.

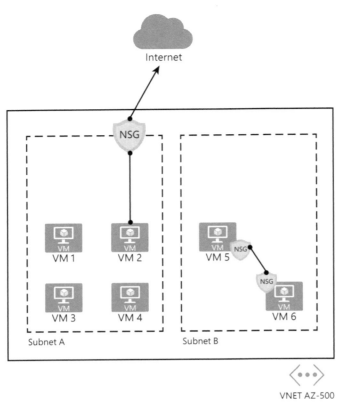

FIGURE 2-14 Different NSG implementations

When you create an NSG, you need to configure a set of rules to harden the traffic. These rules use the following parameters:

- **Name** The name of the rule.
- **Priority** The order in which the rule will be processed. Lower numbers have high priority, which means that a rule priority 100 will be evaluated before rule priority 300. Once the traffic matches the rule, it will stop moving forward to evaluate other rules. When configuring the priority, you can assign a number between 100 and 4096.
- **Source** Define the source IP, CIDR Block, Service Tag, or Application Security Group.
- **Destination** Define the destination IP, CIDR Block, Service Tag, or Application Security Group.
- **Protocol** Define the TCP/IP protocol that will be used, which can be set to **TCP**, **UDP**, **ICMP**, or **Any**.
- **Port Range** Define the port range or a single port.
- **Action** This determines the action that will be taken once this rule is processed. This can be set to **Allow** or **Deny**.

Before creating a new NSG and adding new rules, it is important to know that Azure automatically creates default rules on NSG deployments. Following is a list of the inbound rules that are created:

- **AllowVNetInBound**
  - **Priority**   65000
  - **Source**   VirtualNetwork
  - **Source Ports**   0–65535
  - **Destination**   VirtualNetwork
  - **Destination Ports**   0–65535
  - **Protocol**   Any
  - **Access**   Allow
- **AllowAzureLoadBalancerInBound**
  - **Priority**   65001
  - **Source**   AzureLoadBalancer
  - **Source Ports**   0–65535
  - **Destination**   0.0.0.0/0
  - **Destination Ports**   0–65535
  - **Protocol**   Any
  - **Access**   Allow
- **DenyAllInbound**
  - **Priority**   65500
  - **Source**   0.0.0.0/0
  - **Source Ports**   0–65535
  - **Destination**   0.0.0.0/0
  - **Destination Ports**   0–65535
  - **Protocol**   Any
  - **Access**   Deny

Below is a list of outbound rules that are created:

- **AllowVNetOutBound**
  - **Priority**   65000
  - **Source**   VirtualNetwork
  - **Source Ports**   0–65535
  - **Destination**   VirtualNetwork
  - **Destination Ports**   0–65535
  - **Protocol**   Any
  - **Access**   Allow

- **AllowInternetOutBound**
  - **Priority** 65001
  - **Source** 0.0.0.0/0
  - **Source Ports** 0–65535
  - **Destination** Internet
  - **Destination Ports** 0–65535
  - **Protocol** Any
  - **Access** Allow
- **DenyAllOutBound**
  - **Priority** 65500
  - **Source** 0.0.0.0/0
  - **Source Ports** 0–65535
  - **Destination** 0.0.0.0/0
  - **Destination Ports** 0–65535
  - **Protocol** Any
  - **Access** Deny

> **IMPORTANT DEFAULT RULES CANNOT BE REMOVED**
>
> Keep in mind that these default rules cannot be removed, though if necessary, you can override them by creating rules with higher priorities.

Follow the steps below to create and configure an NSG, which in this example will be associated with a subnet:

1. Navigate to the Azure portal by opening *https://portal.azure.com*.
2. In the search bar, type **network security**, and under **Services**, click **Network Security Groups**; the **Network Security Groups** page appears.
3. Click the **Add** button; the **Create Network Security Group** page appears, as shown in Figure 2-15.
4. In the **Subscription** field, select the subscription where this NSG will reside.
5. In the **Resource Group** field, select the resource group in which this NSG will reside.
6. In the **Name** field, type the name for this NSG.
7. In the **Region** field, select the Azure region in which this NSG will reside.
8. Click the **Review + Create** button, review the options, and click the **Create** button.
9. Once the deployment is complete, click the **Go To Resource** button. The NSG page appears.

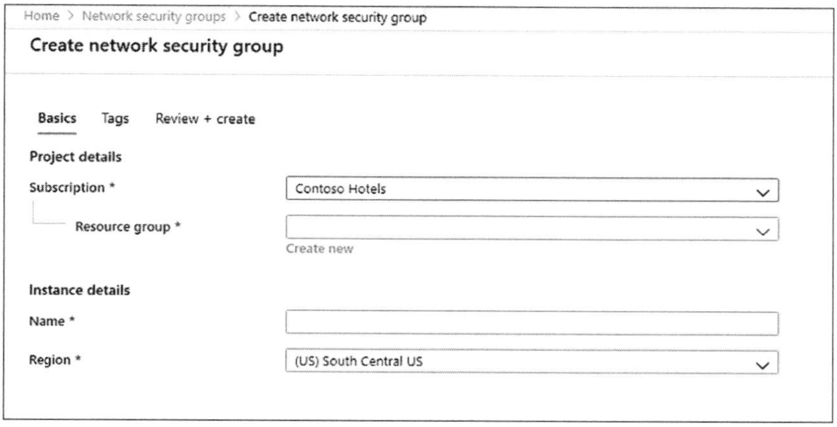
Home > Network security groups > Create network security group
Create network security group
Basics
Tags
Review + create
Project details
Subscription *
Contoso Hotels
Resource group *
Create new
Instance details
Name *
Region *
(US) South Central US

FIGURE 2-15 Initial parameters of the network security group

At this point, you have successfully created your NSG, and you can see that the default rules are already part of it. The next step is to create the custom rules, which can be inbound or outbound. (This example uses inbound rules.) The same operation could be done using the `New-AzNetworkSecurityGroup` PowerShell cmdlet, as shown in the following example:

```
New-AzNetworkSecurityGroup -Name "AZ500NSG" -ResourceGroupName "AZ500RG"  -Location
"westus"
```

Follow these steps to create an inbound rule that allows FTP traffic from any source to a specific server using Azure portal:

1. On the NSG page, under **Settings** in the left navigation pane, click **Inbound Security Rules**.
2. Click the **Add** button; the **Add Inbound Security Rule** blade appears, as shown in Figure 2-16.
3. On this blade, you start by specifying the source, which can be an IP address, a service tag, or an ASG. If you leave the default option (**Any**), you are allowing any source. For this example, leave this set to **Any**.
4. In the **Source Port Ranges** field, you can harden the source port. You can specify a single port or an interval. For example, you can allow traffic from ports 50 to 100. Also, you can use a comma to add another condition to the range, such as `50-100, 135`, which specifies ports 50 through 100 and 135. Leave the default selection (*), which allows any source port.
5. In the **Destination** field, the options are nearly the same as the **Source** field. The only difference is that you can select the VNet as the destination. For this example, change this option to **IP Addresses** and enter the internal IP address of the VM that you created at the beginning of this chapter.

6. In the **Destination Port Ranges** field, specify the destination port that will be allowed. The default port is 8080; for this example, change it to 21.

FIGURE 2-16 Creating an inbound security rule for your NSG

7. In the **Protocol** field, you can select which protocol you are going to allow; in this case, change it to **TCP**.

8. Leave the **Action** field set to **Allow**, which is the default selection.

9. You can also change the **Priority** of this rule. Remember that the lowest priority is evaluated first. For this example, change it to **101**.

10. In the **Name** field, change it to **AZ500NSGRule_FTP** and click the **Add** button.

The NSG will be created, and a new rule will be added to the inbound rules. At this point, your inbound rules should look like the rules shown in Figure 2-17.

Priority	Name	Port	Protocol	Source	Destination	Action
101	AZ500NSGRule_FTP	21	TCP	Any	10.3.0.50	✓ Allow
65000	AllowVnetInBound	Any	Any	VirtualNetwork	VirtualNetwork	✓ Allow
65001	AllowAzureLoadBalancerInBound	Any	Any	AzureLoadBalancer	Any	✓ Allow
65500	DenyAllInBound	Any	Any	Any	Any	⊘ Deny

FIGURE 2-17 List of inbound rules

While these are the steps to create the inbound rule, this NSG has no use if it is not associated with a subnet or a virtual network interface. For this example, you will associate this NSG to a subnet. The intent is to block all traffic to this subnet and only allow FTP traffic to this specific server. Use the following steps to create this association:

1. At the left hand side of the **NSG Inbound Security Rules** page, in the navigation pane of the Network security group, under **Settings**, click **Subnets**.

2. Click the **Associate** button, and in the **Virtual Network** drop-down menu, select the VNet where the subnet resides.

3. After this selection, you will see that the **Subnet** drop-down menu appears; select the subnet and click the **OK** button.

You could also use PowerShell to create an NSG and then associate the NSG to a subnet. To create an NSG using PowerShell, use the New-AzNetworkSecurityRuleConfig cmdlet, as shown in the following example:

```
$MyRule1 = New-AzNetworkSecurityRuleConfig -Name ftp-rule -Description "Allow FTP"
-Access Allow -Protocol Tcp -Direction Inbound -Priority 100 -SourceAddressPrefix *
-SourcePortRange * -DestinationAddressPrefix * -DestinationPortRange 21
```

Application security group

If you need to define granular network security policies based on workloads that are centralized on application patterns instead of explicit IP addresses, you need to use the application security group (ASG). An ASG allows you to group VMs and secure applications by filtering traffic from trusted segments of your network, which adds an extra level of micro-segmentation.

You can deploy multiple applications within the same subnet and isolate traffic based on ASGs. Another advantage is that you can reduce the number of NSGs in your subscription. For example, in some scenarios, you can use a single NSG for multiple subnets of your virtual network and perform the micro-segmentation on the application level by using ASG. Figure 2-18 shows an example of how ASG can be used in conjunction with NSG.

In the example shown in Figure 2-18, two ASGs have been created to define the application pattern for a web application and another ASG to define the application pattern for a SQL database. Two VMs are part of each group, and the ASG is used in the routing table of the NSG located in subnet A. In the NSG routing table, you can specify one ASG as the source and destination, but you cannot specify multiple ASGs in the source or destination.

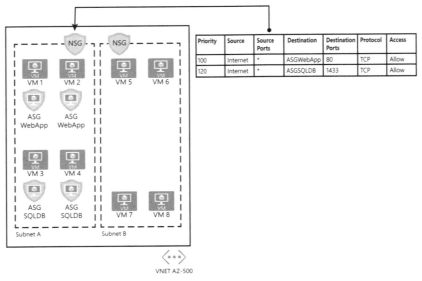

FIGURE 2-18 ASG used as the destination in the NSG routing table

When you deploy VMs, you can make them members of the appropriate ASGs. In case your VM has multiple workloads (Web App and SQL, for example), you can assign multiple ASGs to each application. This will allow you to have different types of access to the same VM according to the workload. This approach also helps to implement a zero-trust model by limiting access to the application flows that are explicitly permitted. Follow these steps to create an ASG:

1. Navigate to the Azure portal at *https://portal.azure.com*.

2. In the search bar, type **application security**, and under **Services**, click **Application Security Groups**.

3. In the **Application Security Groups** dashboard, click the **Add** button, which makes the **Create An Application Security Group** page appear, as shown in Figure 2-19.

FIGURE 2-19 Create An Application Security Group

4. In the **Subscription** drop-down menu, select the appropriate subscription for this ASG.

5. In the **Resource Group** drop-down menu, select the resource group in which this ASG will reside.

6. In the **Name** field, type a name for this ASG.

7. In the **Region** drop-down menu, select the appropriate region for this ASG and click the **Review + Create** button.

8. On the **Review + Create** button page, click the **Create** button.

Now that the ASG is created, you need to associate this ASG to the network interface of the VM that has the workload you want to control. Follow these steps to perform this association:

1. Navigate to the Azure portal at *https://portal.azure.com*.

2. In the search bar, type **virtual**, and under **Services**, click **Virtual Machines**.

3. Click in the VM that you want to perform this association.

4. On the VM's page, in the **Settings** section, click the **Networking** option.

5. Click the **Application Security Group** tab, and the page shown in Figure 2-20 appears.

FIGURE 2-20 Associating the ASG to the virtual network interface card

6. Click the **Configure The Application Security Groups** button, and the **Configure The Application Security Groups** blade appears, as shown in Figure 2-21.

FIGURE 2-21 Selecting the ASG

7. Select the appropriate ASG and click the **Save** button.

You can also use the `New-AzApplicationSecurityGroup` cmdlet to create a new ASG, as shown in the following example:

```
New-AzApplicationSecurityGroup -ResourceGroupName "MyRG" -Name "MyASG" -Location "West US"
```

Now when you create your new NSG rule for inbound or outbound traffic, you can select the ASG as source or destination.

Create and configure Azure Firewall

While NSG provides stateful package flow and custom security rules, you will need a more robust solution when you need to protect an entire virtual network. If your company needs a fully stateful, centralized network firewall as a service (FWaaS) that provides network and application-level protection across different subscriptions and virtual networks, you should choose Azure Firewall.

Also, Azure Firewall can be used in scenarios where you need to span multiple availability zones for increased availability. Although there's no additional cost for an Azure Firewall deployed in an availability zone, there are additional costs for inbound and outbound data transfers associated with Availability Zones. Figure 2-22 shows an Azure Firewall in its own VNet and subnet, allowing some traffic and blocking other traffic based on a series of evaluations.

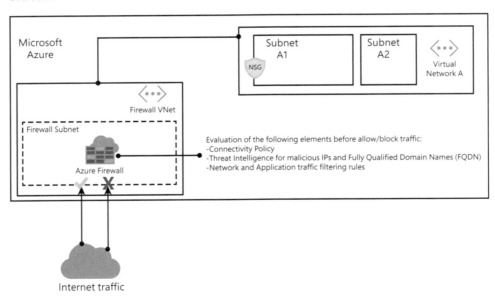

FIGURE 2-22 Azure Firewall topology

As shown in Figure 2-22, the Azure Firewall will perform a series of evaluations prior to allowing or blocking the traffic. Just as with an NSG, the rules in Azure Firewall are processed according to the rule type in priority order (lower numbers to higher numbers). A rule collection name may contain only letters, numbers, underscores, periods, or hyphens. You can configure NAT rules, network rules, and applications rules on Azure Firewall. Keep in mind that Azure Firewall uses a static public IP address for your virtual network resources, and you need that before deploying your firewall. Azure Firewall also supports learning routes via Border Gateway Protocol (BGP).

To evaluate outbound traffic, Azure Firewall will query the network and application rules. Just as with an NSG, no other rules are processed when a match is found in a network rule. Azure Firewall will use the infrastructure rule collection if there is no match. This collection is created automatically by Azure Firewall and includes platform-specific fully qualified domain names (FQDN). If there is still no match, Azure Firewall denies outgoing traffic.

Azure Firewall uses rules based on Destination Network Address Translation (DNAT) for incoming traffic evaluation. These rules are also evaluated in priority and before network rules. An implicit corresponding network rule to allow the translated traffic is added if a match is found. Although this is the default behavior, you can override this by explicitly adding a network rule collection with deny rules that match the translated traffic (if needed).

> **IMPORTANT** **WEB APPLICATION FIREWALL (WAF)**
>
> Application rules aren't applied for inbound connections. Microsoft recommends using Web Application Firewall (WAF) if you want to filter inbound HTTP/S traffic.

In Figure 2-22, you also saw that Azure Firewall leverages Microsoft Threat Intelligence during the traffic evaluation. The Microsoft Threat Intelligence is powered by Intelligent Security Graph and is used by many other services in Azure, including Microsoft Defender for Cloud.

Azure Firewall is available in two tiers, Premium and Standard. The Standard tier includes the following capabilities:

- Built-in high availability
- Availability Zones
- Unrestricted cloud scalability
- Application FQDN filtering rules
- Network traffic filtering rules
- FQDN tags
- Service tags
- Threat intelligence
- Outbound SNAT support
- Inbound DNAT support
- Multiple public IP addresses
- Azure Monitor logging
- Forced tunneling

- Web categories
- Certifications

While these features are enough for many organizations, there will be scenarios where the environment is highly sensitive and regulated, which requires features only available in the next generation Firewall. These features are part of the Azure Firewall Premium tier, which includes:

- **TLS inspection**   With this capability it is possible to decrypt outbound traffic, analyze the data, and then encrypt the data again before sending it to the destination.
- **Intrusion detection and prevention system (IDPS)**   This is a network-based IDPS that enables you to monitor network traffic for malicious activity. In addition, IDPS enables you to log information about these activities, report it, and optionally create a mechanism to attempt to block it.
- **URL filtering**   This capability enhances the Azure Firewall's FQDN filtering feature to consider an entire URL. For example, *www.fabrikam.com/a/b* instead of `www.fabrikam.com`.
- **Web categories**   This feature allows you to control user access to websites by categories such as gambling websites, social media websites, and others.

> **IMPORTANT   AZURE FIREWALL PREMIUM SUPPORT**
>
> Azure Firewall Premium is supported in many regions; for the latest list of supported regions and more information about the supported features, visit *http://aka.ms/az500fwpremium*.

Now that you know the key components of the Azure Firewall, use the following steps to deploy and configure it:

1. Navigate to the Azure portal at *https://portal.azure.com*.
2. In the main dashboard, click **Create A Resource**.
3. Type **firewall** and click **Firewall** in the drop-down menu.
4. On the **Firewall** page, click the **Create** button, and the **Create A Firewall** blade appears, as shown in Figure 2-23.
5. If you have multiple subscriptions, make sure to click the **Subscription** drop-down menu and select the one that you want to use to deploy Azure Firewall.
6. In the **Resource Group** drop-down menu, select the resource group in which you want to deploy your Azure Firewall.
7. In the **Instance Details** section's **Name** field, type the name for this Azure Firewall instance. There is a 50-character limit for the name.
8. In the **Region** drop-down menu, select the region where the Azure Firewall will reside.
9. In the **Availability Zone** drop-down menu, select the availability zone in which the firewall will reside.

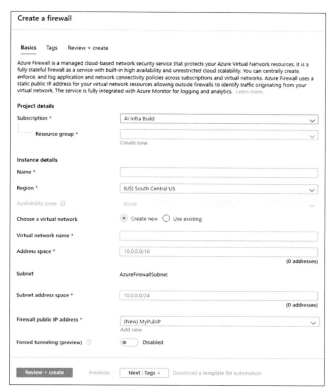

FIGURE 2-23 Creating a new Azure Firewall

10. In the **Firewall Tier** you can select the plan you can use.

11. In the **Firewall Management** section, you can select the use of Firewall policy or classic Firewall rules. Keep in mind that if you use a Firewall policy, you will need to select an existing policy or create a new one.

12. For the **Choose Virtual Network** option, select **Use Existing** and select an existing VNet.

13. In the **Virtual Network** drop-down menu, select the VNet to which you want to deploy Azure Firewall.

14. In the **Firewall Public IP Address** field, select an existing unused public IP address or click **Add New** to create a new one in case all your public IPs are already allocated.

15. You can either enable or disable **Force Tunneling**. The default option is **Disabled**. By enabling this option, you are instructing Azure Firewall to route all Internet-bound traffic to a designated next hop instead of going directly to the Internet. Keep in mind that if you configure Azure Firewall to support forced tunneling, you can't undo this configuration. Leave the default selection and click the **Review + Create** button.

16. The creation of the Azure Firewall will take several minutes. After the deployment is complete, you can click the **Go To Resource** button.

You can also deploy a new Azure Firewall using the `New-AzFirewall` cmdlet, as shown in the following example:

```
New-AzFirewall -Name "azFw" -ResourceGroupName MyRG -Location centralus -VirtualNetwork MyVNet -PublicIpAddress MyPubIP
```

Creating an application rule

Now that the Azure Firewall is created, you can start creating rules. To start, you are going to create an application rule to allow outbound access to *www.bing.com*. Follow these steps to create a rule:

1. On the page that you have open for the firewall you created, click **Rules**, as shown in Figure 2-24.

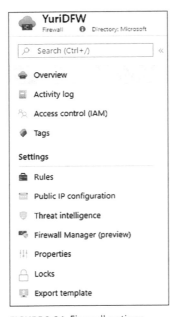

FIGURE 2-24 Firewall options

2. Click the **Application Rule Collection** tab and then click the **+ Add Application Rule Collection** option. The **Add Application Rule Collection** page appears, as shown in Figure 2-25.

3. In the **Name** field, type a name for the rule; for this example, type **Bing**.

4. In the **Priority** field, type the priority for this rule; for this example, type **100**.

5. In the **Action** drop-down menu, leave the default option (**Allow**).

FIGURE 2-25 Creating a new application rule collection

6. No changes are necessary in the **FQDN Tags** field.

7. In the **Target FQDNs field**, type **AllowBing** and leave the **Source Type** set to **IP Address**.

8. Type * in the **Source** field.

9. In the **Protocol:Port** field, type **http,https**.

10. In the **Target FQDNs field**, type **www.bing.com**.

11. Click the **Add** button.

In case you want to perform the same configuration using PowerShell, you can use the `New-AzFirewallApplicationRule` cmdlet, as shown here:

```
$MyAppRule = New-AzFirewallApplicationRule -Name AllowBing -SourceAddress * '
  -Protocol http, https -TargetFqdn www.bing.com
$AppCollectionRule = New-AzFirewallApplicationRuleCollection -Name App-Coll01 '
  -Priority 100 -ActionType Allow -Rule $MyAppRule
$Azfw.ApplicationRuleCollections = $AppRuleCollection
Set-AzFirewall -AzureFirewall $Azfw
```

> **TIP AZURE WEB APPLICATION FIREWALL (WAF)**
>
> If your organization needs inbound HTTP/S protection, it is recommended that you use a web application firewall such as Azure Web Application Firewall (WAF) instead of creating an application rule for port 443.

Creating a network rule

Creating a network rule is very similar to creating an application rule. For this example, you are going to create an outbound network rule that allows access to an external DNS Server. Follow these steps to create your network rule:

1. On the **Firewalls** rules page, click the **Network Rule Collection** tab.

2. Click the **Add Network Rule Collection** option; the **Add Network Rule Collection** blade appears, as shown in Figure 2-26.

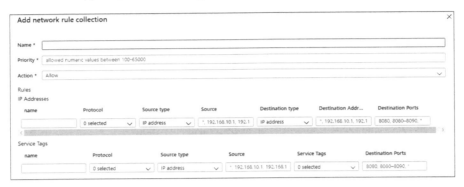

FIGURE 2-26 Creating a new network rule collection

3. In the **Name** field, type **DNS**.

4. In the **Priority** field, type **200**.

5. In the **Action** field, leave the default selection (**Allow**).

6. Under the **IP Addresses** section, type **DNSOutbound** in the **Name** field.

7. Select **UDP** in the **Protocol** field.

8. Leave **IP Address** selection in the **Source Type** field.

9. In the **Source** field, type the range of your subnet, such as **10.30.0.0/24**.

10. Leave the **IP Address** selection in the **Destination Type** field.

11. In the **Destination Address** field, type the IP address of the external DNS.

12. In the **Destination Port**, type **53**.

13. Click the **Add** button.

In case you want to perform the same configuration using PowerShell, you can use the `New-AzFirewallNetworkRule` cmdlet, as shown here:

```
New-AzFirewallNetworkRule -Name "DNSOutbound" -Protocol UDP -SourceAddress
"10.30.0.0/24" -DestinationAddress IP_of_the_DNSSErver -DestinationPort 53
```

Firewall logs

When system admins need to audit configuration changes in the Azure Firewall, they should use Azure Activity logs. For example, the creation of those two rules (application and network) will appear in the Activity Log, which will look similar to Figure 2-27.

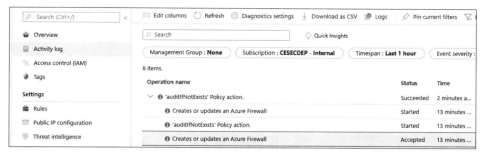

FIGURE 2-27 Activity logs showing the changes in the Azure Firewall

While these actions are automatically logged in the Azure Activity Log, the diagnostic logging for application and network rules are not enabled by default. You can also enable Firewall metrics. These metrics are collected every minute and can be useful for alerting because they can be sampled frequently. When you enable metrics collection, the following metrics will be available for Azure Firewall:

- Application rules hit count
- Network rules hit count
- Data processed
- Firewall health state
- SNAT port utilization

These metrics and the diagnostic logging for application and network rules can be enabled in the Azure Firewall dashboard. Use the following steps to enable these logs:

1. On the **Firewalls** page, in the left navigation pane, under the **Monitoring** section, click **Diagnostic Settings**. The **Diagnostic Settings** page appears, as shown in Figure 2-28.

FIGURE 2-28 Diagnostic settings page

2. Click the **Add Diagnostic Setting** option, which makes the **Diagnostic Settings** blade appear, as shown in Figure 2-29.

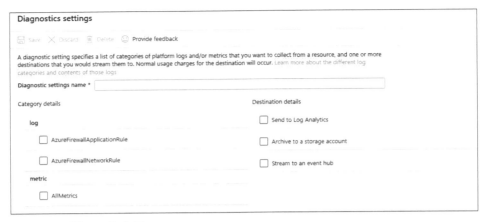

Diagnostics settings

Save ✕ Discard 🗑 Delete ☺ Provide feedback

A diagnostic setting specifies a list of categories of platform logs and/or metrics that you want to collect from a resource, and one or more destinations that you would stream them to. Normal usage charges for the destination will occur. Learn more about the different log categories and contents of those logs

Diagnostic settings name * _____

Category details   Destination details

  log   ☐ Send to Log Analytics

    ☐ AzureFirewallApplicationRule   ☐ Archive to a storage account

    ☐ AzureFirewallNetworkRule   ☐ Stream to an event hub

  metric

    ☐ AllMetrics

FIGURE 2-29 Diagnostic Settings page

3. In the **Diagnostic Settings Name** field, type a name for this setting.

4. In the **Log** section, enable **AzureFirewallApplicationRule** and **AzureFirewallNetworkRule**.

5. In the **Metric** section, enable **AllMetrics**.

6. In the **Destination Details** section, you can choose where you want to send the logs: **Log Analytics**, **Storage Account**, or **Event Hub**. If you need to retain logs for a longer duration for review as needed, choosing **Storage Account** is the best option. If you need to send the logs to a security information and event management (SIEM) tool, the Event Hub is the best option. If you need more real-time monitoring, **Log Analytics** is a better fit. Notice that you can select multiple options, which allows you to address multiple needs.

7. For this example, select **Send To Log Analytics**, and select the workspace in which the logs will reside.

8. Click **Save** and once it is saved, close the blade.

9. Notice that the name of your logging configuration now appears on the **Diagnostic Settings** page.

10. You can use the Set-AzDiagnosticSetting cmdlet to enable diagnostic logging, as shown in the following example:

```
Set-AzDiagnosticSetting  -ResourceId /subscriptions/<subscriptionId>/
resourceGroups/<resource group name>/providers/Microsoft.Network/
azureFirewalls/<Firewall name> '
-StorageAccountId /subscriptions/<subscriptionId>/resourceGroups/<resource group
name>/providers/Microsoft.Storage/storageAccounts/<storage account name> '
-Enabled $true
```

11. Now that the diagnostic logging is configured, click **Logs** in the left navigation pane in the **Monitoring** section. The **Log Analytics** workspace appears with the Azure Firewall schema, as shown in Figure 2-30.

FIGURE 2-30 Schema for the Azure Firewall in Log Analytics

12. To query on the Log Analytics workspace, you use Kusto Query Language (KQL). You can use the sample query to retrieve the logs that are related to the network rules:

```
AzureDiagnostics
| where Category == "AzureFirewallNetworkRule"
```

Create and configure Azure Firewall Manager

Azure Firewall Manager can be used when the organization needs a security management solution that enables centralized security policy and route management. Azure Firewall Manager can provide this type of benefit for two types of Azure network architecture:

- Secured virtual hub: this type of network is utilized when the organization uses an Azure Virtual WAN Hub to create hub-and-spoke architectures. When security and routing policies are associated with such a hub, it is referred to as a secured virtual hub.

- Hub virtual network: this type of network is utilized when the organization is using an Azure virtual network that they create and manage on their own. When security policies are associated with such a hub, it is referred to as a hub virtual network.

When designing the architecture of your Azure network, consider the technical require-ments of the scenario. If these requirements include one or more of the items shown below, then you should use Azure Firewall Manager:

- Centralized deployment and configuration of multiple Azure Firewall instances that span through different Azure regions and subscriptions

- Centralized management of Azure Firewall policies across multiple secured virtual hubs
- Ability to integrate with third-party Security-as-a-Service (SECaaS) providers to obtain additional network protection for VNet and branch Internet connections
- Ability to route traffic to a secured hub for filtering and logging purposes without having to manually set up User Defined Routes (UDR) on spoke virtual networks

> **TIP AZURE FIREWALL MANAGER PRICING**
> Azure Firewall Manager has different components, and some of these components have their own pricing. Make sure to review the Azure Firewall Manager pricing page for the latest information regarding pricing at *http://aka.ms/az500fwmanprice*.

One of the main components of Azure Firewall Manager is the Firewall policy. This policy contains NAT, network and application rule collections, and Threat Intelligence settings. A Firewall policy is a global resource that can be used across multiple Azure Firewall instances and across regions and subscriptions. You can create a policy using Azure portal, REST API, templates, Azure PowerShell, and CLI. You can also migrate existing rules from Azure Firewall using the portal or Azure PowerShell to create policies.

You can create new policies, or you can create a policy inherited from other existing policies. Policies created with non-empty parent policies inherit all rule collections from the parent policy. It is important to mention that when you inherit a policy, any changes to the parent policy will be automatically applied down to associated firewall child policies.

When taking the AZ-500 exam, make sure to carefully read the scenario description and the organization's requirements. Depending on the organization's requirements, you will either create an Azure Firewall Manager to a virtual hub or a hub virtual network.

If you need to secure your cloud network traffic destined to private IP addresses, Azure PaaS, and the Internet, then you should deploy Azure Firewall Manager to a virtual hub. If you need to connect your on-premises network to an Azure virtual network to create a hybrid network, you can create a hub virtual network. By deploying Azure Firewall Manager to this hub virtual network, you are securing your hybrid network traffic destined to private IP addresses, Azure PaaS, and the Internet.

The main use case scenario for Azure Firewall Manager is the centralized management of policies across multiple secured virtual hubs. Azure Firewall Manager supports both classic rules and policies, though when designing your deployment, we recommend that you use policies. Azure Firewall Manager also supports Standard and Premium policies. If your deployment needs any of the components below, you should choose Standard policy:

- NAT rules, Network rules, Application rules
- Custom DNS, DNS proxy
- IP Groups
- Web Categories
- Threat Intelligence

More advanced deployments may require capabilities that will only be available in the Premium policies, which are: TLS Inspection, Web Categories, URL Filtering, and IDPS.

Another scenario supported by Azure Firewall Manager is to leverage third-party security as a service (SECaaS) offerings to protect Internet access for your users. By using this integration, you can secure a hub with a supported security partner. Also, you can route and filter Internet traffic from your Virtual Networks (VNets) or branch locations within a region. The supported security partners are Zscaler, Check Point, and iboss.

> **TIP   SECURITY PROVIDERS**
>
> To see an example of how to deploy a supported third-party security provider to a new or existing hub, visit *http://aka.ms/az500FWMSECaaS*.

The general deployment steps will also vary according to the deployment selection. If you decided to deploy Azure Firewall Manager for hub virtual networks, the overall steps are shown below:

1. Create a Firewall policy.
2. Create a hub-and-spoke architecture.
3. Select the supported provider, which in this case only Azure Firewall is supported.
4. Configure the appropriate routes.

> **TIP   AZURE FIREWALL MANAGER DEPLOYMENT**
>
> To secure a virtual hub using Azure Firewall Manager, follow the steps at *http://aka.ms/az500fwmvhub*. To secure a hub virtual network using Azure Firewall Manager, follow the steps at *http://aka.ms/az500fwhvnet*.

Create and configure Azure Front Door

Consider an Azure deployment across different regions that needs to provide a high-performance experience for applications, and it is resilient to failures. For this type of scenario, Azure Front Door is the best solution.

Azure Front Door works at layer 7 (HTTP/HTTPS) and uses the anycast protocol with split TCP, plus Microsoft's global network for improving global connectivity. By using split TCP-based anycast protocol, Front Door ensures that your users promptly connect to the nearest Front Door POP (point of presence).

> **IMPORTANT   FRONT DOOR TIERS**
>
> By the time this book was written, the Front Door Standard and Premium tiers were in Public Preview. To see the difference between those two tiers, visit *http://aka.ms/az500frontdoortier*.

You can configure Front Door to route your client requests to the fastest and most available application back end, which is any Internet-facing service hosted inside or outside of Azure. Some other capabilities included in Front Door are listed here:

- **Intelligent health probe**   Front Door monitors your back ends for availability and latency. According to its results, it will instant failover when a back end goes down.
- **URL-based routing**   Allows you to route traffic to the back end based on the URL's path of the request. For example, traffic to www.fabrikam.com/hr/* is routed to a specific pool, whereas www.fabrikam.com/soc/* goes to another.
- **Multiple-site hosting**   Enables you to configure a more efficient topology for your deployments by adding different websites to a single Front Door and redirecting to different pools.
- **Session affinity**   Uses cookie-based session affinity to keep the session in the same back end.
- **TLS termination**   Support for TLS termination at the edge.
- **Custom domain, SSL offloading, and certificate management**   You can let Front Door manage your certificate, or you can upload your own TLS/SSL certificate.
- **Application layer security**   Allows you to author your own custom web application firewall (WAF) rules for access control, and it comes with Azure DDoS Basic enabled. Front Door is also a layer 7 reverse proxy, which means it only allows web traffic to pass through to back ends and blocks other types of traffic by default.
- **URL redirection**   Allows you to configure different types of redirection, which includes HTTP to HTTPS redirection, redirection to different hostnames, redirection to different paths, or redirections to a new query string in the URL.
- **URL rewrite**   Allows you to configure a custom forwarding path to construct a request to forward traffic to the back end.

> **TIP   APPLICATION GATEWAY**
> If your scenario requires a layer 7 (HTTP/HTTPS) load balancer just for one region, you can use Azure Application Gateway. If you need a global service that works across multiple regions, you should use Azure Front Door. For more information, see *https://aka.ms/AzDecideLB*.

The diagram shown in Figure 2-31 reflects some of the features that were mentioned previously and gives you a better topology view of the main use case for Azure Front Door.

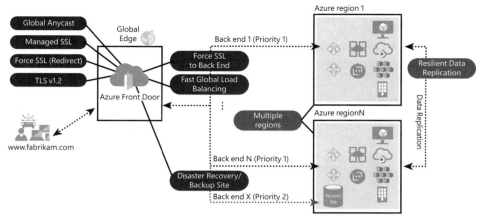

FIGURE 2-31 A sse case for Azure Front Door

Follow the steps below to configure your Azure Front Door:

1. Navigate to the Azure portal at *https://portal.azure.com*.

2. In the search bar, type **front** and under **Services**, click **Front Doors**.

3. On the **Front Doors** page, click the **Add** button; the **Create A Front Door** page appears, as shown in Figure 2-32.

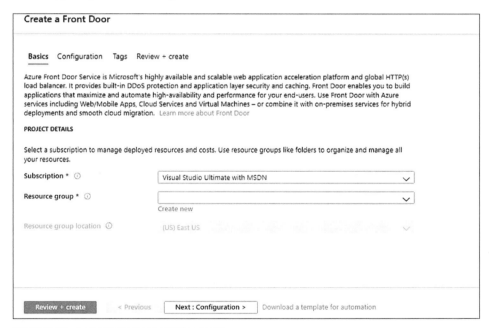

FIGURE 2-32 Azure Front Door creation page

4. In the **Subscription** drop-down menu, select the subscription that you want to use to create the Front Door.

5. In the **Resource Group** drop-down menu, select the resource group that you want for this Front Door.

6. Click the **Next: Configuration** button; the **Configuration** tab appears, as shown in Figure 2-33.

FIGURE 2-33 Initial Front Door configuration

7. Click the plus sign (**+**) in the first square, **Frontends/Domains**; the **Add Front End Host** blade appears, as shown in Figure 2-34.

FIGURE 2-34 Add A Frontend Host

8. In the **Host Name** field, type a unique name for this front end.

9. Front Door forwards requests originating from the same client to different back ends based on load-balancing configuration, which means that Front Door doesn't use session affinity by default. However, some stateful applications usually prefer that subsequent requests from the same user land on the same back end that processed the initial request. In this case, you need to enable session affinity. For this example, leave the default selection in **Session Affinity (Enabled)**.

10. If you want to use Web Application Firewall (WAF) to protect your web application, you can take advantage of the centralized management provided by Front Door. For this example, leave the default **Disabled** setting for **Web Application Firewall** and click the **Add** button.

11. Click the plus sign (**+**) in the second square, **Back End Pools**; the **Add Back End Pool** blade appears, as shown in Figure 2-35.

12. In the **Name** field, type a unique name for the back-end pool.

13. In the **Back Ends** section, click **Add A Back End**; the **Add A Back End** blade appears, as shown in Figure 2-36.

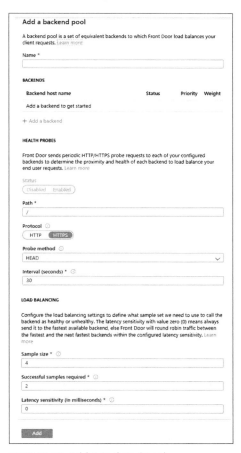

FIGURE 2-35 Add A Back End Pool

14. In the **Back End Host Type** drop-down menu, you can choose the type of resource you want to add. Select **App Service** in the drop-down menu.

15. Once you make this selection, the remaining parameters should be automatically filled with the default options. Review the values and click the **Add** button.

16. Now that you are back to the **Add Back End Pool** blade, review the options under the **Health Probes** section and notice that the default setting for **Probe Method** is HEAD. The HEAD method is identical to GET; the difference is that the server must not return a message-body in the response. This is also the recommended setting to lower the load on your back ends (as well as the cost).

FIGURE 2-36 Configuring a new backend

17. The **Load Balancing** settings for the back-end pool define how health probes are evaluated. These settings are used to determine whether the back end is healthy or unhealthy. The **Sample Size** is used to determine how many sample health probes are necessary to consider the state of the back end (health evaluation). The **Successful Samples Required** is the threshold for how many samples must succeed to be

considered successful. The **Latency Sensitivity** (in milliseconds) option is used when you want to send requests to back ends within the established latency measurement sensitivity range.

18. Leave the default selections and click the **Add** button.

19. Click the plus sign (**+**) in the third square; **Routing Rules**; the **Add Rule** blade appears, as shown in Figure 2-37.

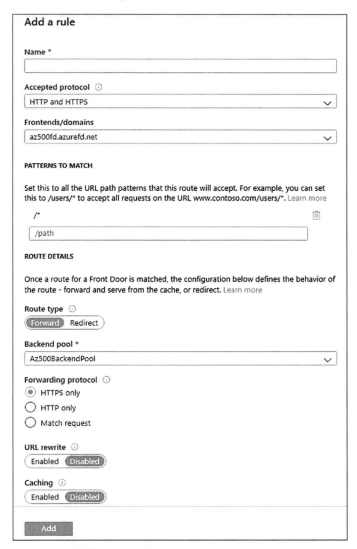

FIGURE 2-37 Adding a new rule

20. In the **Name** field, type a unique name for this routing rule.

21. Under the **Patterns To Match** section, you can add a specific pattern that you want to use. When Front Door is evaluating the request, it looks for any routing with an exact match on the host. If no exact front-end hosts match, it rejects the request and sends a 400 Bad Request error. After determining the specific front-end host, Front Door will filter the routing rules based on the requested path. For this example, leave the default selections.

22. Under the **Route Details** section, you can configure the behavior of the route. In the **Route Type** option, you can select whether you want to forward to the back-end pool or redirect to another place. For this example, leave this set to **Forward**, which is the default. Enable the **URL Rewrite** option if you want to create a custom forwarding path. The **Caching** option is disabled by default, which means that requests that match to this routing rule will not attempt to use cached content. In order words, requests will always fetch from the back end. Leave all the default selections in this section and click the **Add** button.

23. Click the **Review + Create** button, review the summary of your configuration, and click the **Create** button to finish.

24. Wait until the deployment is finished. Once it is finished, click the **Go To Resource** button to see the Front Door dashboard.

It will take a few minutes for the configuration to be deployed globally everywhere after you finish creating your Front Door.

> **IMPORTANT   FRONT DOOR ROUTE**
>
> Routes for your Front Door are not ordered. A specific route is selected based on the best match.

Web application firewall

Web Application Firewall (WAF) can be used on Front Door. Azure also allows you to deploy WAF in other ways, so it is important to understand the design requirements before deciding which WAF deployment you should use.

Review the flowchart available at *http://aka.ms/wafdecisionflow* to better understand WAF's features, which include Azure Load Balancer, Application Gateway, and Azure Front Door. If your scenario has the following characteristic, WAF with Front Door is a good choice:

- Your app uses HTTP/HTTPS.
- Your app is Internet-facing.
- Your app is globally distributed across different regions.
- Your app is hosted in PaaS (such as an Azure App Service).

Consider deploying WAF on Front Door when you need a global and centralized solution. When using WAF with Front Door, the web applications will be inspected for every incoming request delivered by Front Door at the network edge.

Create and configure Web Application Firewall (WAF)

In a scenario where you need to protect your web applications from common threats, such as SQL injection, cross-site scripting, and other web-based exploits, using Azure Web Application Firewall (WAF) on Azure Application Gateway is the most appropriate way to address these needs. WAF on Application Gateway is based on Open Web Application Security Project (OWASP) core rule set 3.1, 3.0, or 2.2.9. These rules will be used to protect your web apps against the top 10 OWASP vulnerabilities, which you can find at *https://owasp.org/ www-project-top-ten*.

You can use WAF on Application Gateway to protect multiple web applications. A single instance of Application Gateway can host up to 40 websites, and those websites will be protected by a WAF. Even though you have multiple websites behind the WAF, you can still create custom policies to address the needs of those sites. The diagram shown in Figure 2-38 has more details about the different components of this solution.

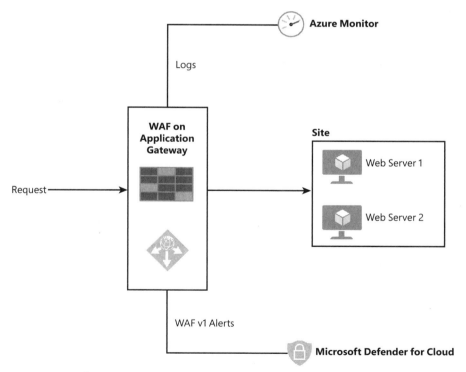

FIGURE 2-38 Different integration components for WAF on Application Gateway

In the example shown in Figure 2-38, a WAF Policy has been configured for the back-end site. This policy is where you define all rules, custom rules, exclusions, and other customizations, such as a file upload limit.

WAF on Application Gateway supports Transport Layer Security (TLS) termination, cookie-based session affinity, round-robin load distribution, and content-based routing. The diagram shown in Figure 2-38 also highlights the integration with Azure Monitor, which will receive all logs related to potential attacks against your web applications. WAV v1 alerts will also be streamed to Microsoft Defender for Cloud, and they will appear in the Security Alert dashboard.

Depending on the scenario requirement, you can configure WAF on the Application Gateway to operate in two different modes:

- **Detection mode**   This mode will not interfere with traffic when suspicious activity occurs. Rather than blocking suspicious activity, this mode only detects and logs all threat alerts. For this mode to work properly, diagnostic logging and the WAF log must be enabled.
- **Prevention mode**   As the name implies, this mode blocks traffic that matches the rules. Blocked requested generate a 403 Unauthorized Access message. At that point, the connection is closed, and a record is created in the WAF logs.

When reviewing the WAF log for a request that was blocked, you will see a message that contains some fields that are similar to this example:

```
Mandatory rule. Cannot be disabled. Inbound Anomaly Score Exceeded (Total Inbound Score:
5 - SQLI=0,XSS=0,RFI=0,LFI=0,RCE=0,PHPI=0,HTTP=0,SESS=0): Missing User Agent Header;
individual paranoia level scores: 3, 2, 0, 0
```

The anomaly score comes from the OWASP 3.x rules, which have a specific severity: Critical, Error, Warning, or Notice. The previous message indicates that the total inbound score is 5, which translates to a severity equal to Critical. It is important to emphasize that the traffic will not be blocked until it reaches the threshold, which is 5. This means that if traffic matches the block rule but has an anomaly score of 3, it will not be blocked, though the message that you will see in the WAF log says that it is blocked. The severity levels are 5 (Critical), 4 (Error), 3 (Warning), and 2 (Notice).

> *TIP*   **APPLICATION GATEWAY**
>
> To create an application gateway with a Web Application Firewall using the Azure portal, use the steps from this article: *https://aka.ms/az500wafag*.

Configure resource firewall

In addition to Azure Firewall, you can also leverage the native firewall-related capabilities for different services. Azure Storage and SQL Database are examples of Azure services that have this functionality.

When you leverage this built-in functionality to harden your resources, you are adding an extra layer of security to your workload and following the defense in depth strategy, as shown in Figure 2-39.

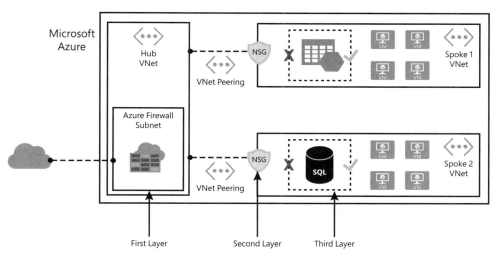

FIGURE 2-39 Multiple layers of protection to access the resource

Azure storage firewall

When you enable this feature in Azure Storage, you can better control the level of access to your storage accounts based on the type and subset of networks used. When network rules are configured, only applications requesting data over the specified set of networks can access a storage account.

You can create granular controls to limit access to your storage account to requests coming from specific IP addresses, IP ranges, or from a list of subnets in an Azure VNet. The firewall rules created on your Azure Storage are enforced on all network protocols that can be used to access your storage account, including REST and SMB.

Because the default storage accounts configuration allows connections from clients on any other network (including the Internet), it is recommended that you configure this feature to limit access to selected networks. Follow these steps to configure Azure Storage firewall:

1. Navigate to the Azure portal at *https://portal.azure.com*.
2. In the search bar, type **storage**, and under **Services**, click **Storage Accounts**.
3. Click the storage account for which you want to modify the firewall settings.
4. On the storage account page, under the **Settings** section in the left navigation pane, click the **Firewalls And Virtual Networks** option; the page shown in Figure 2-40 appears.

FIGURE 2-40 Azure storage firewall and virtual network settings

5. Under **Allow Access From**, click **Selected Networks**; the options shown in Figure 2-41 will become available.

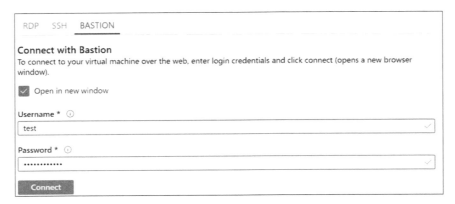

FIGURE 2-41 Azure storage firewall settings

6. Under the **Virtual networks** section, you could either add a new VNet or assign this storage account to a specific VNet.

7. Under the **Firewall** section, you can harden the address range that can have access to this storage account. For that, you need to type the IP addresses or the range using CIDR format. Keep in mind that services deployed in the same region as the storage account use private Azure IP addresses for communication. Therefore, you cannot restrict access to specific Azure services based on their public outbound IP address range.

8. Under the **Exceptions** section, you can enable or disable the following options:

   ■ **Allow Trusted Microsoft Services To Access This Storage Account** Enabling this option will grant access to your storage account from Azure Backup, Azure Event Grid, Azure Site Recovery, Azure DevTest Labs, Azure Event Hubs, Azure Networking, Azure Monitor, and Azure SQL Data Warehouse.

   ■ **Allow Read Access To Storage Logging From Any Network** Enable this point if you want to allow this level of access.

   ■ **Allow Read Access To Storage Metrics From Any Network** Enable this option if you need the storage metrics to be accessible from all networks.

9. Once you finish configuring, click the **Save** button.

If you want to quickly deny network access to the storage account, you can use the Update-AzStorageAccountNetworkRuleSet cmdlet, as shown here:

```
Update-AzStorageAccountNetworkRuleSet -ResourceGroupName "MyRG" -Name "mystorage"
-DefaultAction Deny
```

Azure SQL database firewall

When configuring your Azure SQL database, you can restrict access to a specific network by using the server-level firewall rules or database-level firewall rules. These rules can enable or disable access from clients to all the databases within the same SQL Database server. These rules are stored in the master database.

If your database is accessible from the Internet and a computer tries to connect to it, the firewall first checks the originating IP address of the request against the database-level IP firewall rules for the database that the connection requests. If the address isn't within a range in the database-level IP firewall rules, the firewall checks the server-level IP firewall rules.

The server-level firewall rules can be configured via the Azure portal, whereas the database-level firewall needs to be configured on the database itself by using the sp_set_database_firewall_rule SQL command. To configure the server-level firewall, follow these steps:

1. Navigate to the Azure portal at *https://portal.azure.com*.

2. In the search bar, type **database**, and under **Services**, click **SQL Databases**.

3. Click the database for which you want to modify the server-level firewall settings.

4. In the Overview page, click the **Set Server Rule** button, as shown in Figure 2-42.

FIGURE 2-42 Selecting the option to configure the server-level firewall

5. The Firewall settings page appears, as shown in Figure 2-43.

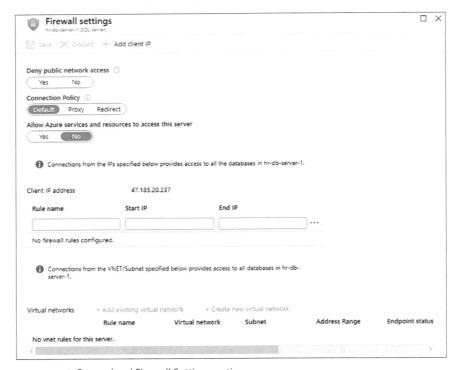

FIGURE 2-43 Server-level Firewall Settings options

6. Under **Deny Public Network Access** option, select **Yes** if you want to prohibit access from the Internet or **No** if you want to allow Internet access to this database.

7. The **Connection Policy** option allows you to configure how clients can connect to Azure SQL. The available options are

   ▪ **Default**   The default policy is basically a redirect for all client connections originating inside of Azure and proxy for all client connections originating outside.

   ▪ **Policy**   By selecting this option, all connections are proxied via the Azure SQL Database gateways (which varies according to the Azure region). This setting will increase latency and reduce throughput.

   ▪ **Redirect**   By selecting this option, all clients will establish connections directly to the node hosting the database, which reduces latency and improves throughput.

8. Under **Allow Azure Services And Resources To Access This Server**, you have the option to **Enable** or **Disable** this type of access.

9. Next are three fields, **Rule Name**, **Start IP**, and **End IP**, which allow you to create filters for client connections.

10. The last option that you can configure is the **Virtual Networks setting**, which allows you to either create or add an existing VNet.

11. Once you finish configuring, click the **Save** button.

Azure Key Vault Firewall

Just like the previous resources, Azure Key Vault also allows you to create network access restrictions by using Key Vault firewall, which applies to Key Vault's data plane. This means that operations such as creating a new vault or deleting or modifying the settings won't be affected by the firewall rules. Below are two use-case scenarios for Azure Key Vault Firewall:

- Contoso needs to implement Azure Key Vault to store encryption keys for its applications. Contoso wants to block access to its keys for requests coming from the Internet.

- Fabrikam implemented Azure Key Vault, and now it needs to lock down access to its keys and enable access only to Fabrikam's applications and a shortlist of specific hosts.

To configure Azure Key Vault Firewall, you should first enable the Key Vault Logging using the following sequence of PowerShell commands:

```
$storagea = New-AzStorageAccount -ResourceGroupName ContosoResourceGroup -Name
fabrikamkeyvaultlogs -Type Standard_LRS -Location 'East US'
$kvault = Get-AzKeyVault -VaultName 'ContosoKeyVault'
Set-AzDiagnosticSetting -ResourceId $kvault.ResourceId -StorageAccountId $storagea.Id
-Enabled $true -Category AuditEvent
```

In this sequence, you will create a new storage account to store the logs, obtain the Key Vault information, and finally, configure the diagnostic setting for your Key Vault.

After finishing this part, you can go to the Azure portal, open your Key Vault, and in the left navigation pane under the **Settings** section, click **Networking** > **Private Endpoint And Selected Networks**, as shown in Figure 2-44.

On this page, you can click the **Add Existing Virtual Networks** or **Add New Virtual Networks** options to start building your list of allowed virtual networks to access your Key Vault. Keep in mind that once you configure those rules, users can only perform Key Vault data plane operations when their requests originate from this list of allowed virtual networks. The same applies when users are trying to perform data plane operations from the portal, such as listing the keys.

> **IMPORTANT   IP NETWORK RULES**
>
> If you are creating IP network rules, you can only use public IP addresses. Reserved IP address ranges are not allowed in IP rules. Private networks include addresses defined with RFC 1918.

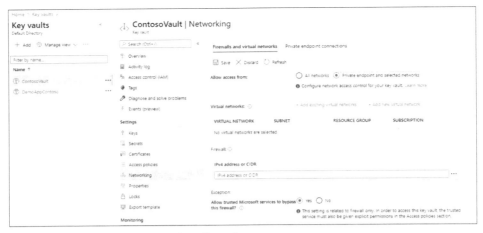

FIGURE 2-44 Azure Key Vault Firewall configuration

In Figure 2-44, notice the **Allow Trusted Microsoft Services To Bypass This Firewall** option, which is set to **Yes** by default. This will allow the following services to have access to your Key Vault regardless of the firewall configuration: Azure Virtual Machines deployment service, Azure Resource Manager template deployment service, Azure Application Gateway v2 SKU, Azure Disk Encryption volume encryption service, Azure Backup, Exchange Online, Share-Point Online, Azure Information Protection, Azure App Service, Azure SQL Database, Azure Storage Service, Azure Data Lake Store, Azure Databricks, Azure API Management, Azure Data Factory, Azure Event Hubs, Azure Service Bus, Azure Import/Export, and Azure Container Registry.

Azure App Service Firewall

You might also want to harden the network access for your apps that are deployed via Azure App Service. Although the terminology used in this section refers to "Azure App Service Firewall," what you are really implementing is a network-level access-control list. The access restrictions capability in Azure App Service is implemented in the App Service front-end roles. These front-end roles are upstream of the worker hosts where your code runs.

A common exam scenario for the implementation of this capability is when you need to restrict access to your app from certain VNets or the Internet. On the AZ-500 exam, make sure to carefully read the scenario because, in this case, you are adding restrictions to access the app itself, not the host.

To configure access restrictions on your Azure App Services, open the Azure portal, open the **App Services** dashboard, click your app service or Azure function, and in the **Settings** section, click **Networking**. The **Access Restrictions** option is shown at the right (see Figure 2-45).

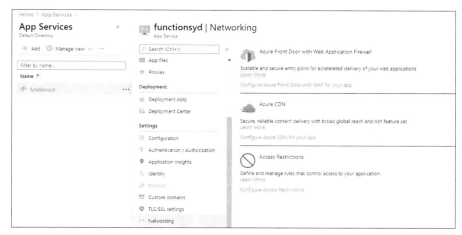

FIGURE 2-45 Azure App Services access restriction

To start the configuration, click **Configure Access Restrictions** in the **Access Restriction** section. You will see the **Access Restriction** page, as shown in Figure 2-46. The initial table is blank (no rules), and you can click **Add Rule** to start configuring your restrictions.

FIGURE 2-46 Adding Access Restrictions

It is recommended that you schedule a maintenance window to configure these restrictions because any operation (add, edit, or remove) in those rules will restart your app for changes to take effect.

Implement Azure service endpoints

You can also have a VNet that has only PaaS services and allow these services to be accessible outside of the VNet in which they reside. For example, the database admin needs to access the Azure SQL Database from the Internet. In this scenario, the database admin needs to create a service endpoint to allow secure access to the database.

At the time this chapter was written, the following Azure services supported service endpoint configuration:

- Azure Storage
- Azure SQL Database
- Azure SQL Data Warehouse
- Azure Database for PostgreSQL server
- Azure Database for MySQL server
- Azure Database for MariaDB
- Azure Cosmos DB
- Azure Key Vault
- Azure Service Bus
- Azure Event Hubs
- Azure Data Lake Store Gen 1
- Azure App Service
- Azure Container Registry

> **IMPORTANT   NETWORK UPDATES**
>
> For the most updated list of supported service endpoints, see *https://docs.microsoft.com/ en-us/azure/virtual-network/virtual-network-service-endpoints-overview.*

From a security perspective, service endpoints provide the ability to secure Azure service resources to your VNet by extending the VNet identity to the service. After enabling service endpoints in your VNet, you can add a VNet rule to secure the Azure service resources to your VNet. By adding this rule, you are enhancing the security by fully removing public Internet access to resources and allowing traffic only from your virtual network.

Another advantage of using a service endpoint is traffic optimization. Service endpoint always takes service traffic directly from your VNet to the service on the Microsoft Azure backbone network, which means that the traffic is kept within the Azure backbone network. By having this control, you can continue auditing and monitoring outbound Internet traffic from your VNet without affecting service traffic.

> **IMPORTANT   DEPLOYMENT MODEL**
>
> This feature is available only to virtual networks deployed through the Azure Resource Manager deployment model.

The VNet service endpoint allows you to harden the Azure service access to only allowed VNet and subnet access. This adds an additional level of security to the network and isolates the Azure service traffic. All traffic using VNet service endpoints flows over the Microsoft backbone, thus providing another layer of isolation from the public Internet. You can also fully remove public Internet access to the Azure service resources and allow traffic only from their virtual networks through a combination of IP firewall and access control list on the VNet, which protects the Azure service resources from unauthorized access.

To configure a virtual network service endpoint, you will need to perform these two main actions:

- Enable service endpoint in the subnet
- Add a service endpoint to your VNet

If you are configuring Azure Storage, you also need to configure a service endpoint policy.

> **NOTE VNET SERVICE POLICY**
>
> For more information on Azure VNet service endpoint policies for Azure Storage, see *https:// docs.microsoft.com/en-us/azure/virtual-network/virtual-network-service-endpoint-policies-overview*.

Enabling a service endpoint on the subnet can be done during the creation of the subnet or after the subnet is created. In the proprieties of the subnet, you can select the service endpoint in the **Services** drop-down menu, as shown in Figure 2-47.

FIGURE 2-47 Service Endpoints configuration on the subnet

To configure virtual network service endpoints on your virtual network, use the following steps:

1. Navigate to the Azure portal at *https://portal.azure.com*.
2. In the search bar, type **virtual networks**; under **Services**, click **Virtual Networks**.
3. Click the virtual network for which you want to configure the service endpoint.
4. In the left pane, click **Service Endpoint**, as shown in Figure 2-48.
5. Click the **Add** button.
6. In the **Add Service Endpoints** page, click the drop-down menu and select the Azure Service that you want to add.

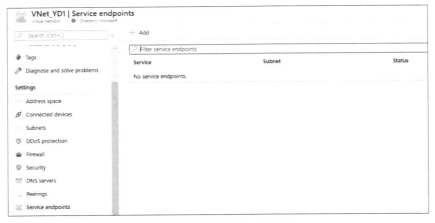

FIGURE 2-48 Configuring a VNet service endpoint

Azure private endpoints and Private Links

When referring to a private endpoint in Azure, you are basically referring to a network interface that has a private IP address obtained from a virtual network. This network interface is then connected privately and securely to an Azure service via a Private Link. In this case, the Azure service can be an Azure Storage, Azure SQL, an Azure Cosmos DB, or your own service using Private Link service.

When you use private endpoints, the traffic is secured to a Private Link resource. An access control validation is done by the platform to check the network connections are reaching only the specified Private Link resource. If you need to access more resources within the same Azure service, you will need extra private endpoints.

> **MORE INFO** **PRIVATE LINK RESOURCES**
>
> For more information about the available Private Link resources, see *http://aka.ms/az500plink*.

It is very important to mention that a private endpoint enables connectivity between the consumers from the same virtual network, regionally peered virtual networks, globally peered virtual networks, on-premises using VPN or ExpressRoute, and services powered by Private Link. Another important consideration is that network connections will only be allowed to be initiated by clients that are connecting to the private endpoint. Service providers don't have a routing configuration to create connections into service consumers.

> **NOTE** **DEPLOYMENT CONSIDERATIONS**
>
> Although the Private Link resource can be deployed in a different region than the virtual network and private endpoint, the private endpoint must be deployed in the same region and subscription as the virtual network.

An Azure Private Link service is the reference to your service that is powered by Azure Private Link. After you create a Private Link service, Azure will generate a globally unique, named moniker called "alias" based on the name you provide for your service.

> **MORE INFO MORE ABOUT PRIVATE LINK**
>
> For more information about Private Link, see *http://aka.ms/a500privatelink*.

Implement Azure DDoS protection

By default, Azure Distributed denial of service (DDoS) basic protection is already enabled on your subscription. This means that traffic monitoring and real-time mitigation of common network-level attacks are fully covered and provide the same level of defense as the ones utilized by Microsoft's online services.

While the basic protection provides automatic attack mitigations against DDoS, there are some capabilities that are only provided by the DDoS Standard tier. The organization's requirements will lead you to determine which tier you will utilize. If Contoso needs to implement DDoS protection on the application level, it needs to have real-time attack metrics and resource logs available to its team. Contoso also needs to create post-attack mitigation reports to present to upper management. These requirements can only be fulfilled by the DDoS Standard tier. Table 2-2 provides a summary of the capabilities available for each tier:

TABLE 2-2 Azure DDoS Basic versus Standard

Capability	DDoS Basic	DDoS Standard
Active traffic monitoring and always-on detection	X	X
Automatic attack mitigation	X	X
Availability guarantee	Per Azure region.	Per application.
Mitigation policies	Tuned per Azure region volume.	Tuned for application traffic volume.
Metrics and alerts	Not available.	X
Mitigation flow logs	Not available.	X
Mitigation policy customization	Not available.	X
Support	Yes, but it is a best-effort approach. In other words, there is no guarantee support will address the issue.	Yes, and it provides access to DDoS experts during an active attack.
SLA	Azure region.	Application guarantee and cost protection.
Pricing	Free.	Monthly usage.

To configure Azure DDoS, your account must be a member of the Network Contributor role, or you can create a custom role that has read, write, and delete privileges under `Microsoft.Network/ddosProtectionPlans` and action privilege under `Microsoft.Network/ddosProtectionPlans/join`. Your custom role also needs to have read, write, and delete privileges under `Microsoft.Network/virtualNetworks`. After you grant access to the user, use the following steps to create a DDoS Protection plan:

1. Navigate to the Azure portal at *https://portal.azure.com*.

2. In the search bar, type **DDoS**, and under **Services**, click **DDoS Protection Plans**.

3. On the **DDoS Protection Plans** page, click the **Add** button; the **Create A DDoS Protection Plan** page appears, as shown in Figure 2-49.

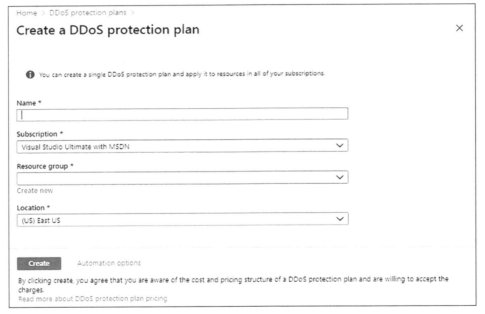

FIGURE 2-49 Create A DDoS Protection Plan

4. In the **Name** field, type the name for this DDoS protection.

5. In the **Subscription** field, select the appropriate subscription.

6. In the **Resource group** field, click the drop-down menu and select the resource group that you want.

7. In the **Location** field, select the region for the DDoS.

8. Before you click the **Create** button, read the note that is located under this button. This note emphasizes that by clicking **Create**, you are aware of the pricing for DDoS protection. Because there is no trial period for this feature, you will be charged during the first month of utilizing this feature.

9. After clicking **Create**, go to the search bar, type **network**, and click **Virtual Networks**.

10. Click the virtual network for which you want to enable the DDoS Standard.

11. In the left navigation pane, click the **DDoS Protection** option.

12. Click the **Standard** option, as shown in Figure 2-50.

FIGURE 2-50 Enabling DDoS Standard on the VNet

13. Click the **DDoS Protection Plan** drop-down menu and select the DDoS protection plan that you created in step 9.

14. Click the **Save** button.

At this point, you can configure Azure Monitor to send alerts by leveraging DDoS protection metrics. To do that, open Azure Monitor, click **Metrics**, select the scope of the public IP address located in the VNet where DDoS Standard is enabled, click the **Metric** drop-down menu, and select **Under DDoS Attack Or Not**, as shown in Figure 2-51.

To access a DoS attack mitigation report, you need to first configure diagnostic settings. This report uses the Netflow protocol data to provide detailed information about the DDoS attack on your resource. To configure this option, click **Diagnostic Settings** in the **Settings** section in the Azure Monitor blade, as shown in Figure 2-52.

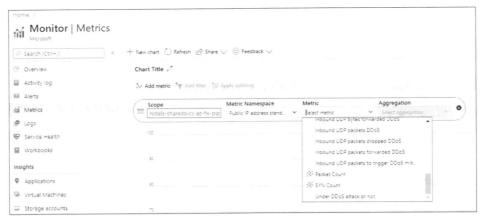

FIGURE 2-51 Monitoring DDoS activity

FIGURE 2-52 Configuring diagnostic logging

As you can see in the bottom part of the right blade, this page allows you to configure diagnostic logging for `DDoSProtectionNotifications`, `DDoSMitigationFlowLogs`, and `DDoSMitigationReports`. Just like any other diagnostic setting, you can store this data in a storage account, Event Hub, or a Log Analytics workspace.

EXAM TIP

For the AZ-500 exam, always make sure to review the details of the use case to ensure you are selecting the most appropriate option according to the scenario description.

Besides these options, is important to mention that Microsoft Defender for Cloud will also surface security alerts generated by DDoS Protection. There are two main alerts that could be triggered by this service and surfaced in Defender for Cloud:

- DDoS Attack detected for Public IP
- DDoS Attack mitigated for Public IP

Skill 2.2: Configure advanced security for compute

This section of the chapter covers the skills necessary to configure advanced security for compute, according to the Exam AZ-500 outline.

Configure Azure endpoint protection for virtual machines (VMs)

Endpoint protection is an imperative part of your security strategy, and these days, you can't have endpoint protection without an antimalware solution installed on your computer.

Consider a scenario in which you provision a new VM that doesn't have an endpoint protection configured. Wouldn't it be ideal to have a solution that alerts you to the fact that an endpoint protection is missing in that VM? This is exactly what happens when you have Microsoft Defender for Cloud enabled in your subscription.

Follow these steps to access Defender for Cloud and review the endpoint protection recommendations:

1. Navigate to the Azure portal at *https://portal.azure.com*.
2. In the search bar, type **security**, and under **Services**, click **Microsoft Defender for Cloud**.
3. In Defender for Cloud main dashboard, under the **Resource Security Hygiene** section, click **Compute & Apps**.
4. In the resulting list, click the **Install Endpoint Protection Solution On Virtual Machines** option; the **Endpoint Protection Not Installed On Azure VMs** page appears, as shown in Figure 2-53.

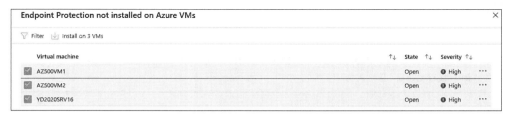

FIGURE 2-53 List of VMs that don't have an endpoint protection solution installed

5. Select the VM on which you want to install the endpoint protection and click the **Install On 1 VM** button. The **Select Endpoint Protection** page appears, as shown in Figure 2-54.

FIGURE 2-54 Selecting the available endpoint protection solution to install

6. Defender for Cloud automatically suggests that you install the Microsoft Antimalware for Azure, which is a free real-time protection that helps identify and remove viruses, spyware, and other malicious software. Click the **Microsoft Antimalware** option; the **Microsoft Antimalware** page appears, as shown in Figure 2-55.

FIGURE 2-55 Microsoft Antimalware installation

7. Click the **Create** button; the **Install Microsoft Antimalware** blade appears, as shown in Figure 2-56.

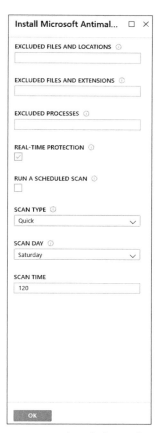

FIGURE 2-56 Installation options

8. If you need to create an endpoint protection exclusion list, this is where you would do that. For example, let's say you are aware that you want to avoid issues caused by anti-malware scans of the files used by your app. You can add the paths used by this application in the exclusion list. This blade contains the following options:

- **Excluded Files And Locations**   Here, you can specify any paths or locations to exclude from the scan. To add multiple paths or locations, separate them with semicolons. This is an optional setting.

- **Excluded Files And Extensions**   This box lets you specify filenames or extensions to exclude from the scan. Again, to add multiple names or extensions, you separate them with a semicolon. Note that you should avoid using wildcard characters.

- **Excluded Processes**   Use this box to specify any processes that should be excluded from the scan. Again, use semicolons to separate multiple processes.

- **Real-Time Protection**   By default, this check box is enabled. Unless you have a good business reason to do otherwise, you should leave it that way.

- **Run a Scheduled Scan** Selecting this check box enables you to run a scheduled scan.
- **Scan Type** If you selected the **Run A Scheduled Scan** check box, you can use this drop-down menu to specify the type of scan. (A quick scan is run by default.)
- **Scan Day** If you selected the **Run A Scheduled Scan** check box, you can use this drop-down menu to specify the day that the scan will run.
- **Scan Time** If you selected the **Run A Scheduled Scan** check box, you can use this drop-down menu to specify what time the scan will run. The time is indicated in increments of 60 minutes (60 = 1 AM, 120 = 2 AM, and so on).

9. After you customize the options according to your needs, click the **OK** button.

10. After this step, the installation process will start. You can close the **Defender for Cloud** dashboard at this point.

Often, you will want to see an immediate reflection of the changes you made in the dashboard. However, be aware that the Defender for Cloud dashboard has different refresh times, which vary according to the objects. For example, operating system security configurations data are updated within 48 hours, and Endpoint Protection data is updated within 8 hours. This means that even if the installation of the endpoint succeeds in the next five minutes after you started, the dashboard will only reflect that installation in the next refresh cycle.

Having said that, it is important to mention that if the antimalware that was installed on the machine identifies a malicious code running, it will immediately trigger an alert. This alert will appear in the Security Alerts dashboard, as shown in Figure 2-57.

FIGURE 2-57 The Alert that appears in the Security Alert dashboard when Microsoft Antimalware takes an action

When you open this alert, you will see more details about the operation, which include the attacked resource, subscription, threat status, and file path, as shown in Figure 2-58.

Having an endpoint protection installed is only the first step to enhance the overall protection of your VM. There are many other aspects of VM security that need to be taken into consideration, and hardening is one of those. (See the next section.) Beyond hardening, what else can be implemented to secure a VM? Let's start with access control. In a scenario in which an organization has multiple subscriptions, you might need a way to manage access efficiently. Establishing a good access control policy is one way to do just that.

In Azure, you can use Azure policies to create conventions for resources and create customized policies to control access. You can apply these policies to resource groups and the VMs that belong to those resource groups will inherit those policies. You can implement those policies at the management group level if you have multiple subscriptions that should receive the same policy.

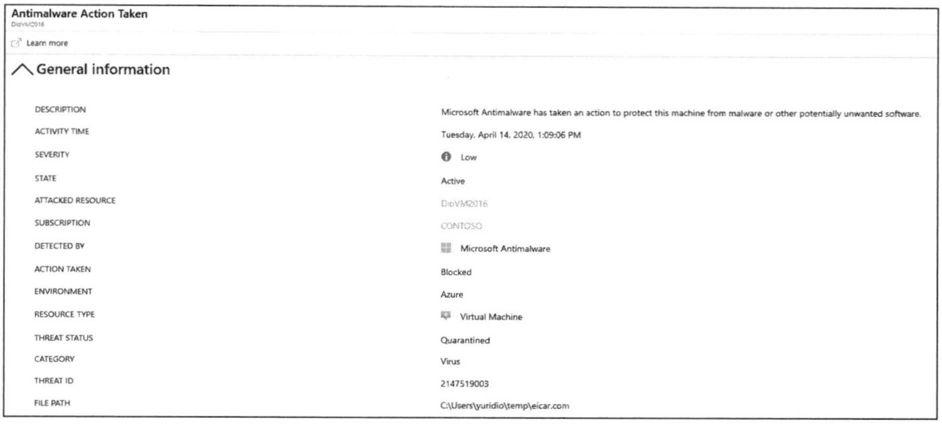

Antimalware Action Taken
DevVM2016

Learn more

General information

DESCRIPTION	Microsoft Antimalware has taken an action to protect this machine from malware or other potentially unwanted software.
ACTIVITY TIME	Tuesday, April 14, 2020, 1:09:06 PM
SEVERITY	ℹ Low
STATE	Active
ATTACKED RESOURCE	DevVM2016
SUBSCRIPTION	CONTOSO
DETECTED BY	Microsoft Antimalware
ACTION TAKEN	Blocked
ENVIRONMENT	Azure
RESOURCE TYPE	Virtual Machine
THREAT STATUS	Quarantined
CATEGORY	Virus
THREAT ID	2147519003
FILE PATH	C:\Users\yuridio\temp\eicar.com

FIGURE 2-58 Details about an alert are triggered in Microsoft Defender for Cloud when malware is detected.

When configuring access control, always make sure to use the least-privilege approach. You can leverage built-in Azure roles to allow users to access and set up VMs. Instead of giving a higher level of access, you can assign a user to the Virtual Machine Contributor role, and that user will inherit the rights to manage VMs, though the user won't be able to manage the virtual network or storage account to which he or she is connected. The same applies for users who need access to Microsoft Defender for Cloud to visualize the recommendations for their VMs; they should have the Security Reader role, which will enable them to see recommendations but will not allow them make changes to the configuration.

While the Defender for Cloud provides good insights regarding the current security posture of your workloads, you should also consider the threat detection for VMs that comes with Defender for Servers. Defender for Servers has Virtual Machine Behavioral Analysis (VMBA) that uses behavioral analytics to identify compromised resources based on an analysis of the virtual machine (VM) event logs, such as processing creation events and log-in events. If your scenario requires detection of attacks against your VMs, Defender for Servers must be enabled.

VMs threat detections in Defender for Servers are applicable for Windows and Linux operating systems. Figure 2-59 shows an example of a threat detection based on VMBA in Defender for Servers. This alert appears in the **Security Alerts** dashboard.

Threat detection is an important security control, though there are other security controls that must also be in place and that are categorized as proactive measures or proactive security controls.

Disk encryption should also be applied to your VMs. Consider a scenario where the organization needs to ensure that encryption is in place no matter where the data is located (at rest or in-flight), and you need to quickly identify whether data is encrypted. Defender for Cloud can give you this level of visibility.

FIGURE 2-59 Example of a VM threat detection in Defender for Servers

Defender for Cloud will trigger a recommendation when it identifies VMs that don't have disk encryption enabled. Another aspect of VM security is the identification of resource abuse. When VM processes consume more resources than they should, this could also be an indication of suspicious activity. Without a doubt, performance issues could happen for a variety of issues, including an application that was not well-written. Performance issues might also happen because the VM is running out of resources because the valid load is high. (In this case, you need to upgrade the VM with more resources.) Whatever the cause may be, the bottom line is that a VM's performance can lead to service disruption, which directly violates the security principle of availability.

You can use Azure Monitor to obtain visibility of your VM's health. By leveraging Azure Monitor's features, such as resource diagnostic log files, you can identify potential issues that might compromise performance and availability. Azure Monitor and diagnostic logging are covered in more detail in Chapter 3, "Manage security operations."

Implement and manage security updates for VMs

Keeping the system up to date is another imperative measure for any organization that wants to implement host security. The good news is that in Azure, you have two major services that can be used to ensure that your VMs are fully up to date.

Consider a scenario where you need to manage operating system updates for your Windows and Linux VMs, not only in Azure but also on-premises and in any other cloud environment. You can use the Update Management solution in Azure Automation to manage your VMs. Following are the components used by Update Management:

- **Log Analytics agent for Windows or Linux**   This is the same agent used by Defender for Cloud, which means you should have it already installed if you are using Defender for Cloud.

- **PowerShell Desired State Configuration (DSC) for Linux**   The management platform in PowerShell running on Linux.

- **Automation Hybrid Runbook Worker**   Each Windows machine that is managed by the solution is listed in the Hybrid worker groups.

- **Microsoft Update or Windows Server Update Services (WSUS) for Windows machines**   The update management platform managed by Microsoft (Microsoft Update) or managed by your organizations (WSUS).

Update management collection is done via a scan that is performed twice per day for each managed Windows server (clients are not supported) and every hour for Linux machines. The following versions of the operating systems are supported by this solution:

- Windows Server 2019 (Datacenter/Datacenter Core/Standard)
- Windows Server 2016 (Datacenter/Datacenter Core/Standard)
- Windows Server 2012 R2 (Datacenter/Standard)
- Windows Server 2012
- Windows Server 2008 R2 RTM and SP1 Standard (assessment only, patching is not supported)
- CentOS 6, 7, and 8
- Red Hat Enterprise 6, 7, and 8
- SUSE Linux Enterprise Server 12, 15, and 15.1
- Ubuntu 14.04 LTS, 16.04 LTS, 18.04 LTS, and 20.04 LTS

You can enable the Update Management solution directly from the VM's properties, which is a good approach if you only need to enable this solution for one VM. If you need to deploy to all VMs, you can select all VMs at once from the **Virtual Machines** dashboard and deploy to all VMs from there. VMs can be spread across up to three resources groups when enabling this solution for multiple VMs. Follow these steps to enable this feature for multiple VMs:

1. Navigate to the Azure portal at *https://portal.azure.com*.
2. In the search bar, type **virtual machine**, and under **Services**, click **Virtual Machines**.
3. Click the check box next to the field **Name** to select all VMs.
4. Click the **Services** button and click **Update Management**; the **Enable Update Management** page appears, as shown in Figure 2-60.

FIGURE 2-60 Enabling Update Management for VMs

5. Notice that the default configuration has the **AUTO** option selected. This option will auto-configure Log Analytics workspace and automation account based on your VM's subscription and location. If you already have VMs deployed with the Log Analytics and the agent is already configured to report to a specific workspace, the auto-configuration won't work; you need to select **CUSTOM** and from there select the workspace where the VM resides as well as the Azure automation account that will be used by Updated Management.

6. For this example, leave the default selection and click the **Enable** button.

The deployment of this solution can take some time, depending on the amount of VMs that you select; wait until it is fully finished before proceeding.

Managing updates

Now that the Update Management solution is deployed to your VMs, you can access its dashboard to visualize the list of missing updates and scheduled update deployments. To access the Update Management dashboard, use the following steps:

1. Navigate to the Azure portal at *https://portal.azure.com*.

2. In the search bar, type **automate**, and under **Services**, click **Automated Accounts**.

3. Click the automation account that is used by your Update Management solution.

4. In the left pane, click **Update Management**, and if the scan is completed, the list of updates will appear, as shown in Figure 2-61.

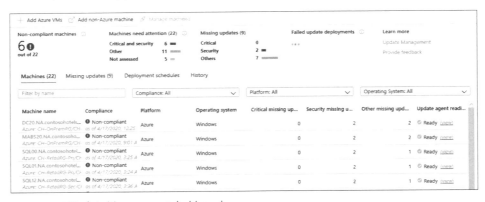

FIGURE 2-61 Update Management dashboard

5. Click the **Missing Updates** tab to visualize the updates that are currently missing on the machines (see Figure 2-62).

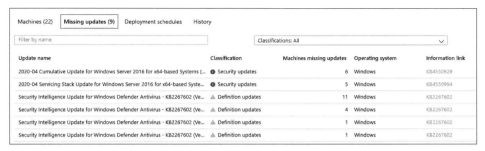

FIGURE 2-62 List of missing updates

In the example given in the previous steps, you saw an environment that was already in production, with machines already reporting to Update Management and a deployment schedule already created. In a new deployment, you will see that there is a **Schedule Update Deployment** button in the main **Update Management** dashboard, as shown in Figure 2-63.

FIGURE 2-63 Option to schedule the deployment of the updates

Configure security for containers services

Azure Container Registry (ACR) is a private registry of Docker and Open Container Initiative (OCI) images, based on open-source Docker Registry 2.0. Developers can pull (download) images from an Azure container registry, and they can also push (upload) to a container registry as part of a container development workflow. ACR pricing tiers are

- **Basic** More suitable for developers learning about ACR
- **Standard** Increased storage and image throughput and more suitable for a production environment
- **Premium** More suitable for high-volume scenarios and high image throughput

EXAM TIP

On the exam, you might need to select the best pricing tier (also known as a SKU) according to the given scenario.

You can use an Azure AD service principal to provide container image *docker push* and *pull* access to your container registry. Azure AD service principals provide access to Azure resources within your subscription. Think of a service principal as a user identity for a service.

Manage access to Azure Container Registry

To manage access to your Azure Container Registry (ACR) you must add a user to a specific role that will allow the user to perform certain tasks. Table 2-3 provides the mapping of the roles for the allowed tasks that can be executed in the ACR:

TABLE 2-3 Azure Container Registry RBAC roles

Role	Tasks that can be executed
Owner	Access resource manager, create and delete the registry, push images, pull images, delete image data, and change policies
Contributor	Access resource manager, create and delete the registry, push images, pull images, delete image data, and change policies
Reader	Access resource manager and pull images
ArcPush	Push and pull images
ArcPull	Pull image
ArcDelete	Delete image data
ArcImageSigner	Sign images

For CI/CD automation scenarios, you need *docker push* capabilities. For this type of scenario, we recommend that you assign the *AcrPush* role. This recommendation comes from the application of the principle of least privilege because this role, unlike the broader *Contributor* role, prevents the user from performing other registry operations or accessing Azure Resource Manager. Using the same rationale, nodes running containers need the *AcrPull* role but shouldn't require *Reader* capabilities.

To pull or push images to an Azure container registry, a client must interact over HTTPS with two different endpoints: the Registry REST API endpoint and the storage endpoint. By default, an ACR accepts connections over the Internet from hosts on any network. If you are using ACR Premium, you can leverage Azure VNet network access rules to control access to your ACR.

When managing ACR, it is a good practice to implement a vulnerability assessment solution that scans all pushed images. You can leverage Microsoft Defender for Containers to have the vulnerability assessment functionality.

When this capability is enabled, Microsoft Defender for Containers scans the image that was pushed using a Qualys scanner, which is fully integrated with the Microsoft Defender for Containers, and there is no additional cost for the Qualys engine. Figure 2-64 shows a diagram of how vulnerability management for ACR is done using Microsoft Defender for Containers.

If an issue is found during this scanning process, Microsoft Defender for Containers generates an actionable recommendation that appears in Microsoft Defender for Cloud dashboard with guidance for remediating the issue. Figure 2-65 shows an example of the type of recommendations you might see.

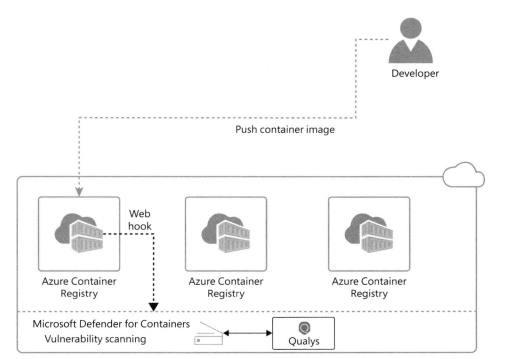

FIGURE 2-64 Vulnerability scanning process in Defender for Containers

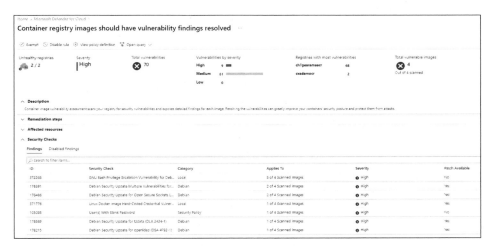

FIGURE 2-65 Container registry image recommendation in Microsoft Defender for Cloud

Configure security for serverless compute

A growing type of serverless compute is Azure Kubernetes (AKS), and when it comes to security for Kubernetes, one of the first aspects you need to address is isolation. This isolation is applicable for scenarios that you need to isolate workloads or teams. AKS provides capabilities for multitenant clusters and resource isolation. Natively, Kubernetes already creates a logical isolation boundary by using a namespace, which is the logical group of resources (such as pods).

Also, the following Kubernetes features should be used in scenarios that require isolation and multitenancy:

- **Scheduling**   The AKS scheduler allows you to control the distribution of compute resources and to limit the impact of maintenance events. This component includes the use of features such as resource quotas and pod-disruption budgets.
- **Networking**   AKS networking enables you to leverage the network policy's capability to allow or deny traffic flow to pods.
- **Authentication and authorization**   As mentioned earlier in the chapter, the use of RBAC and Azure AD integration is imperative to enhance the security of your authentication and authorization.
- **Other features**   These features include pod-security policies, pod-security contexts, scanning images, and runtimes for vulnerabilities.

> *IMPORTANT*   **LEAST PRIVILEGE**
>
> An important design consideration when planning your AKS is to provide the least number of privileges that are scoped to the resources each team needs.

There are two main types of isolation for AKS clusters: logical and physical. You should use logical isolation to separate teams and projects. Using logical isolation, a single AKS cluster can be used for multiple workloads, teams, or environments.

It is also recommended that you minimize the number of physical AKS clusters you deploy to isolate teams or applications. Figure 2-66 shows an example of this logical isolation.

Logical isolation can help minimize costs by enabling autoscaling and run only the number of nodes required at a time.

Physical isolation is usually selected when you have a hostile multitenant environment where you want to fully prevent one tenant from affecting the security and service of another. The physical isolation means that you need to physically separate AKS clusters. In this isolation model, teams or workloads are assigned their own AKS clusters. While this approach usually looks easier to isolate, it adds additional management and financial overhead.

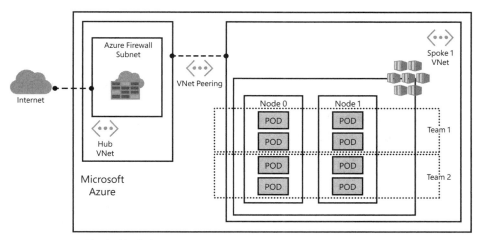

FIGURE 2-66 AKS logical isolation

There are many built-in capabilities in AKS that help ensure that your AKS Cluster is secure. Those built-in capabilities are based on native Kubernetes features, such as network policies and secrets, with the addition of Azure components, such as NSG and orchestrated cluster upgrades.

The combination of these components is used to keep your AKS cluster running the latest OS security updates and Kubernetes releases, secure pod traffic, and provide access to sensitive credentials. Figure 2-67 shows a diagram with the core AKS security components.

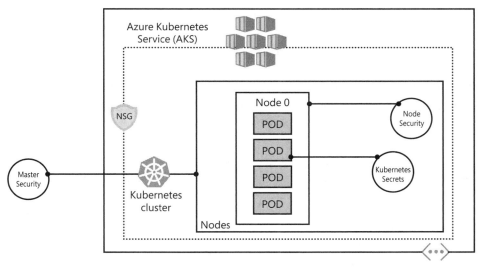

FIGURE 2-67 Core AKS security components

When you deploy AKS in Azure, the Kubernetes master components are part of the managed service provided by Microsoft. Each AKS cluster has a dedicated Kubernetes master. This master is used to provide API Server, Scheduler, and so on. You can control access to the API server using Kubernetes RBAC controls and Azure AD.

While the Kubernetes master is managed and maintained by Microsoft, the AKS nodes are VMs that you manage and maintain. These nodes can use Linux OS (optimized Ubuntu distribution) or Windows Server 2019. The Azure platform automatically applies OS security patches to Linux nodes on a nightly basis, but on Windows nodes, Windows Update does not automatically run or apply the latest updates. This means that if you have Windows nodes, you need to maintain the schedule around the update lifecycle and enforce those updates.

From the network perspective, these nodes are deployed into a private virtual network subnet with no public IP addresses assigned to it. SSH is enabled by default and should only be used for troubleshooting purposes because it is only available using the internal IP address. In Figure 2-67, you also have an NSG, which can also be used to enhance network protection.

AKS nodes use Azure Managed Disks, and the data is automatically encrypted at rest within the Azure platform. To fulfill the security principle of availability, these disks are also securely replicated within the Azure datacenter.

> **IMPORTANT PLANNING AKS**
>
> When you are planning AKS high availability, consider the process of upgrading an AKS Cluster. Read this article for more information about the upgrade process: *https://docs.microsoft.com/en-us/azure/aks/upgrade-cluster*.

The diagram shown in Figure 2-67 shows the Kubernetes secret element, which is used to inject sensitive data into pods, such as credentials or keys. The use of secrets reduces the sensitive information that is defined in the pod or service YAML manifest. You can read more about secrets in Kubernetes at *https://kubernetes.io/docs/concepts/configuration/secret*.

In addition to the native capabilities in Kubernetes and Azure that were described previously, you can enhance the security posture of your AKS deployment by leveraging Microsoft Defender for Cloud recommendations.

Microsoft Defender for Cloud constantly monitors the AKS and Docker configurations and then generates security recommendations that reflect industry standards. In addition to that, if you use Microsoft Defender for Containers, you will also have threat detections that are created based on the continuous analysis of raw security events, such as network data and process creation and the Kubernetes audit log. Based on this information, Microsoft Defender for Containers will alert you if threats and malicious activity detected at the host and AKS cluster level. Figure 2-68 shows an example of an alert that notifies you about an exposure of Kubernetes services.

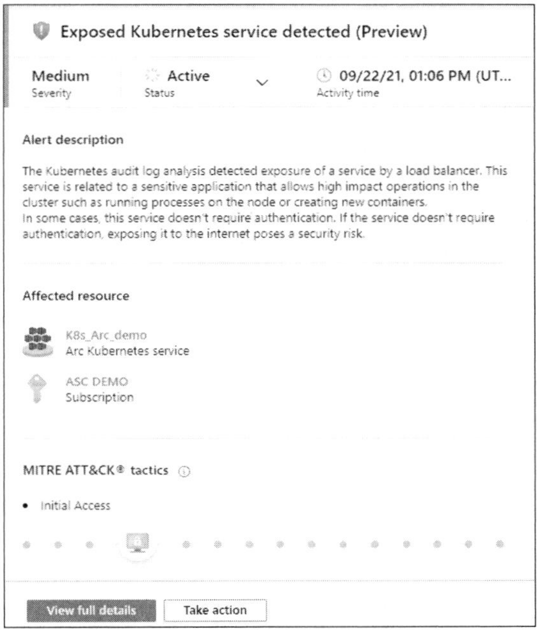

FIGURE 2-68 Alert for AKS generated by Defender for Containers

Configure security for Azure App Service

Azure App Service is an HTTP-based service for hosting web applications, REST APIs, and mobile back ends. Azure App Service Environment (ASE) is an Azure App Service feature that provides an isolated and dedicated environment for securely running App Service apps in the cloud. You can create multiple ASEs to host multiple apps running in Windows, Linux, Docker, mobile, and function apps.

> **IMPORTANT** **PRICING TIER**
>
> All pricing tiers run your apps on the shared network infrastructure in the Azure App Service, except for the Isolated pricing tier, which gives you complete network isolation by running your apps inside a dedicated App Service environment.

To configure security for Azure App Service, you need to understand the variety of options available. Azure App Service has built-in security controls that can be leveraged to enhance the overall security posture of your apps. Essentially, some of these controls are Azure components that were described throughout this chapter. Table 2-4 provides a summary of the security controls that can be used with Azure App Service.

TABLE 2-4 Advantages and limitations

Layer	Security control	Description
Network	Service Endpoint	You can use access restrictions to define a priority-ordered allow/deny list that controls network access to your app. This is an important practice to limit exposure to inbound network traffic.
	VNet injection support	This security control is used for ASE, which is a private implementation of App Service dedicated to a single customer and injected into that customer's VNet.
	Network Isolation and Firewalling support	You can configure network access control list (ACL) to lock down allowed inbound traffic.
	Forced tunneling support	Although ASE outbound dependency traffic must go through the VIP that is provisioned with the ASE, you can configure it to customize the network routing.
Monitoring	Azure monitoring support	You can review quotas and metrics for an app and the App Service plan. You can also configure alerts and auto-scale rules-based metrics.
	Control and management plane logging and audit	Because all management operations performed on App Service objects occur via Azure Resource Manager (ARM), you will be able to see historical logs of these operations. Keep in mind that there is no data-plane logging and auditing available for App Service.
Identity	Authentication	Supports integration with Azure AD and other OAuth providers.
	Authorization	Controlled by Azure AD and RBAC.
Data Protection	Server-side encryption at rest: Microsoft-managed keys	The App Service site file content is stored in Azure Storage, which automatically encrypts the content at rest, and the customer's supplied secrets are encrypted at rest.
	Server-side encryption at rest: customer-managed keys (BYOK)	Supports the storage of an application's secret in Key Vault, so that it can be retrieved during runtime.
	Encryption in transit	Supports the use of HTTPS for inbound traffic.
	API calls encrypted	Also supported via calls over HTTPS.
Configuration management	Configuration management support	The state of an App Service configuration can be exported as an ARM template.

Besides the available security controls that are inherited from Azure, you should also ensure that you are always developing your apps using the latest versions of supported platforms, programming languages, protocols, and frameworks. It is very important that throughout the development lifecycle, you properly configure the authentication for these apps. Always make sure that authentication is required and that anonymous access is disabled unless the scenario's description clearly states that it must be enabled. You can also enhance your authentication security by requiring clients to use a certificate to authenticate. This practice improves security by allowing connections only from clients that can authenticate using certificates that you provide.

As part of your secure configuration of App Service, make sure that data in transit is protected, which means that you should always redirect HTTP to HTTPS traffic and that you enforce the latest version of the TLS protocol. Communications from your Azure App Service and other Azure resources, such as Azure Storage, should also be encrypted. If the scenario description requires you to transfer files from your Azure app for another location using FTP, make sure that you are utilizing FTPS instead.

Some of the overall security recommendations for Azure App Service will also be surfaced in Microsoft Defender for Cloud, as shown in Figure 2-69.

Microsoft Defender for Cloud will perform this security assessment on your apps, which is part of the Microsoft Defender for Cloud security posture management. However, if you enable Defender for App Service plan, you will also get threat detection for App Service. Microsoft Defender for App Service threat detection includes analytics and machine-learning models that cover all interfaces that allow customers to interact with their applications, whether it's over HTTP or through one of the management methods.

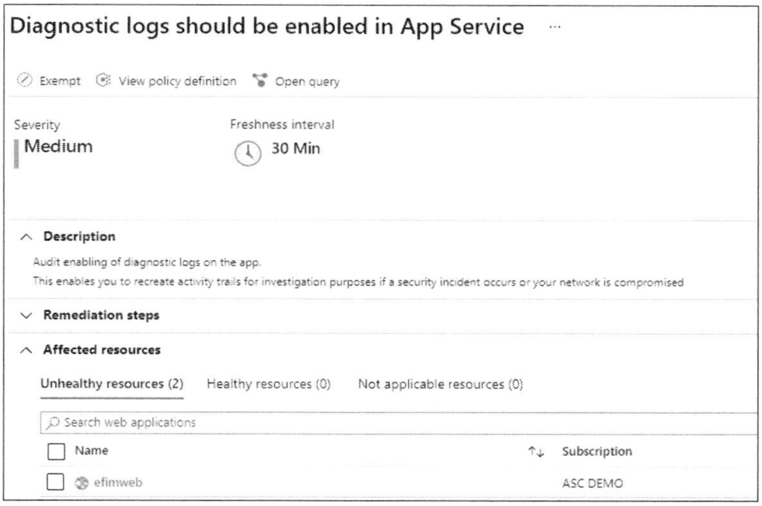

FIGURE 2-69 Defender for Cloud recommendations for App Service

To ensure your App Service is secure, you also need to address the authentication. By default, authentication and authorization are disabled. Upon enabling it, every incoming HTTP request passes through it before being handled by your application code. The authentication and authorization module runs separately from your application code and is configured using app settings.

The authentication and authorization modules are responsible for handling the authentication of users based on the selected provider, and it validates, stores, and refreshes tokens. They also manage the authenticated session and inject identity information into request headers. To configure authentication in App Service, you need to switch the **App Service Authentication** toggle to **ON**, and under **Authentication / Authorization**, the authentication options will appear, as shown in Figure 2-70.

FIGURE 2-70 Authentication and authorization options

Because App Service uses federated identity in which a third-party identity provider manages the user identities and authentication flow, the next step is to configure the type of authentication provider that will answer to requests that are not authenticated. Click the **Action To Take When Request Is Not Authenticated** drop-down menu and select the appropriate option. The option that you selected in the drop-down menu should match with the provider that you select in the **Authentication Providers** section. Once you select the appropriate provider, its sign-in endpoint is available for user authentication and for validation of authentication tokens from the selected provider.

> **TIP** **END-TO-END AUTHENTICATION AND AUTHORIZATION**
>
> For an example of how to authenticate and authorize users end to end in Azure App Service, see *http://aka.ms/az500AppServiceAuth*.

If you select the **Allow Anonymous Requests (No Action)** option in the drop-down menu, this option will defer authorization of unauthenticated traffic to your application code; in other words, you need to write the authentication code in your app. If it is an authenticated request,

App Service will pass along authentication information in the HTTP headers. Table 2-5 shows a summary of each identity provider:

TABLE 2-5 App Service identity providers

Identity provider	Sign-in endpoint	Configuration requirements
Azure AD	/.auth/login/aad	You can create a new Azure AD App or use an existing one. Allows you to enable Common Data Services (CDS) Permissions.
Microsoft Account	/.auth/login/microsoftaccount	Requires the Client ID and Client Secret. You can select different scopes that are responsible for enabling different operations.
Facebook	/.auth/login/facebook	Requires the App ID and App Secret. You can select different scopes that are responsible for enabling different operations.
Google	/.auth/login/google	Requires a Client ID and a Client Secret.
Twitter	/.auth/login/twitter	Requires an API key and an API secret.

> **IMPORTANT COMMON DATA SERVICE (CDS)**
>
> Common Data Service (CDS) enables you to securely store and manage data that's used by your apps. Standard and custom entities within CDS provide a secure and cloud-based storage option for your data. For more information about CDS, see *https://docs.microsoft.com/en-us/powerapps/maker/common-data-service/data-platform-intro*.

If Contoso administrator's requirement is to securely store and manage the data that is used by the company's app, Azure AD is the identity provider that addresses this requirement because Azure AD allows you to use CDS.

Because App Service is a Platform as a Service (PaaS), the operating system (OS) and application stack are managed for you by Azure, which means you don't need to worry about software updates. Azure manages OS patching on two levels: the physical servers and the guest VMs that run the App Service resources. Both will follow the regular Microsoft Patch Tuesday update cycle, which is once a month, unless it is a zero-day patch, which will be handled with higher priority and probably out of band (outside the regular Patch Tuesday cycle). When a new major or minor version is added to App Service, it is installed side by side with the existing versions.

App Service preserves its Service Level Agreement (SLA) even during the patch updates, which means that even if a patch requires a VM to restart, it will not affect App Service production because there always will be a buffer in capacity.

Access to patches in the registry at `HKEY_LOCAL_MACHINE\SOFTWARE\Microsoft\Windows\CurrentVersion\Component Based Servicing\Packages` is locked down, though basic info regarding OS and runtime updates can be queried using Kudu Console at *https://github.com/projectkudu/kudu/wiki/Kudu-console*. For example, if you want to see the Windows version, you can access this URL: *https://<appname>.scm.azurewebsites.net/Env.cshtml*.

Configure encryption at rest

Data encryption at rest is an extremely important part of your overall VM security strategy. Defender for Cloud will even trigger a security recommendation when a VM is missing disk encryption. You can encrypt your Windows and Linux virtual machines' disks using Azure Disk Encryption (ADE). For Windows OS, you need Windows 8 or later (for client) and Windows Server 2008 R2 or later (for servers).

ADE provides operating system and data disk encryption. For Windows, it uses BitLocker Device Encryption; for Linux, it uses the DM-Crypt system. ADE is not available in the following scenarios:

- Basic A-series VMs
- VMs with a less than 2 GB of memory
- Generation 2 VMs and Lsv2-series VMs
- Unmounted volumes

ADE requires that your Windows VM has connectivity with Azure AD to get a token to connect with Key Vault. At that point, the VM needs access to the Key Vault endpoint to write the encryption keys, and the VM also needs access to an Azure storage endpoint. This storage endpoint will host the Azure extension repository as well as the Azure storage account that hosts the VHD files.

> **IMPORTANT   URL FILTERING**
>
> If the VM is hardened and there are Internet access restrictions, make sure that this VM can at least access the URL. See *http://aka.ms/az500kvfw*.

Group policy is another important consideration when implementing ADE. If the VMs for which you are implementing ADE are domain joined, make sure to not push any group policy that enforces Trusted Platform Module (TPM) protectors. In this case, you will need to make sure that the **Allow BitLocker Without A Compatible TPM** policy is configured. Also, BitLocker policy for domain-joined VMs with custom group policy must include the following setting: `Configure User Storage Of BitLocker Recovery Information / Allow 256-Bit Recovery Key`.

Because ADE uses Azure Key Vault to control and manage disk encryption keys and secrets, you need to make sure Azure Key Vault has the proper configuration for this implementation. One important consideration when configuring your Azure Key Vault for ADE is that they (VM and Key Vault) both need to be part of the same subscription. Also, make sure that encryption secrets are not crossing regional boundaries; ADE requires that the Key Vault and the VMs are co-located in the same region. When configuring your Azure Key Vault, use `Set-AzKeyVaultAccessPolicy` with `-EnabledForDiskEncryption` to allow Azure platform to access the encryption keys or secrets in your key vault, as shown here:

```
Set-AzKeyVaultAccessPolicy -VaultName "<your -keyvault-name>" -ResourceGroupName
"MyResourceGroup" -EnabledForDiskEncryption
```

While these are the main considerations for Windows VM encryption, Linux VMs have some additional requirements. When you need to encrypt both data and OS volumes where the root (/) file system usage is 4 GB or less, you will need to have at least 8 GB of memory. However, if you need to encrypt only the data volume, the requirement drops to 2 GB of memory. The requirement doubles if Linux systems are using a root (/) file system greater than 4 GB, which means that the minimum memory requirement is root file system usage * 2.

> **MORE INFO**   **SUPPORTED LINUX DISTRIBUTIONS**
>
> To see the list of supported Linux distributions for ADE implementation, visit *http://aka.ms/ az500ADELinux*.

EXAM TIP

Understanding those considerations before implementing ADE is very important, mainly when reading a scenario in the AZ-500 exam. The scenario description will give you the requirements and the constraints, which means that in some scenarios, it won't be possible to implement ADE unless some other task is executed prior to the ADE implementation.

Assuming that you have the right prerequisites in place to implement ADE, you can use the Set-AzVmDiskEncryptionExtension PowerShell cmdlet to implement the encryption in a VM, as shown in the following example:

```
$AKeyVault = Get-AzKeyVault -VaultName MyAKV -ResourceGroupName MyRG
Set-AzVMDiskEncryptionExtension -ResourceGroupName MyRG -VMName MyVM
-DiskEncryptionKeyVaultUrl $AKeyVault.VaultUri -DiskEncryptionKeyVaultId $AKeyVault.
ResourceId
```

Wait a few minutes, and the output will show the field IsSuccessStatusCode as True, and the StatusCode as OK. You can also check the encryption status using Get-AzVmDiskEncryption Status cmdlet. If it was encrypted successfully you should see a result similar to this:

```
OsVolumeEncrypted            : Encrypted
DataVolumesEncrypted         : NoDiskFound
OsVolumeEncryptionSettings   : Microsoft.Azure.Management.Compute.Models.
DiskEncryptionSettings
ProgressMessage              : Provisioning succeeded
```

> **MORE INFO**   **DISK ENCRYPTION**
>
> For more disk encryption scenarios for Windows VM, see *http://aka.ms/az500ADEWin*.

Configure encryption in transit

To ensure that you are always protecting the data in transit, you should configure your App Service to use an SSL/TLS certificate. To create a TLS bind of your certificate to your app or enable client certificates for your App Service app, your App Service plan must be configured to the Basic, Standard, Premium, or Isolated tiers.

The App Service enables different scenarios to handle certificates, which include the capability to buy a certificate; import an existing certificate from the App Service; upload an existing certificate that you might have already; import a certificate from Key Vault (from any subscription on the same tenant); or create a free App Service custom certificate. (This last option does not provide support for naked domains.)

With the exception of buying a certificate—which is available via the **Buy Certificate** button—all other options are surfaced under the **Private Key Certificates (.pfx)** tab in the **TLS/SSL Settings** option in the right-hand navigation pane of the App Service that you selected. Figure 2-71 shows an example of this tab.

FIGURE 2-71 Options to configure a private key certificate for App Service

For the purpose of the AZ-500 exam, the scenario description is what leads you to choose one option over the other. For example, let's say that a Contoso administrator needs to secure data in transit for their App Service, but the administrator needs to save costs, leverage the existing Public Key Infrastructure (PKI) on-premises, and support naked domains. In this case, the most appropriate option would be to upload an existing certificate. This will save costs because it will leverage the existing PKI (which already met the second requirement), and it supports naked domains. When uploading an existing certificate, make sure you have the password for the protected PFX file; the private key must be at least 2048 bits long, and it must contain all intermediate certificates in the certificate chain.

Another important scenario is when you need to respond to requests to a specific hostname over HTTPS. In this case, you need to secure a custom domain in a TLS binding. In this scenario, you would use the **Add TLS/SSL Binding** option, which is available in the **Bindings** tab, as shown in Figure 2-72.

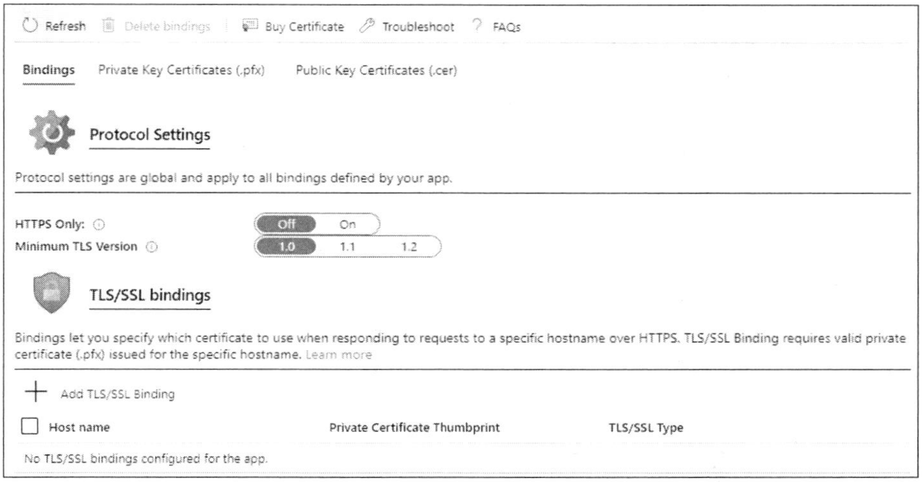

FIGURE 2-72 Options to add a TLS/SSL binding

The certificate that will be used to bind TLS/SSL needs to contain an `ExtendedKeyUsage` for server authentication object identifier (OID), which is `1.3.6.1.5.5.7.3.1`, and it must be signed by a trusted certificate authority. Also, notice that on this page, you can also configure your App Service to only answer to HTTPS, and you can configure the TLS version that will be used.

> **TIP   CERTIFICATES**
>
> **For the detailed steps to configure the different types of certificates, see *https://aka.ms/ az500AppCertificates*.**

Thought experiment

In this thought experiment, demonstrate your skills and knowledge of the topics covered in this chapter. You can find answers to this thought experiment in the next section.

Advanced security for compute at Tailwind Traders

You are one of the Azure administrators for Tailwind Traders, an online general store that specializes in a variety of products for the home. Tailwind Traders is deploying new VMs in Azure to increase the compute capacity because the company is forecasting an increase in online store shopping during the upcoming holiday season. Before releasing those VMs for use, they need to ensure that these VMs are configured to use security best practices, which include secure configurations, endpoint protection installation, and ensuring that the operating system is fully up to date.

Currently, Tailwind Traders does not have any cloud security posture management in place, but the company is interested in trying Microsoft Defender for Cloud. To improve security, they also need to continuously monitor those servers to identify potential attacks, and they want to receive an alert in case there are suspicious activities or indications of an attack against those servers. Another goal of Tailwind Traders is to allow the Security Operation Center (SOC) analysts to have read-only access to the Defender for Cloud dashboard in order to view the alerts. With this information in mind, answer the following questions:

1. Will Microsoft Defender for Cloud meet those requirements?
2. What Azure role should the SOC analysts have to accomplish their goals?
3. Where in Microsoft Defender for Cloud should the administrator go to identify whether the servers have an endpoint protection solution installed?

Thought experiment answers

This section contains the solution to the thought experiment. Each answer explains why the answer choice is correct.

1. Microsoft Defender for Cloud will only accomplish partial results of the desired requirements. It will enable the administrator to see security recommendations and improve the security posture of the workloads, but to have continuous monitoring of threat detection, the administrator needs to enable Microsoft Defender for Servers.
2. You should assign Security Reader role to the SOC analysts.
3. To identify whether the servers have an endpoint protection solution installed, you should go to the **Recommendations** dashboard in Microsoft Defender for Cloud.

Chapter summary

- There are different types of Azure VPNs that will be selected according to the organization's requirement, including site-to-site VPN, point-to-site VPN, VNet-to-VNet, and multi-site VPN.
- Consider using ExpressRoute if your connectivity scenario requires a higher level of reliability, faster speeds, consistent latencies, and higher security than typical Internet connections.
- Network security group (NSG) in Azure allows you to filter network traffic by creating rules.
- Consider using Azure Firewall when your organization requires a fully stateful firewall, centralized management, with network- and application-level protection.
- Consider using Azure Front Door when your organization's requirements include Azure deployment across different regions with a high-performance experience for applications and that it is resilient to failures.

- When you need resource-level filtering to enhance the security of your workloads, make sure to use a resource-level firewall.

- Enable Azure DDoS Standard when you need to tune application traffic volume, and you want to ensure an SLA level that provides application guarantee and cost protection.

- To receive threat alerts in Microsoft Defender for Cloud, you need to enable a Microsoft Defender for Cloud plan for the appropriate workload.

- You can use Microsoft Defender for Cloud to monitor the security posture of Azure Kubernetes and Azure Container registry.

- Azure Disk Encryption requires that your Windows VM has connectivity with Azure AD to get a token to connect with Key Vault.

- To ensure that you are always protecting the data in transit, you should configure your App Service to use an SSL/TLS certificate.

CHAPTER 3

Manage security operations

The main goal of security operations is to maintain and restore the security assurances of the systems as adversaries attack them. The National Institute of Standards and Technology (NIST) describes the tasks of security operations in their Cybersecurity Framework, which are Detect, Respond, and Recover. To be able to execute those functions in a cloud environment, you not only need the correct approach, but you also need to understand how the native tools work to provide you the data you need to limit the time and access an attacker can get to valuable systems and data.

Azure has native capabilities that you can leverage to continuously monitor your environment's security operations, allowing you to quickly identify potential threats to your workloads.

Skills in this chapter:

- Skill 3.1: Configure centralized policy management
- Skill 3.2: Configure and manage threat protection
- Skill 3.3: Configure and manage security monitoring solutions

Skill 3.1: Configure centralized policy management

While security monitoring is critical for any organization that wants to continue improving its security posture, governance is foundational for any organization that wants to establish deployment standards and ensure that security is applied at the beginning of the deployment pipeline. This section of the chapter covers the skills necessary to configure centralized policy management according to the Exam AZ-500 outline.

Configure a custom security policy

It's well-known in all areas of IT (enterprise, small business, and even start-ups) that policy-based management streamlines and increases the effectiveness of IT operations. This is especially true in security, where the combination of technologies and processes becomes a potent weapon. In fact, it's recognized by many that if the right policies are in place, and those policies are carried out assiduously, then even less than optimal technology can be effective at protecting the organization.

Azure Policy allows you to create, assign, and manage a variety of policy definitions. Policy definitions can be compared with your current configuration, and any resources that do not meet the requirements of your policy can then be determined to be "out of compliance." You can then focus on the out-of-compliance assets and bring them into compliance.

A "policy assignment" is a policy definition that has been assigned to take place within a specific "scope." For example, a scope might range from an Azure management group to a resource group. A management group enables you to manage access, policy, costs, and compliance across subscriptions. The term "scope" refers to all the resource groups, subscriptions, or management groups to which the policy definition is assigned. Policy assignments are inherited by all child resources.

An "initiative definition" is a collection of policy definitions tailored toward achieving a singular overarching goal. Initiative definitions simplify the management and assignment of policy definitions. They simplify policy definition assignments by grouping a set of policies into a single initiative definition. Figure 3-1 shows these components:

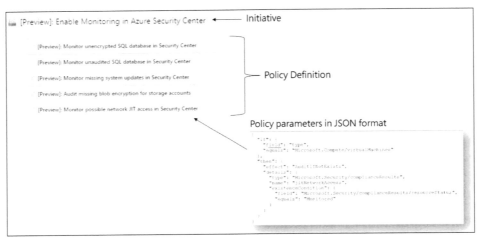

FIGURE 3-1 Azure Policy components

If you need to create a new custom security policy, you can leverage Microsoft Defender for Cloud or Azure Policy to do that. From a terminology perspective, if you use Microsoft Defender for Cloud, you always refer to a *custom security policy*. However, if you use the Azure Policy dashboard, you refer to a *custom policy*. When you use Microsoft Defender for Cloud to create a custom policy, you are creating a custom initiative that will be reflected in Microsoft Defender for Cloud as a recommendation.

Create a policy initiative

Using the built-in policy initiative in your Microsoft Defender for Cloud deployment has several advantages. The most obvious advantage is that you don't need to care about enabling recommendations because they will automatically apply to every subscription you enroll in Microsoft Defender for Cloud. Though it is less obvious, it is important to point out that the built-in policy definitions and the initiative definition are both maintained by Microsoft. In other words, if there are changes to the resource providers used within these policy definitions, or if new definitions are created, these changes will be automatically incorporated into the built-in initiative definition. However, there are cases when you want to have custom policies in your environment, either because you want to tailor the existing policy or because you want to add more assessments to your environment.

To add a custom policy initiative to Microsoft Defender for Cloud, follow these steps:

1. Open the Azure portal and sign in with an account that has **Security Admin** privileges.

2. In the left navigation pane, select **Microsoft Defender For Cloud**.

3. In Microsoft Defender for Cloud left navigation pane, click **Environment settings**.

4. Select the subscription that you want to change the policy, and in the left navigation click **Security Policy**.

5. Click **Add A Custom Initiative**. The **Add Custom Initiatives** blade appears, as shown in Figure 3-2.

FIGURE 3-2 Add a custom policy initiative to Microsoft Defender for Cloud

6. You can either click **Add** to assign an existing custom initiative or click **+ Create New** to build a new custom initiative definition from scratch and assign it to your subscription.

7. You can add a combination of custom and built-in policy definitions to your custom initiative. Once you've created it, click **Save** > **Add** to assign it to your subscription.

8. When assigning the custom initiative from Microsoft Defender for Cloud, you can assign it to a subscription, a particular resource group within that subscription, or both. (Remember, you can only assign the built-in default initiative on management groups and subscriptions.) Also, you can define an exclusion for either a resource group or a particular resource so the policies won't apply to the excluded scope. See Figure 3-3.

The policies with your custom initiative will be grouped under the new security control Custom Recommendation in the Microsoft Defender for Cloud **Recommendations** dashboard, as shown in Figure 3-4.

FIGURE 3-3 Assign a custom policy definition with scope and exclusions

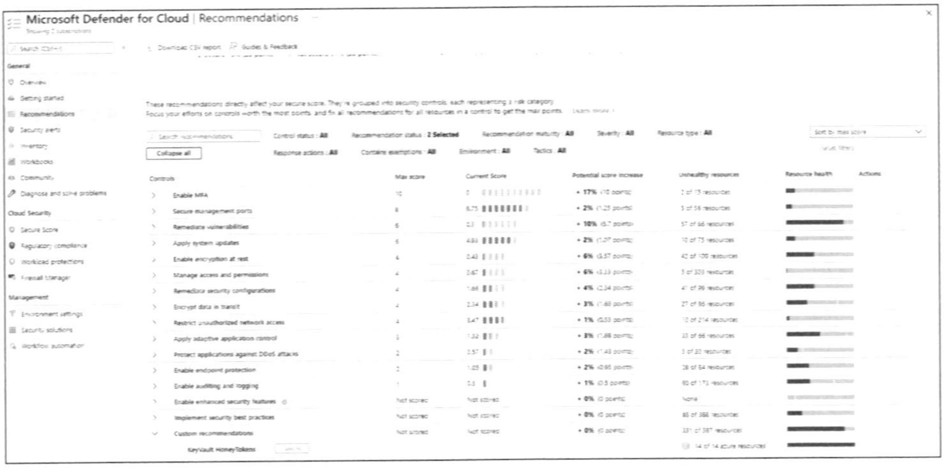

FIGURE 3-4 Custom recommendations based on a custom policy initiative

As mentioned before, you can use custom, built-in policy definitions (or both) within your custom initiative definition. If you choose to use built-in policies, they still are maintained by Microsoft, whereas custom policy definitions are not automatically updated. So, if you are using custom policies in a custom initiative, you need to establish a process that helps you to keep track of backend changes related to the policies' intent and to update your custom policies accordingly.

Configure security settings and auditing by using Azure Policy

A policy definition can have different effects on the scope it is assigned to. The *append* mode is used to add additional fields to a resource when it is created or updated. For example, you can use append to add a list of allowed IP addresses to a storage resource. A policy definition in audit mode will report resources that are non-compliant regarding the settings within your definition. For example, if you have an internal agreement that organizational resources are only deployed to Azure regions within Europe, you can use an audit policy to report resources that are deployed in a US region. A similar effect is auditifnotexists, which will report resources that do not have a particular configuration or setting. For example, you would use auditifnotexists mode if you want to see resources that do not have a particular tag configured.

If you configure a definition in deployifnotexists (DINE) mode, once you deploy a resource, a particular setting or configuration will be automatically remediated if it has not already been defined when configuring the resource to be deployed. For example, to ensure that the Azure Monitoring Agent is installed on all VMs that are created within your Azure environment, you can use a DINE policy.

A definition that is configured in deny mode will prevent the deployment of resources that are noncompliant regarding a particular setting. In the first example with the Azure regions, you can use a deny policy to not only audit but to prevent the deployment of resources to a US region. Finally, there is the modify mode that is used to add, update, or remove properties or tags on a resource when it is created or updated. This effect is commonly used to update tags on resources. Also, modify mode allows you to remediate existing resources using remediation tasks. In addition to the effects mentioned previously, the following effects are currently supported in a policy definition:

- **Append**   Adds additional fields to the requested resource during creation or update. For example, you could use this effect if you want to specifify a list of allowed IPs during the storage creation.

- **Disabled**   This effect is useful for testing scenarios where the policy definition has parameterized the effect.

- **Modify**   Adds, updates, or removes properties or tags on a subscription or resource during creation or update.

The first step to achieving governance in Azure is to ensure that you are leveraging Azure Policy for policy enforcement. You can also enforce data residency and sovereignty using Azure Policy. For example, use Azure Policy if you need to enforce all new resources to be created to use a specific region. As mentioned earlier in this chapter, from the centralized management perspective, it's always recommended that you assign a policy to a management group and move the subscriptions that you want to inherit that policy to that management group.

Many built-in roles grant permission to Azure Policy resources. You can use the Resource Policy Contributor role, which includes most Azure Policy operations. The Owner role has full rights to perform all actions, and both Contributor and Reader roles have access to all Azure Policy Read operations. You can use the Contributor role to trigger resource remediation, but you can't use it to create definitions or assignments.

When you are enforcing policies, you need to ensure that your policy initiative is using the right type of effect. If the scenario's requirement is that you avoid provisioning certain workloads if certain attributes are not set, your policy effect should be **Deny**. The **Deny** attribute is used to prevent a resource request that doesn't match defined standards through a policy definition and fails the request.

If your scenario's requirement is to change parameters if they were not set during provision time, then your policy effect should be `DeployIfNotExists`. For example, if a Contoso administrator wants to deploy Azure Network Watcher when a virtual network is created, the administrator should enforce the `DeployIfNotExists` effect for that policy. `DeployIfNotExists` runs about 15 minutes after a resource provider has handled a create or update resource request and has returned a success status code. When you configure a policy with this type of effect, you also create a remediation task. The goal of this remediation task is to configure the resource with the desired parameter.

Updating tags on a resource during creation or update is common. For example, let's say a Contoso administrator needs to update the cost center for all resources during creation. For this scenario, you need to use the `Modify` effect. Just like the `DeployIfNotExists` effect, you also need to configure a remediation task to run the desired change. Keep in mind that when you are creating this remediation task for both effects, you will need to check the **Create A Managed Identity** option. You can use the identity to authenticate to any service that supports Azure AD authentication—including Key Vault—without any credentials in your code.

Follow the steps below to configure policy enforcement using Azure Policy:

1. Navigate to the Azure portal at *https://portal.azure.com*.
2. In the search bar, type **policy**, and under **Services**, click **Policy**.
3. On the **Policy** page, click **Assignments** under **Authoring** in the left pane. Figure 3-5 shows an example of the **Assignments** page.

FIGURE 3-5 Policy assignments page

4. Notice on this page, you can assign an initiative or a policy. For this example, click the **Assign Policy** button. The **Assign Policy** page appears (see Figure 3-6).

FIGURE 3-6 Selecting the policy to assign

5. On the **Basics** tab, you can select the **Scope** in which this policy should be assigned. If your scenario requires centralized management, you can assign it to a management group. If the scenario requires that you only assign it to the subscription level, then leave the default selection.

6. In the **Exclusion** field, you can optionally select resources that you want to exclude from this policy. For example, if you have certain resource groups that should be exempted from this policy, add those resource groups to this list.

7. In the **Policy Definition** field, click the ellipsis to open the available policies.

8. On the **Available Definitions** blade, a list of all policy definitions is shown. For this example, type **SQL** in the **Search** field.

9. Select the **Deploy SQL DB Transparent Data Encryption** policy and click the **Select** button.

10. Notice that both the **Policy Definition** and **Assignment Name** fields have been populated with the name of the policy.

11. Click the **Parameters** tab and notice that for this policy, there are no parameters or effects.

12. Click the **Remediation** tab to configure the additional options. Figure 3-7 shows the available options.

13. Click the **Create A Remediation Task** check box.

14. The **Policy To Remediate** drop-down menu will automatically select the policy that needs to be used for remediation.

15. Notice that the **Create A Managed Identity** option is automatically selected with the **System Assigned Managed Identity** option. The **Managed Identity Location** is also set to East US by default, but you can change it.

16. Also, in the **Permission** section under **This Identity Will Also Be Given The Following Permissions**, the **SQL DB Contributor** permission is selected by default.

17. Click the **Review + Create** button.

18. Click the **Create** button.

Now that the policy and the remediation task are created, you have the full extent of policy enforcement. You can monitor the compliance of this policy by using the **Overview** dashboard in Azure Policy; then, you click the policy to see more details about the assignment. Figure 3-8 shows the **Assignment Details** dashboard.

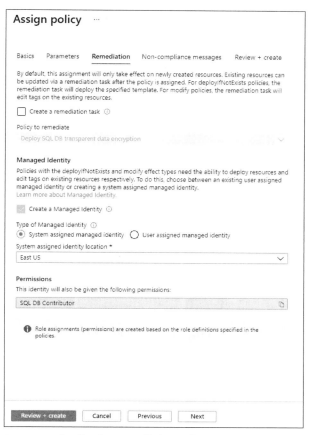

FIGURE 3-7 Configuring remediation tasks

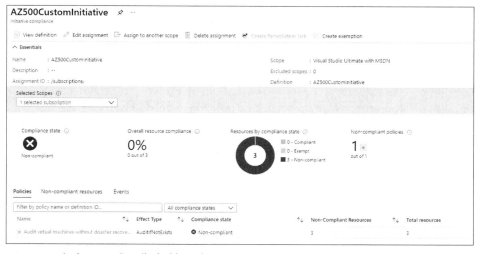

FIGURE 3-8 Assignment Details dashboard

Skill 3.2: Configure and manage threat protection

Threat protection is imperative for organizations that are proactively managing their security posture and need to reactively take actions when threats are identified. However, to quickly identify threats, you need threat detection that has relevant analytics for different types of workloads. This section of the chapter covers the skills necessary to configure and manage threat protection according to the Exam AZ-500 outline.

Microsoft Defender for servers

When you enable Microsoft Defender for Servers, the following features are available automatically:

- Threat detections for supported versions of Windows and Linux.
- Integration with Microsoft Defender for Endpoint (MDE), which is the Microsoft Endpoint Detection and Response (EDR) solution. In this case, the license is included for Servers only.
- File integrity monitoring.
- Just-in-time VM access.
- Integrated vulnerability assessment with the options to deploy either Qualys or Threat and Vulnerability Management (TVM).
- Adaptive application control.
- Adaptive network hardening.
- Network map.
- Regulatory compliance dashboard.

Microsoft Defender for servers uses advanced security analytics and machine-learning technologies to evaluate events across the entire cloud fabric. The security analytics include data from multiple sources, including Microsoft products and services, the Microsoft Digital Crimes Unit (DCU), the Microsoft Security Response Center (MSRC), and external feeds. This is the core of Defender for Servers threat detection, and on top of that, different detection mechanisms are available based on the workload.

Microsoft Defender for Servers applies known patterns to discover malicious behavior, which is called *behavioral analysis*. It uses statistical profiling to build a historical baseline, which means an alert might be triggered when Defender for Servers detects deviations from established baselines that conform to a potential attack vector. The result will be externalized in the dashboard via a security alert. A security alert contains valuable information about what triggered the alert, the resources targeted, the source of the attack, and suggestions to remediate the threat. Alerts generated by Microsoft Defender for servers are also called Virtual Machine Behavioral Analysis (VMBA). This type of alert uses behavioral analytics to identify compromised resources based on an analysis of the virtual machine (VM) event logs, such as process-creation events, in memory only (fileless attack), and log-in events. While these examples are related to Microsoft Defender for servers, other Microsoft Defender plans might use different methods to identify suspicious activity (and trigger an alert).

Microsoft Defender for servers also identifies suspicious activity in the network layer by collecting security information from your Azure Internet Protocol Flow Information Export (IPFIX) traffic and analyzes it to identify threats. The Suspicious Incoming RDP Network Activity from Multiple Sources alert is an example of an alert that belongs to this category. Microsoft Defender for servers has different threat detections for Windows and Linux, as shown in the following sections.

Windows

Microsoft Defender for servers detection in Windows looks at many events, and once it finds something suspicious, it triggers an alert. For example, if you execute the command below in a VM monitored by Microsoft Defender for servers, it will be considered a suspicious activity:

```
powershell -nop -exec bypass -EncodedCommand "cABvAHcAZQByAHMAaAB1AGwAbAAgAC0AYwBvAG0AbQ
BhAG4AZAAgACIAJgAgAHsAIABpAHcAcgAgAGgAdAB0AHAAcwA6AC8ALwBkAG8Adw6uAGwAbwBhAGQALgBzAHkAcw
BpAG4AdAB1AHIAbgBhAGwAcwAuAGMAbwBtAC8AZgBpAGwAZQBzAC8AUwB5AHMAbQBvAG4ALgB6AGkAcACAAgAC0ATw
B1AHQARgBpAGwAZQAgAGMAOgBcAHQAZQBtAHAAAXABzAHYAYYBoAG8AcwB0AC4AZQB4AGUAIAB9ACIA"
```

PowerShell is a very powerful tool; the Mitre attack's techniques page at *https://attack.mitre.org/techniques/T1086/* shows that PowerShell has been used in many attack campaigns. When Microsoft Defender for servers detects the PowerShell execution with the encoding command, it raises an alert for what the user is trying to hide. In this case, the command above is trying to download the sysmon.zip file from the SysInternals website and save it in the C:\temp folder with the svhost.exe name:

```
powershell -command "& { iwr https://download.sysinternals.com/files/Sysmon.zip -OutFile
c:\temp\svchost.exe }"
```

PowerShell encoding to download malware from command-and-control is a common malicious pattern, so Microsoft Defender for servers will raise an alert.

> **MORE INFO**
>
> You can test Windows Detection in Defender for Servers using the playbook at *http://aka.ms/ASCWindowsDetection*.

Linux

When Linux Detections was first released, there was a dependency in the AuditD to be installed in the Linux operating system. While AuditD provides a significant amount of info that can be used to detect threats, not all Linux distros will have AuditD installed by default. For this reason, the latest change in behavior for Linux Detections was to bake-in the necessary elements that will collect relevant data in the agent (Log Analytics Agent) itself.

Accessing security alerts

The number of security alerts you see in the Security Alerts dashboard might vary depending on the number of resources you are monitoring with Defender for Servers and the business itself. Some organizations receive more attacks than others, and as a result, have more security alerts. If you don't have any security alerts in your environment, you can simulate an alert using the procedure below:

1. Open Azure portal and sign in with a user who has **Security Admin** privileges.
2. In the left navigation pane, click **Microsoft Defender For Cloud**.
3. In the Microsoft Defender for Cloud left navigation pane under **General**, click the **Security Alerts** option.
4. In the top-right corner, click the **Create Sample Alerts** option; the **Create Sample Alerts (Preview)** blade appears, as shown in Figure 3-9.

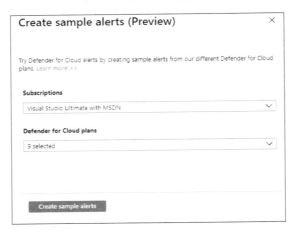

FIGURE 3-9 Creating a sample alert

5. In the **Subscriptions** drop-down menu, select the subscription for which you want to generate the sample alert.
6. Click the **Defender For Cloud** plans drop-down menu, click **Select All** to uncheck all plans, and select only **Virtual Machines**.
7. Click the **Create Sample Alerts** button to generate the sample alerts.

After a few minutes, you will see that six sample alerts will appear in the Security Alert dashboard, as shown in Figure 3-10.

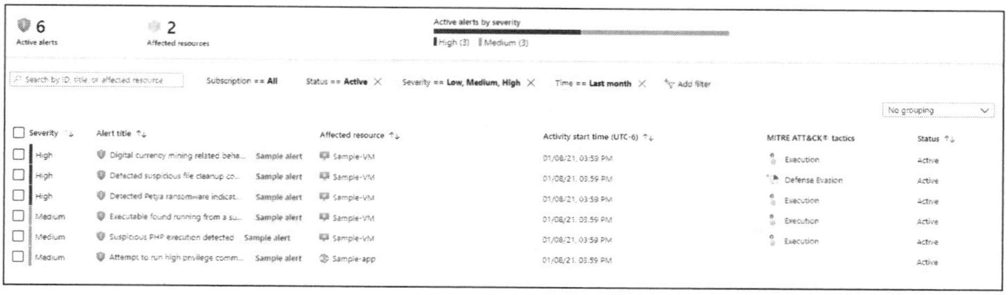

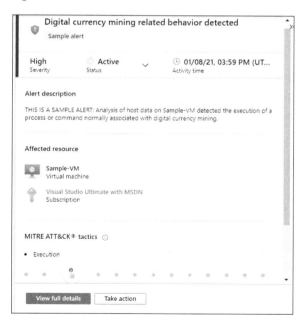

FIGURE 3-10 Security Alert dashboard with the sample alerts for VMs

By default, the Security Alert dashboard presents the alerts indexed by severity, but you can use the filtering options to change the severities that you want to see. You can also filter by:

- **Subscription** If you have multiple subscriptions selected, you can customize which subscriptions you want to see alerts from.
- **Status** By default, only **Active** is selected. You can change it to also see alerts that were dismissed.
- **Time** Allows you to configure the timeline of the alerts that you can see—up to the three last months.
- **Add Filter** Allows you to add more filters that are not visible by default.

In addition to the filters, you can also use the search box to search for alert ID, alert title, or affected resource. Clicking the desired alert opens the **Alert Details** page, as shown in Figure 3-11.

FIGURE 3-11 Alert details page

This initial page allows you to review the alert's details and change the status from **Active** to **Dismissed**. Also, a graphical representation of where the alerts fit into the Mitre ATT&CK Tactics framework is shown.

> **MORE INFO**
>
> You can obtain more information about this framework at *https://attack.mitre.org/versions/v7/*.

After reviewing the alert's details, you can obtain more granular information by accessing the alert's full page. To do that, click the **View Full Details** button, and the full alert page appears, as shown in Figure 3-12.

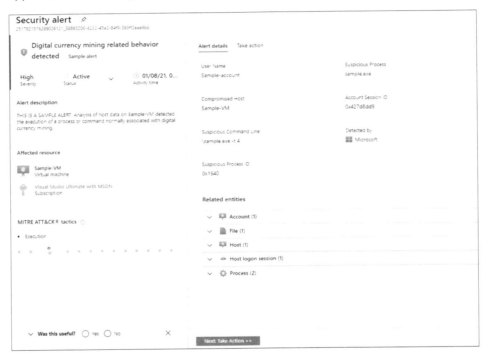

FIGURE 3-12 Alert details page

The right part of the full alert page shows more relevant detail. At the bottom part of the page is the **Related Entities** section, which enumerates the relevant entities (**Account**, **File**, **Host**, **Host Logon Session**, and **Process**) that were used during this attack. Keep in mind that the related entities will vary according to the alert type and whether those entities were used. Although the example shown in Figure 3-12 is from a sample alert, the fields of this alert type are the same as you would see in a live alert.

Another important option on this page is the **Take Action** tab, which contains relevant information to mitigate the highlighted threat in this alert, the recommendations that could be remediated to prevent future attacks, the option to trigger a Logic App automation, and the option to create a suppression rule. Figure 3-13 shows an example of this tab's content.

FIGURE 3-13 Take Action tab with the available options for an alert

Evaluate vulnerability scan from Microsoft Defender for servers

Vulnerability assessment is a key component of any security posture management strategy. Microsoft Defender for servers provides a built-in vulnerability assessment capability for your Azure VMs based on Qualys, an industry-lead vulnerability management solution. Also, it allows you to leverage Threat and Vulnerability Management (TVM), which is the native solution for Microsoft Defender for Endpoint (MDE). If you don't have Microsoft Defender for servers enabled and you are only using Microsoft Defender for Cloud, you will still receive a recommendation for installing the vulnerability assessment on your machine. However, this recommendation (which does not suggest the built-in vulnerability assessment) requires you to have a Qualys or Rapid7 license.

When you enable Microsoft Defender for servers in your subscription, the VMs that don't have a vulnerability assessment solution installed will be identified. Also, a security recommendation will appear, suggesting the built-in vulnerability assessment solution should be installed. This recommendation is similar to the example shown in Figure 3-14.

To install this vulnerability assessment solution, you need Write permissions on the VM to which you are deploying the extension. Assuming that you have the necessary privilege level, you will be able to select the VM from the list shown on the **Unhealthy Resources** tab and click the **Remediate** button. This recommendation has the **Quick-Fix** capability, which means you can trigger the extension installation directly from this dashboard. Like any extension in Azure, the Qualys extension runs on top of the Azure Virtual Machine agent, which means it runs as `Local Host` on Windows systems and as `Root` in Linux systems.

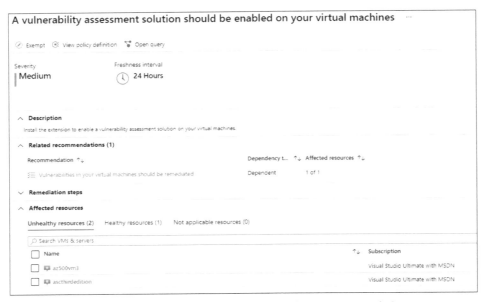

A vulnerability assessment solution should be enabled on your virtual machines   ...

⊘ Exempt   ⊗ View policy definition   ⬚ Open query

Severity   Freshness interval
| Medium   🕐 24 Hours

∧ Description
Install the extension to enable a vulnerability assessment solution on your virtual machines.

∧ Related recommendations (1)

Recommendation ↑↓   Dependency t... ↑↓   Affected resources ↑↓
⋮≣ Vulnerabilities in your virtual machines should be remediated   Dependent   1 of 1

∨ Remediation steps

∧ Affected resources

Unhealthy resources (2)   Healthy resources (1)   Not applicable resources (0)

🔍 Search VMs & servers

☐ Name   ↑↓   Subscription
☐ 🖥 az500vm3   Visual Studio Ultimate with MSDN
☐ 🖥 ascthirdedition   Visual Studio Ultimate with MSDN

FIGURE 3-14 Recommendation to install the built-in vulnerability assessment solution

The VMs that already have the agent installed will be listed under the **Healthy Resources** tab. When Microsoft Defender for Cloud cannot deploy the vulnerability scanner extension to the VMs, it will list those VMs on the **Not Applicable Resources** tab. VMs might appear on this tab if they are part of a subscription using the Free pricing tier or if the VM image is missing the ImageReference class (which is used on custom images and VMs restored from backup). Another reason for a VM to be listed on this tab is if the VM is not running one of the supported operating systems:

- Microsoft Windows (all versions)
- Red Hat Enterprise Linux (versions 5.4+, 6, and 7.0 through 7.7, 8)
- Red Hat CentOS (versions 5.4+, 6, and 7.0 through 7.7)
- Red Hat Fedora (versions 22 through 25)
- SUSE Linux Enterprise Server (versions 11, 12, and 15)
- SUSE OpenSUSE (versions 12 and 13)
- SUSE Leap (version 42.1)
- Oracle Enterprise Linux (versions 5.11, 6, and 7.0 through 7.5)
- Debian (versions 7.x through 9.x)
- Ubuntu (versions 12.04 LTS, 14.04 LTS, 15.x, 16.04 LTS, and 18.04 LTS)

If you are deploying this built-in vulnerability assessment on a server that has restricted access to the Internet, it is important to know that during the setup process, a connectivity check is done to ensure that the VM can communicate with Qualys's cloud service on the following two IP addresses: 64.39.104.113 and 154.59.121.74.

Once the extension is installed in the target VM, the agent will perform the vulnerability assessment of the VM through a scan process. The scan result will be surfaced in another security recommendation, which is called **Vulnerabilities In Your Virtual Machines Should Be Remediated**. A sample of this recommendation is shown in Figure 3-15.

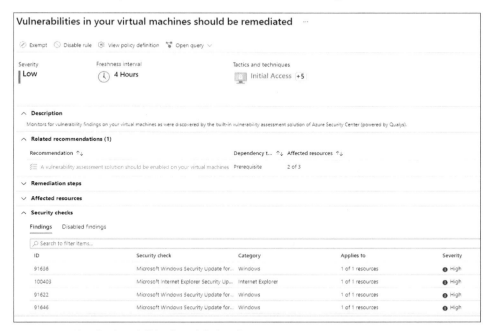

FIGURE 3-15 List of vulnerabilities found during the scan

On this page, you can see the list of findings in the **Security Checks** section. If you click a specific security check, Microsoft Defender for Cloud will show another blade with the details of that vulnerability, which include the **Impact**; **Common Vulnerabilities**; **Exposure (CVE)** (located under the **General Information** section); the **Description** of the type of threat; the **Remediation** steps; **Additional References** for this security check; and the list of **Affected Resources**. See Figure 3-16.

The deployment of these recommended remediations is done out-of-band; in other words, you will deploy them outside Microsoft Defender for Cloud. For example, suppose a security check requires you to install a security update on your target computer. In that case, you will need to deploy that security update using another product, such as Update Management. Some other remediations will be more about security best practices. For example, security check 105098 (Users Without Password Expiration) recommends that you create a password policy with an expiration date. This is usually deployed using Group Policy in Active Directory.

FIGURE 3-16 Vulnerability details blade

Vulnerability scanning for SQL

Assessing the vulnerability of SQL servers is also natively available in Microsoft Defender for Cloud as part of Microsoft Defender for SQL.

When you enable Microsoft Defender for SQL, you will have threat protection for Azure SQL Database, which detects anomalous activities that indicate unusual and potentially harmful attempts to access or exploit databases. For example, this feature could generate an alert about a possible vulnerability to SQL Injection attacks. Usually, there are two possible reasons for a faulty statement: A defect in application code might have constructed the faulty SQL statement, or the application code or stored procedures didn't sanitize the user input.

When Microsoft Defender for Cloud identifies databases that don't have this feature enabled, it will trigger a security recommendation, as shown in Figure 3-17.

FIGURE 3-17 Security recommendation to enable Defender for SQL

After this feature is enabled, Microsoft Defender for Cloud also indicates that you need to enable the vulnerability assessment for your SQL servers (see Figure 3-18).

FIGURE 3-18 Security recommendation to enable vulnerability assessment in SQL

EXAM TIP

For the AZ-500 exam, make sure to remember the vulnerability scanning options and that the built-in vulnerability assessment for VMs in Microsoft Defender for Cloud can be deployed using the Quick-Fix feature.

Configure Microsoft Defender for SQL

Microsoft Defender for SQL is a protection plan that helps you mitigate potential database vulnerabilities and detect anomalous activities that can indicate threats to your databases. Defender for SQL has evolved over the years and currently has two major plans:

- Microsoft Defender for Azure SQL database servers, which includes Azure SQL Database, Azure SQL Managed Instance, and Dedicated SQL Pool in Azure Synapse.

- Microsoft Defender for SQL Servers on Machines, which includes SQL Server running on VMs in Azure, on-premises, or in another cloud provider. Microsoft Defender for SQL provides threat detection for anomalous activities indicating unusual and potentially harmful attempts to access or exploit databases. Figure 3-19 shows an example of an alert triggered by this plan.

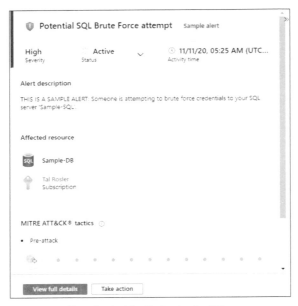

FIGURE 3-19 Sample alert for Defender for SQL

The Microsoft Defender for Azure SQL database servers can be easily enabled on the subscription level on any Azure SQL database that you want; no agent is required. However, to use Microsoft Defender for SQL Servers on Machines, you need to enable the plan at the subscription level, and you must onboard the server, which means provisioning the Log Analytics Agent on SQL Server. If your VMs are in Azure, you just need to use the auto-provisioning option in Microsoft Defender for Cloud to automatically onboard the Log Analytics Agent to your Azure VMs.

Another scenario is the integration with Azure Arc, which allows a deeper integration across different scenarios. It is recommended to use Azure Arc for your SQL Servers on-premises or in different cloud providers (AWS and GCP), and once they are fully on board, you can deploy the Log Analytics Agent. In summary, follow the sequence below to fully onboard:

1. Enable Azure Arc on your machines (follow the steps at *http://aka.ms/az500enablearc*).

2. Install the Log Analytics agent on this machine. You can easily identify which machines are missing the agent by reviewing the Log Analytics agent should be installed on your Windows-based Azure Arc machines recommendation in Microsoft Defender for Cloud.

3. Enable the **SQL Servers On Machines** pricing plan on the **Pricing And Settings** page of Microsoft Defender for Cloud. The plan will be enabled on all SQL servers and will be fully active after the first restart of the SQL Server instance.

> ***TIP*** **IDENTIFYING ARC-ENABLED MACHINES**
>
> You can quickly identify which machines are Azure Arc-enabled by using the Inventory dashboard. Create a filter based on **Resource Type** and change the criteria to **See Only Servers–Azure Arc**.

Skill 3.3: Configure and manage security monitoring solutions

Microsoft Sentinel is a Microsoft Security Information and Event Management (SIEM) and Security Orchestration, Automation, and Response (SOAR) solution. You can use this solution to ingest data from different data sources, create custom alerts, monitor incidents, and respond to alerts. This section of the chapter covers the skills necessary to configure and manage security monitoring solutions according to the Exam AZ-500 outline.

Introduction to Azure Monitor

Although an introduction to Azure Monitor is not part of the official AZ-500 outline, it is important to understand Azure Monitor components before diving into more details about alerts.

When it comes to using Azure Monitor, one common question is, "How do I enable it?" Azure Monitor is automatically enabled when you create a new Azure subscription. At that point, activity log and platform metrics are automatically collected. The other common question is, "Can Azure Monitor also monitor resources that are on-premises?" Although Azure Monitor implies (by the name) that the resources are in Azure, it also collects data to monitor from virtual machines and applications in other clouds and on-premises.

For this reason, before making any sort of configuration in Azure Monitor, it is important to understand some foundational concepts of this platform. The following section covers some key principles.

Reviewing Azure Monitor concepts

The diagram shown in Figure 3-20 helps you better understand the breadth of Azure Monitor and the different areas that it touches.

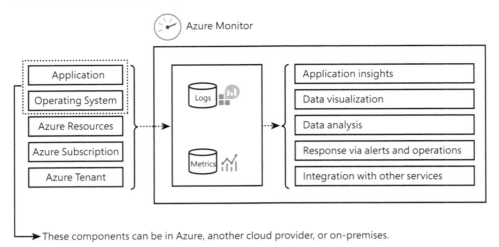

FIGURE 3-20 Architecture diagram of the Azure Monitor solution

On the left side of the diagram shown in Figure 3-20, you have the different layers that represent the components that will generate logs, which can be ingested by Azure Monitor. From the application and operating system perspective, the machine can be physically located on-premises, in Azure, or another cloud provider. Aside from these data sources, you can also ingest data from different Azure resources, subscriptions, and the Azure tenant itself. This data is ingested into the Log Analytics Workspace, which is part of the Azure Monitor solution, and once the data is there, you can query it using Kusto Query Language, which uses schema entities that are organized in a hierarchy similar to SQL's databases, tables, and columns.

The last three layers that appear on the left side of the diagram shown in Figure 3-20 represent the three major layers in Azure where you can obtain logging information. The definition of each layer is shown here:

- **Azure Resources** Here, you will be able to obtain resource logs, which have operations that were executed in the data plane level of Azure, such as getting a secret from Azure Key Vault. These logs are also referred to as diagnostic logs.

- **Azure Subscription** Here, you will be able to obtain activity logs, which have operations that were executed in the management plane. You should review these logs when you need to determine the answer for the *what* (what operation was made), *who* (who made this operation), and *when* (when this operation was made). For example, if a VM was deleted, you should go to Azure Activity Log to find out the answer of the *what*, *who*, and *when* regarding the deleted VM operation.

- **Azure Tenant** Here, you will be able to obtain the Azure Active Directory logs. In this layer, you have the history of sign-in activity and see an audit trail of changes made in the Azure Active Directory.

It is very important to understand those layers when studying for the AZ-500 exam because you may have scenarios where you will need to select the right option regarding where to look for specific information. For example, if the Contoso administrator wants to identify the user who stopped the virtual machine two weeks ago, where should they search for this information? If you answered *Azure Activity Log*, you are correct. As mentioned before, in Activity Log, you will find management plane operations and the identification of the *what*, *who*, and *when* an operation was performed.

Metrics are another type of information that can be ingested. Metrics are numerical values that describe some aspect of a system at a particular point in time. Telemetry, such as events and traces, and performance data are stored as logs so that they can all be combined for analysis. This type of information can be used during scenarios where you need to collect security-related performance counters from multiple VMs and create alerts based on certain thresholds.

Because Azure Monitor starts collecting data from a resource upon the creation of that resource, it is important to know where to look when you need information about those resources. Many resources will have a summary of performance data that is relevant for that resource; usually, this summary is located in the **Overview** page of that resource. For example, in the **Overview** option of an Azure storage account, you will see insights regarding the average latency, egress data, and requests, as shown in Figure 3-21.

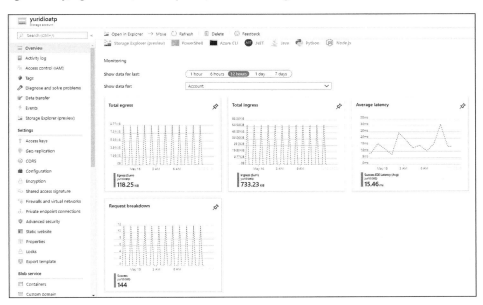

FIGURE 3-21 Summary of storage account performance insights

If you need to query logs that have operations that were executed in the management plane, you should use the Azure Activity Log. To access the Activity Log, follow these steps:

1. Navigate to the Azure portal at *https://portal.azure.com*.

2. In the search bar, type **activity**, and under **Services**, click **Activity Log**. The **Activity Log** page appears, as shown in Figure 3-22.

FIGURE 3-22 Activity log initial page

3. Here, you can use the **Timespan** filter to adjust the timeline that you want to perform your query. For this example, this filter was changed for the last hour, and after applying the change, the result appears, as shown in Figure 3-23.

FIGURE 3-23 Activity log results after filtering

4. The result shows a summary of the operation, including the **Status**, **Time**, **Time Stamp**, **Subscription**, and **Event Initiated By**. If you want more detailed information about the operation, you can expand the **Operation Name** field and click it. There, you can see the details of the operation in the JSON tab.

As mentioned in the previous section, the other type of data that you might want to use is metric. If you are monitoring a virtual machine and you need more metrics beyond the ones that appear in the **Overview** page, you can go to the **Metrics** page and from there, customize the metrics that you want to monitor, as shown in Figure 3-24.

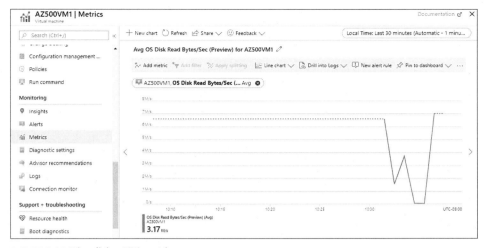

FIGURE 3-24 Visualizing VM metrics

Create and customize alert rules in Azure Monitor

Another important feature in Azure Monitor is the ability to create alerts for different types of events. You can use the following types of data to generate alerts with the data that was collected for the past 30 days (by default):

- Metric values
- Log search queries
- Activity log events
- Health of the underlying Azure platform
- Tests for website availability

In Figure 3-24, you can see the **OS Disk Read Bytes/Sec** option right above the **New Alert Rule** chart. This option allows you to go from this dashboard directly to the **Alert** dashboard and create an alert rule using the metric that is currently shown on screen: **OS Disk Read Bytes/Sec**. See Figure 3-25.

The **Create Alert Rule** page has some important parameters that must be filled, but when you activate this page from the **Metrics** page (where you already configured the metrics that you want to monitor), the **Create Alert Rule** page prepopulates the **Scope** (which is the target resource that you want to monitor) and the **Condition** (which is the rule logic that will be used to trigger the alert). While the scope has the resource that you want to monitor, the condition might need some adjustments according to your needs. To customize the condition, just click the condition name, and the **Configure Signal Logic** blade appears, as shown in Figure 3-26.

Create alert rule
Rules management

Create an alert rule to identify and address issues when important conditions are found in your monitoring data. Learn more
When defining the alert rule, check that your inputs do not contain any sensitive content.

Scope
Select the target resource you wish to monitor.

Resource	Hierarchy
AZ500VM1	Visual Studio Ultimate with MSDN > ContosoCST

Edit resource

Condition
Configure when the alert rule should trigger by selecting a signal and defining its logic.

Condition name	Estimated monthly cost (USD)
Whenever the avg os disk read bytes/sec (preview) is greater than <logic undefined>...	$ 0.10

Select condition

Total $ 0.10

Action group
Send notifications or invoke actions when the alert rule triggers, by selecting or creating a new action group. Learn more

Action group name	Contains actions
No action group selected yet	

Select action group

Create alert rule

FIGURE 3-25 Creating an alert rule

FIGURE 3-26 Customizing the alert logic

The first part of this blade has the performance counter name that you are using for this rule and a sample chart with data over the last 6 hours. The second part of this blade is where you configure the threshold. In the **Alert Logic** section, you can change the toggle to one of these options:

- **Static**   You provide a specific value as the threshold.
- **Dynamic**   Uses machine learning to continuously learn about the behavior pattern.

In this case, the Contoso administrator wants to receive an alert if the average OS Disk Read Bytes/Sec counter is higher than 3 MB, which means **Static** is the best option to use. In this case, the operator remains greater than, the **Aggregation Type** remains average, and you just need to enter the value (in this case, 3) in the **Threshold Value** field. The **Condition Preview** section explains the logic, so you can confirm that this is what you want to do. The **Evaluated Based On** section is where you can configure the **Aggregation Granularity (Period)** option, which defines the interval over which the data points are grouped. You can also configure the **Frequency Evaluation**, which defines how often this alert rule should be executed. The **Frequency Evaluation** should be the same as the **Aggregation Granularity** or higher. Once you finish, click the **Done** button.

Next, configure the **Action Group** section, which allows you to configure the type of notification that you want to receive. To configure this option, click **Select Action Group**, and in the **Select An Action Group To Attach To This Alert Rule** blade, click the **Create Action Group** option; the **Add Action Group** blade appears, as shown in Figure 3-27.

On this blade, you should start by typing a name for this action group; this can be a long name that helps you identify what this group does. In the **Short Name** field, add a short name, which appears in emails or messages that might be sent by this alert. Select the subscription and resource group to where this action group resides; under **Action Name**, type a name for the first action. Notice that there are many fields for actions; that's because you can have actions such as sending an email, sending an SMS message, or running a runbook, among others. In his case, the Contoso administrator wants to send an email to a distribution list and send an SMS message to the on-call phone. For the action type, select **Email/SMS Message/Push/Voice**, and the **Email/SMS Message/Push/Voice** blade appears. In this blade, type the email and the SMS number, and then click **OK** twice.

To finish the alert creation, you just need to add an **Alert Rule Name** and a brief **Description**, and then choose the **Severity** of the alert from the drop-down menu. The severity should represent the level of criticality that you want to assign for this rule. In this case, the Contoso administrator understands that when this threshold is reached, an important (not critical) alert should be raised, which, in this case, could be represented by **Sev 2**, as shown in Figure 3-28.

FIGURE 3-27 Action group configuration

FIGURE 3-28 Configuring the alert rule details

Ideally, you should enable this rule upon creation, which is why the **Enable Alert Rule Upon Creation** check box is selected by default. To commit all the changes, click the **Create Alert Rule** button.

Once you finish creating the rule, you should receive an email advising you that you were added to the action group. A sample of this email is shown in Figure 3-29.

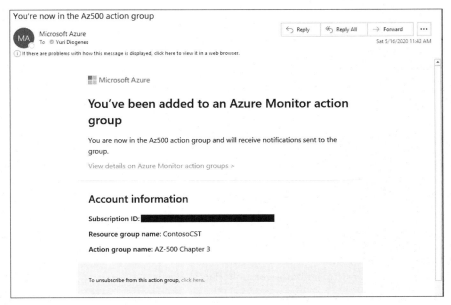

FIGURE 3-29 Email notification generated by Azure Monitor

You should also receive the SMS message. Notice that the short name that you used appears in the message, as shown in Figure 3-30.

FIGURE 3-30 SMS notification generated by Azure Monitor

Now that you created an alert based on a metric that you used previously, the question is, "What if I need to change the alert rule?" If you want to be able both to see and change alerts, you can use the **Alerts** dashboard. Follow the steps below to access this dashboard.

1. Navigate to the Azure portal at *https://portal.azure.com*.

2. In the search bar, type **alert**, and under **Services**, click **Alerts**.

3. Click the **Manage Alert Rules** button, and the **Rules** page appears, as shown in Figure 3-31.

FIGURE 3-31 Activity log results after filtering

4. The alert rule that you created appears in the list. To edit the rule, you just need to click it. If you need to create a new alert rule, click the **New Alert Rule** button. Both steps will lead you to the **Create Alert Rule** page, which was previously shown in Figure 3-25.

> **IMPORTANT RBAC ROLES REQUIRED**
>
> The consumption and management of alert instances requires the user to have the built-in RBAC roles of either monitoring contributor or monitoring reader.

Once an alert is fired, the status of the alert is set to **New**, which means the rule was detected, but it hasn't been reviewed. Keep in mind that the **Alert State** is different and independent of the **Monitor Condition**. While the **Alert State** is set by the user, the **Monitor Condition** is automatically set by the system. When an alert is fired, the alert's **Monitor Condition** is set to **Fired**. When the underlying condition that caused the alert to fire clears, the monitor condition is set to **Resolved.** (For example, the alert clears if your condition was to send an alert if the CPU reaches 80 percent utilization, and then the CPU utilization drops to 50 percent.) You can see this information in the email—assuming you configured the rule to send an email—as shown in Figure 3-32.

FIGURE 3-32 Email notification stating that an alert was resolved

Configure diagnostic logging and log retention by using Azure Monitor

In Azure, each resource requires its own diagnostic setting. In these settings, you define the categories of logs and metric data that should be sent to the destinations defined in the setting. Also, you need to define the destination of the log, which includes sending it to the Log Analytics workspace, Event Hubs, and Azure Storage.

It is important to mention that each resource can have up to five diagnostic settings. If the scenario requirement states that you need to send logs to a Log Analytics workspace and Azure Storage, you will need two diagnostic settings. Follow these steps to configure the diagnostic settings:

1. Navigate to the Azure portal at *https://portal.azure.com*.

2. In the search bar, type **monitor**, and under **Services**, click **Monitor**. The **Monitor | Overview** page appears.

3. In the left navigation pane, under **Settings**, click **Diagnostics Settings**; the **Monitor | Diagnostic** settings page appears, as shown in Figure 3-33.

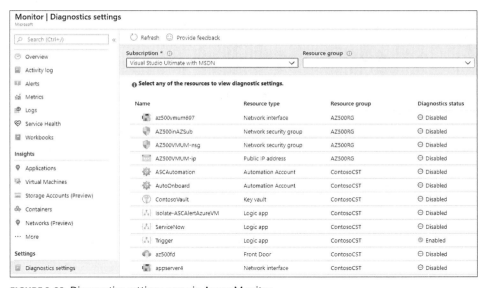

FIGURE 3-33 Diagnostics settings page in Azure Monitor

4. As you can see, all resources that can have diagnostic settings appear in this list. For this example, click the Front Door resource that was created in Chapter 2.

5. Click the **Add Diagnostic Setting** option; the **Diagnostics Settings** page appears, as shown in Figure 3-34.

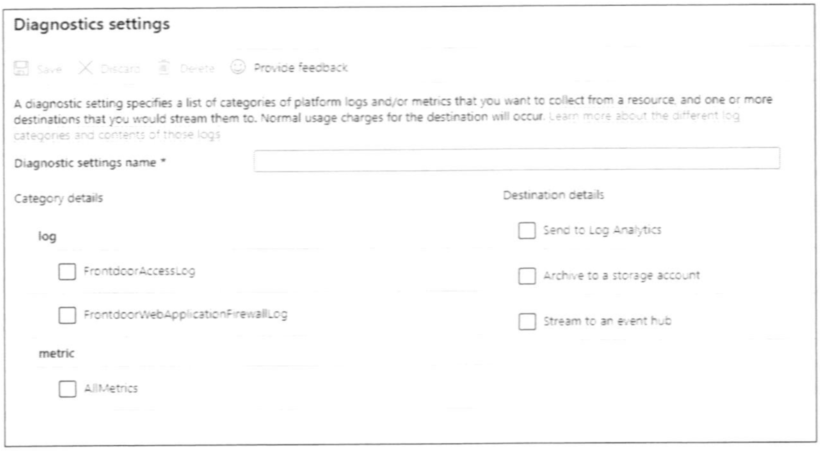

FIGURE 3-34 Diagnostic settings for a Front Door resource

6. In the **Diagnostic Setting Name** field, type a comprehensive name for this setting.

7. For this specific resource, you have two types of logs. The first is a metric log in which you can only select the ones that you need for your scenario; the second is the destination log, which can be Log Analytics, a storage account, or an Event Hub.

8. In this case, the Contoso Administrator needs to be able to easily query Front Door access logs and WAF logs using a comprehensive query language. To meet this requirement, you need to select **Log Analytics**, which utilizes Kusto Query Language (KQL) to perform queries.

9. When you select the **Send To Log Analytics** option, you will see the option to select the subscription and the Log Analytics workspace that you want to utilize (assuming you have one). Make a selection and click the **Save** button.

10. After saving, the **Save** button is no longer available, which indicates that the changes have been committed.

While the previous sample configuration describes the steps to configure a Log Analytics workspace as the diagnostic settings destination, the overall settings can vary according to the destination. For example, if you select storage account, the options shown in Figure 3-35 will appear.

Notice that when configuring a storage account as your destination, you can customize the retention policy for each log. In a scenario where the requirement is to store the Front Door access logs for 50 days and the WAF logs for 40 days, the best destination for this setting is the storage account because it allows this type of granular configuration.

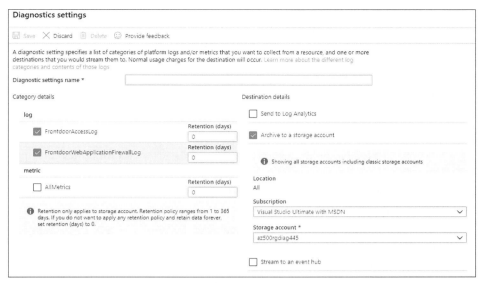

FIGURE 3-35 Storage account Diagnostic Settings

Consider selecting **Event Hub** as the destination when you need to stream the data to another platform. For example, you might do this if you need to send the Front Door (could be any other Azure resource) access logs to a third-party security information and event management (SIEM) solution, such as Splunk. In this case, using Event Hub is the best option because it allows the logs to be easily streamed to a SIEM solution.

EXAM TIP

For the AZ-500 exam, make sure you understand the capabilities of each destination because the requirements of each scenario will lead to different storage options.

Monitoring security logs by using Azure Monitor

Because each Azure resource can have different sets of logs and configurations, you need to ensure that you are collecting all logs that affect your security monitoring. For Platform as a Service (PaaS) services such as Azure Key Vault, you just need to configure the diagnostic settings to the target location (Log Analytics workspace, storage account, or Event Hub) where the log will be stored. For Infrastructure as a Service (IaaS) VMs, you need more steps because you want to ensure that you are collecting the relevant security logs from the operating system itself.

Data plane logs are the ones that will give you more information about security-related events in IaaS VMs. Assuming that you already have a Log Analytics workspace that will store this data, you will need to do the following actions to configure Azure Monitor to ingest security logs from VMs. First, enable the Log Analytics VM Extension and collect security events from the operating system. Once the data is collected, you can visualize it using the Log Analytics workspace and perform queries using KQL. Assuming that you already have a Log Analytics workspace created, follow these steps to configure this data collection:

1. Navigate to the Azure portal at *https://portal.azure.com*.

2. In the search bar, type **log analytics**, and under **Services**, click **Log Analytics Workspaces**.

3. On the **Log Analytics Workspaces** page, click the workspace in which you want to store the security logs.

4. In the left navigation pane of the workspace page, under **Workspace Data Sources**, click **Virtual Machines**.

5. Click the virtual machine that you want to connect to this workspace. Notice that the **Log Analytics Connection** status appears as **Not Connected**, as shown for the AZ500VM3 virtual machine in Figure 3-36.

FIGURE 3-36 Virtual Machines that are available in the workspace

6. On the VM's page, click the **Connect** button, as shown in Figure 3-37.

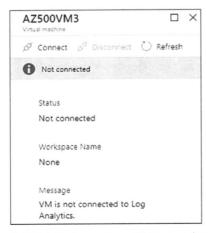

FIGURE 3-37 Connecting a VM to a workspace

7. At this point, the Log Analytics agent will be installed and configured on this machine. This process takes a few minutes, during which time the **Status** shows as `Connecting`. You can close this page, and the process will continue in the background.

8. After the agent is installed, the **Status** will change to `This Workspace`.

9. In the left navigation pane of the main workspace page, under **Settings**, click **Advanced Settings**.

10. On the **Advanced Settings** page, click **Data** > **Windows Event Logs**, as shown in Figure 3-38.

FIGURE 3-38 Configuring the data source for ingestion

11. In the **Collect Events From The Following Event Logs** field, type **System** and select **System** from the drop-down menu. Click the **plus sign** (+) to add this log. Leave the default options selected. If you have specific security events that you want to collect, type **security** and select the appropriate events.

12. Click the **Save** button.

13. Click **OK** in the pop-up window and close this page.

Azure Monitor also has solutions that can enhance the data collection for different scenarios. This can be extremely helpful for security monitoring. You can also leverage an Azure Resource Manager (ARM) template to deploy the agent in scale; when doing so, you will need two parameters: the workspace ID and the workspace key.

Introduction to Microsoft Sentinel's architecture

Although an introduction to Microsoft Sentinel is not part of the official AZ-500 outline, it is important to better understand Microsoft Sentinel's architecture before talking about alerts. The major Microsoft Sentinel components are diagrammed in Figure 3-39.

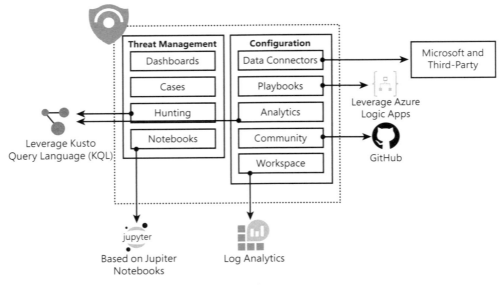

FIGURE 3-39 Major components of Microsoft Sentinel

The components shown in Figure 3-39 are presented in more detail in the following list:

- **Dashboards**   Built-in dashboards provide data visualization for your connected data sources, which enables you to deep dive into the events generated in those services.

- **Cases**   An aggregation of all the relevant evidence for a specific investigation. It can contain one or multiple alerts, which are based on the analytics that you define.

- **Hunting**   A powerful tool to investigators and security analytics who need to pro-actively look for security threats. The searching capability is powered by Kusto Query Language (KQL).

- **Notebooks**   By integrating with Jupyter notebooks, Microsoft Sentinel extends the scope of what you can do with the data that was collected. It combines full programma-bility with a collection of libraries for machine learning, visualization, and data analysis.

- **Data Connectors**   Built-in connectors are available to facilitate data ingestion from Microsoft and partner solutions.

- **Playbook**   A collection of procedures that can be automatically executed upon an alert that is triggered by Microsoft Sentinel. Playbooks leverage Azure Logic Apps, which help you automate and orchestrate tasks and workflows.

- **Analytics**   Enables you to create custom alerts using Kusto Query Language (KQL).

- **Community**   The Microsoft Sentinel Community page is located on GitHub (*https://aka.ms/ASICommunity*), and it contains Detections based on different types of data sources that you can leverage to create alerts and respond to threats in your environ-ment. It also contains hunting queries samples, Playbooks, and other artifacts.

- **Workspace** Essentially, a Log Analytics workspace is a container that includes data and configuration information. Azure Sentinel uses this container to store the data that you collect from the different data sources.

The sections that follow assume that you already have a workspace configured to use with Microsoft Sentinel.

> **IMPORTANT** **SENTINEL IS NOT COVERED IN DEPTH**
>
> This book does not cover Microsoft Sentinel entirely; it only covers the topics that are relevant for the AZ-500 exam. To learn more, see, *Microsoft Azure Sentinel: Planning and implementing Microsoft's cloud-native SIEM solution*, published by Microsoft Press.

Configure Data Sources to Microsoft Sentinel

The first step to configure a SIEM solution such as Microsoft Sentinel is ensuring that the data relevant to your requirements is ingested. For example, if you need to collect data related to conditional access policies and legacy authentication-related details using sign-in logs, you need to configure the Azure Active Directory (AD) connector. Microsoft Sentinel comes with a variety of connectors that enable you to start ingesting data from those data sources with just a couple of clicks. Keep in mind that you need to have those services enabled to start ingesting data using these connectors. Use Table 3-1 to identify some use-case scenarios and to determine which connector is available for each scenario:

TABLE 3-1 Microsoft Sentinel connectors and use-case scenarios

Scenario	Connector
You need to gain insights about app usage; conditional access policies; legacy authentication-related details; and activities like user, group, role, app management.	Azure AD
You need to get details of operations such as file downloads, access requests sent, and changes to group events, and you need to set the mailbox and details of the user who performed the actions.	Office 365
You need to gain visibility into your cloud apps; get sophisticated analytics to identify and combat cyberthreats; and control how your data travels.	Microsoft Defender for Cloud Apps
You need to gain insights into subscription-level events that occur in Azure, including events from Azure Resource Manager operational data; service health events; write operations taken on the resources in your subscription; and the status of activities performed in Azure.	Azure Activity
You need to gain visibility about users at risk, risk events, and vulnerabilities.	Azure AD Identity Protection
You need to gain insights into your security state across hybrid cloud workloads; reduce your exposure to attacks; and respond to detected threats quickly.	Microsoft Defender for Cloud

The connectors shown in this table are considered service-to-service integrations. Also, there are connectors to external solutions using API and others that can perform real-time log streaming using the Syslog protocol via an agent. Following are some examples of external connectors (non-Microsoft) that use agents:

- Check Point
- Cisco ASA
- DLP solutions
- DNS machines - agent installed directly on the DNS machine
- ExtraHop Reveal(x)
- F5
- Forcepoint products
- Fortinet
- Linux servers
- Palo Alto Networks
- One Identity Safeguard
- Other CEF appliances
- Other Syslog appliances
- Trend Micro Deep Security
- Zscaler

To configure data connectors, you will need the right level of privilege. The necessary roles for each connector are determined per connector type. For example, to configure the Azure AD connector, you will need the following permissions:

- **Workspace** Read and write permissions are required.
- **Diagnostic Settings** Required read and write permissions to AAD diagnostic settings.
- **Tenant Permissions** Required Global Administrator or Security Administrator roles on the workspace's tenant.

> **NOTE AZURE AD LOGS**
> To ingest Azure AD logs into the Microsoft Sentinel workspace, you will also need an Azure AD P1/P2 License.

While this connector has a decent list of permission requirements, some others will be simpler. For example, to configure the Azure Activity connector, you just need Read and Write permissions in the workspace. The requirements for each connector will be available on the connector's page in Microsoft Sentinel.

For this initial scenario, let's say that Fabrikam wants to ensure that the following things are ingested in Microsoft Sentinel: all events from Azure Resource Manager operational data; service health events; write operations taken on Fabrikam's subscription resources, and the status of activities performed in Azure. To accomplish that, you need to configure the Azure Activity connector. Follow these steps:

1. Navigate to the Azure portal at *https://portal.azure.com*.

2. In the search bar, type **sentinel**, and under **Services**, click **Microsoft Sentinel**.

3. On the Microsoft Sentinel workspaces page, click the workspace that you want to use with Microsoft Sentinel; the **Microsoft Sentinel | Overview** page appears (see Figure 3-40).

FIGURE 3-40 Microsoft Sentinel Overview page

IMPORTANT   AZURE SENTINEL DASHBOARD

If this is the first time you've launched Microsoft Sentinel after configuring the workspace, your dashboard will not have any data because data collection is not configured yet.

---

4. In the left navigation pane, under **Configuration**, click **Data Connectors**.

5. On the **Data Connectors** page, click **Azure Activity**.

6. On the **Azure Activity** blade, click the **Open Connector Page** button, as shown in Figure 3-41.

FIGURE 3-41 Azure Activity blade

7. On the **Azure Activity** page, click the **Configure Azure Activity Logs** link, as shown in Figure 3-42.

8. On the **Azure Activity Log** blade, click the subscription that you want to connect, and in the **Subscription** blade that appears, click the **Connect** button, as shown in Figure 3-43.

9. Once it finishes connecting, click the **Refresh** button to update the button's status. You will see that now the **Disconnect** button is available.

10. Close the **Subscription** blade, close the **Azure Activity Log** blade, and close the **Azure Activity** connector page.

11. When you return to the **Microsoft Sentinel | Data Connectors** page, make sure to click the **Refresh** button to update the Azure Activity data connector status.

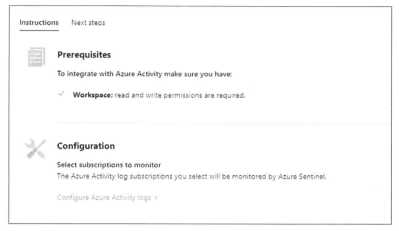

FIGURE 3-42 Azure Activity data connector configuration

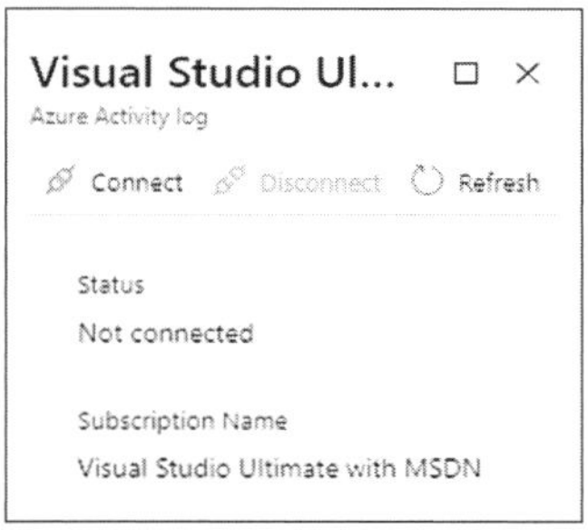

FIGURE 3-43 Subscription blade

The core steps to configure Microsoft Sentinel data connectors are very similar, though depending on the connector, you might need to execute more steps. This is true mainly for external connectors and services in different cloud providers. For example, if you need to connect to Amazon AWS to stream all AWS CloudTrail events, you will need to perform some steps in the AWS account.

Create and customize alerts

After the different data sources are connected to Microsoft Sentinel, you can create custom alerts, which are called Analytics. There are two types of analytics that can be created: a scheduled query rule and a Microsoft incident creation rule. A scheduled query rule allows you to fully customize the parameters of the alert, including the rule logic and the alert threshold. A Microsoft incident creation rule allows you to automatically create an incident in Azure Sentinel for an alert that was generated by a connected service. This type of rule is available for alerts generated by Microsoft Defender for Cloud, Microsoft Defender for IoT, Microsoft Defender for Endpoint Protection, Azure AD Identity Protection, Microsoft Defender for Cloud Apps, and Microsoft Defender for Identity.

When considering which one you need to utilize, make sure to understand the prerequisites for the scenario because those requirements will determine the type of rule that you need to create. For example, if the requirement is to customize the alert with parameters that will determine the query scheduling and alert threshold, then the best option is the scheduled query rule. For this scenario, Fabrikam wants to create a medium severity alert every time a VM is deleted, and an incident should be created for further investigation. Follow these steps to create a scheduled query rule:

1. Navigate to the Azure portal at *https://portal.azure.com*.

2. In the search bar, type **sentinel**, and under **Services**, click **Microsoft Sentinel**.

3. On the Microsoft Sentinel workspaces page, click the workspace that you want to use with Microsoft Sentinel; the **Microsoft Sentinel | Overview** page appears.

4. In the left navigation pane, under **Configuration**, click **Analytics**.

5. Click the **Create** button and select the **Scheduled Query Rule** option. The **Analytic Rule Wizard – Create New Rule** page appears, as shown in Figure 3-44.

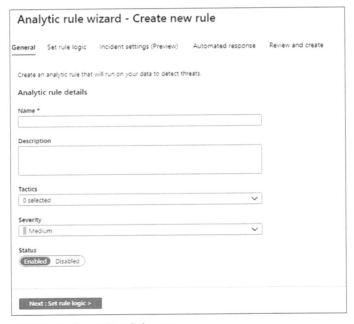

FIGURE 3-44 Create New Rule page

6. In the **Name** field, type a name for this analytic.

7. Optionally, you can write a full description for this analytic and select the tactic. The **Tactics** drop-down menu contains a list of the different phases available in the cyber kill chain. You should select the appropriate phase for the type of alert that you want to create; for this example, select **Impact**.

8. The **Severity** drop-down menu contains a list of all available levels of criticality for the alert. For this example, leave it set to **Medium**.

9. Because you want to activate the rule after creating it, leave the **Status** set to **Enabled**.

10. Click the **Next: Set Rule Logic** button; the **Set Rule Logic** tab appears, as shown in Figure 3-45.

FIGURE 3-45 Configuring the rule logic

11. In the **Rule Query** field, you need to type the KQL query. Because Fabrikam wants to receive an alert when VMs are deleted, type the following sample query:

```
AzureActivity
| where OperationNameValue contains "Microsoft.Compute/virtualMachines/delete"
```

12. In some scenarios, you might need to customize the **Map Entities** options to enable Microsoft Sentinel to recognize the entities that are part of the alerts for further analysis. For this scenario, you can leave the default setting.

13. Under **Query Scheduling**, the first option is to customize the frequency with which you want to run this query. Because this scenario does not have a specifically defined frequency, leave it set to run every 5 hours.

14. Next, you can customize the timeline in which you want to run this query under the **Lookup Data From The Last** option. By default, the query will run based on the last 5 hours of data collected. Because in this scenario, it was not specifically specified, leave the timeline as is.

15. Under **Alert Threshold** is the **Generate Alert When Number Of Query Results** drop-down menu. Because this scenario calls for an alert to be generated every time a VM is deleted, you should leave this set to the default setting, **Is Greater Than 0**.

16. Under **Suppression**, you could choose to stop the query after the alert is generated. In this scenario, leave the default selection, which is **Off**.

17. Click the **Next: Incident Settings (Preview)** button; the **Incident Settings** tab appears, as shown in Figure 3-46.

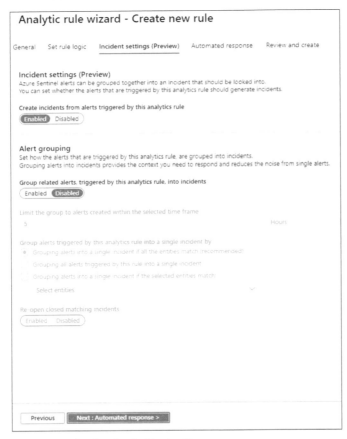

FIGURE 3-46 Configuring incident settings

18. Leave the **Create Incidents From Alerts Triggered By This Analytics Rule** option selected (which is the default setting) because the scenario requires an incident to be created.

19. Under **Alert Grouping**, you can configure how the alerts that are triggered by this analytics rule are grouped into incidents. For this scenario, leave the default selection, which is **Disabled**.

20. Click the **Next: Automated Response** button; the **Automated Response Tab** appears, as shown in Figure 3-47.

FIGURE 3-47 Configuring an Automated Response

21. The **Automation Response** tab contains a list of all Azure Logic Apps available. In a new deployment, it is common to see an empty tab because there will be no Logic Apps available. You will learn more about automated responses in the next section of this chapter.

22. Click the **Next: Review** button, review the options, and click the **Create** button.

23. After the rule is created, you will be taken back to the **Microsoft Sentinel | Analytics** page; the rule appears in the **Active Rules** list. If you click it, you will see the rule's parameters, as shown in Figure 3-48.

FIGURE 3-48 Custom alert after creation

While this rule was created specifically for a particular scenario, you can utilize existing templates, which are located on the **Rule Templates** tab in the main **Microsoft Sentinel | Analytics** page. You can create a scheduled rule type based on different known types of attacks. For example, if you have a scenario in which you need to detect distributed password cracking attempts in Azure AD, you can just create a rule based on the available template, as shown in Figure 3-49.

There are other scenarios in which you might need to simply create an incident in Microsoft Sentinel based on an alert triggered by a connected service. For example, you might want to create an incident every time an alert is triggered from Microsoft Defender for Cloud. The initial steps are the same. The difference is that in step 5 of the earlier instructions, you would select the **Microsoft Incident Creation** rule. When this option is selected, you will see the **Analytic Rule Wizard Create – Create New Rule** page, as shown in Figure 3-50.

In the **Microsoft Security Service** drop-down menu, you can select the connected service that you want to use as the data source. For example, if you select **Microsoft Defender For Cloud** from the list and you do not customize the included or excluded alerts, Microsoft Sentinel will create an incident for all alerts triggered by Microsoft Defender for Cloud.

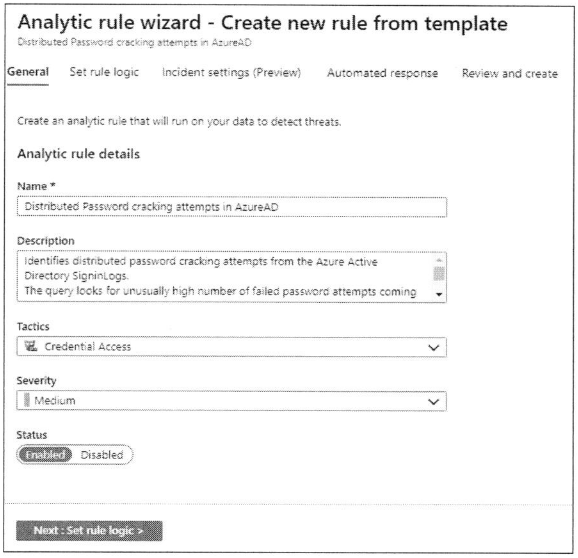

FIGURE 3-49 Creating an alert based on a template

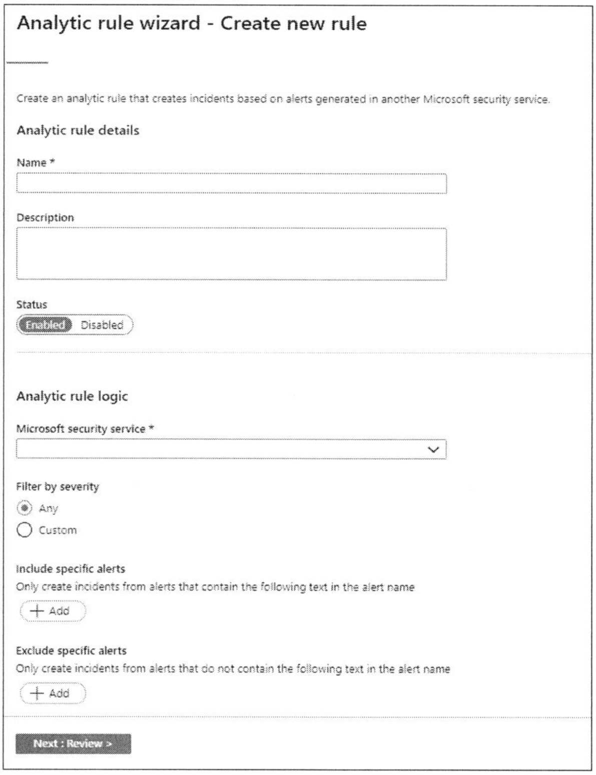

FIGURE 3-50 Creating an alert based on a connected service

Evaluate alerts and incidents in Microsoft Sentinel

Besides the main overview dashboard available in Microsoft Sentinel that displays charts and a summary of the events and alerts, you can also perform direct queries in the Log Analytics workspace or visualize the collected data using Workbooks. If you need to visualize security events quickly, click the **SecurityEvent** option in the **Events And Alerts Over Time** tile; the Log Analytics workspace appears with the query result, as shown in Figure 3-51.

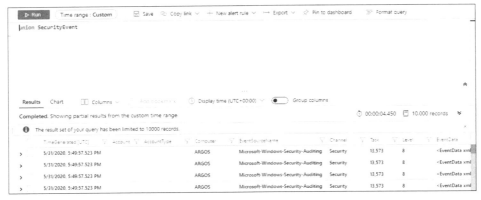

FIGURE 3-51 Security Events

When accessing the information directly from the Log Analytics workspace, you can leverage KQL search to explore further the information that you are trying to find out. This type of approach to query data freely using the Log Analytics workspace is more often used in investigation scenarios (reactive).

> **IMPORTANT NO AUTOMATED INVESTIGATION IN SENTINEL**
>
> Although Microsoft Sentinel has investigation capabilities, it doesn't have automated investigation. This feature is available only in Microsoft Defender for Endpoint.

For more proactive scenarios, one option is to use Azure Workbooks. Microsoft Sentinel Workbooks provide interactive reports that can be used to visualize your security and compliance data. Workbooks combine text, queries, and parameters to make it easy for developers to create mature visualizations, advanced filtering, drill-down capabilities, advanced dashboard navigations, and more. To leverage a specific Workbook template, you must have at least Workbook Reader or Workbook Contributor permissions on the resource group of the Microsoft Sentinel workspace.

Using a Workbook is a great choice for monitoring scenarios where you need data visualization through a dashboard with specific analytics for each data source. Another use case scenario is when you want to build your custom dashboard with data coming from multiple data sources.

For example, if you need to evaluate Azure Activity Log data that is being ingested in Microsoft Sentinel using the **Azure Activity** connector, you can use the **Azure Activity Workbook**. In the main Microsoft Sentinel dashboard, under **Threat Management**, click **Workbooks**. Next, click the **Azure Activity** option and click the **View Template** button at the right; the Azure Activity Workbook appears, as shown in Figure 3-52.

FIGURE 3-52 Security Events

Leveraging the correct option to evaluate results in Microsoft Sentinel can help you save time identifying the relevant information.

Incidents

Another way to evaluate results in Microsoft Sentinel is by looking at incidents. When an incident is created based on an alert that was triggered, you can review this incident in the dashboard, and you can remediate the incident using a Playbook that you previously created. Also, you can investigate the incident.

To access the incidents dashboard, click **Incidents** under the **Threat Management** section on the main Microsoft Sentinel page. Figure 3-53 shows an example of an incident.

When an incident is selected, you will see a summary of the incident details in the right pane. As you triage the incident, you can do the following:

- Change the incident's severity.
- Change incident status. (For example, you can change the severity to **Active** if it is an ongoing investigation.)
- Assign the incident to an owner. (By default, the owner is shown as **Unassigned**.)

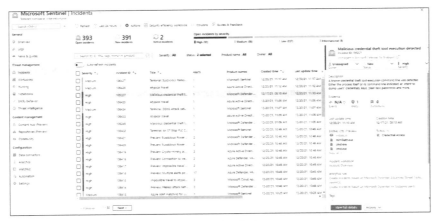

FIGURE 3-53 Visualizing an incident in Azure Sentinel

To see more details about the incident, click the **View Full Details** button. Figure 3-54 shows an example of a full incident.

Depending on the artifacts that are available about the incident, you will also have access to the Investigation dashboard, as shown in Figure 3-54:

FIGURE 3-54 A full incident

Threat hunting

Threat hunting is the process of iteratively searching through a variety of data with the objective of identifying threats in the systems. Threat hunting involves creating hypotheses about the attackers' behavior and researching the hypotheses and techniques that were used to determine the artifacts that were left behind.

In a scenario in which a Contoso administrator wants to proactively review the data that Microsoft Sentinel collected to identify indications of an attack, the threat hunting capability is the recommended way to accomplish this task. Proactive threat hunting can help to identify sophisticated threat behaviors used by threat actors even when they are still in the early stages of the attack. To access the threat **Hunting** dashboard, click **Hunting** in the **Threat Management** section on the main Microsoft Sentinel page. Figure 3-55 shows an example of this dashboard.

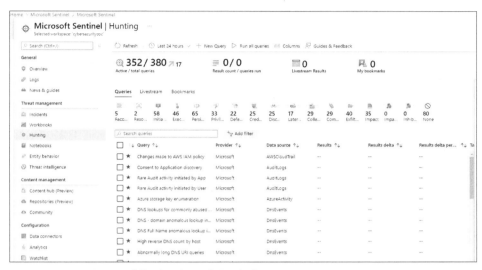

FIGURE 3-55 Hunting capability in Microsoft Sentinel

To start hunting, you just need to select the predefined query, which was created for a specific scenario, and click the **Run Query** button in the right-hand pane. This pane shows a summary of the results. Click the **View Results** button to see the full details of the query.

Thought experiment

In this thought experiment, demonstrate your skills and knowledge of the topics covered in this chapter. You can find answers to this thought experiment in the next section.

Monitoring Security at Tailwind Traders

You are one of the Azure administrators for Tailwind Traders, an online general store specializing in various products for the home. As a part of your duties for Tailwind Traders, you need to work with the Security Operations Center (SOC) to ensure that alerts generated by Microsoft Defender for Cloud are ingested in Microsoft Sentinel. The SOC Team also needs auditing information about VM creation, and this information needs to be streamed to Azure Sentinel.

Tailwind Traders has been using Microsoft Defender for Cloud for a while, primarily to obtain alerts. The company now wants to use other capabilities in Microsoft Defender for Servers to reduce the attack surface of its IaaS VMs. One of the requirements is to ensure that management ports are closed by default and will only open when an explicit request is made for a specific period. Because of some internal auditing, Tailwind Traders database administrators also need to have a vulnerability assessment available for the company's Azure SQL database. With this information in mind, answer the following questions:

1. Which connectors should be used in Microsoft Sentinel to enable this scenario?
2. Which feature in Microsoft Defender for Servers will help to reduce the attack surface based on Tailwind Traders' requirements?
3. What needs to be done first before enabling SQL Vulnerability Assessment for Tailwind Traders' databases?

Thought experiment answers

This section contains the solution to the thought experiment.

1. Microsoft Defender for Cloud and Azure Activity Log.
2. Just-in-Time VM Access.
3. First, you need to enable Microsoft Defender for SQL.

Chapter summary

- Azure resources logs operations that were executed at the data plane level, while activity logs at the subscription level register operations that were executed in the management plane.
- You can customize alerts in Azure Monitor for different data types, including metrics, log search queries, and activity logs events.
- Monitoring solutions leverage services in Azure to provide additional insight into the operation of an application or service.
- Microsoft Defender for Servers provides built-in vulnerability assessment using native integration with Qualys or TVM.
- To enable vulnerability assessment for SQL, you first need to enable the Microsoft Defender for SQL.
- The regulatory compliance dashboard in Microsoft Defender for Cloud can be customized to add other standards that are not available out of the box.
- To ingest data from different data sources into Microsoft Sentinel, you can use service-to-service connectors or external connectors.

CHAPTER 4

Secure data and applications

The security of data stored in Azure, the security of SQL, and the security of your secrets, keys, and certificates is as important as the security of any other element of your cloud deployment. One of the most commonly reported cloud data breach types is the storage container full of important customer data that is left open to the world. You've also likely heard of application passwords and connection strings left exposed in source code repositories and SQL database data exfiltrated by clever attackers who leveraged SQL injection vulnerabilities that went undetected until breached data started showing up on the dark web. In this chapter, you will learn how to secure your organization's Azure Storage deployments, the steps that you can take to protect your organization's SQL Server instances, and how to configure and secure Azure Key Vault so that secrets such as connection strings—as well as keys and certificates—can only be accessed by authorized users and applications.

Skills in this chapter:

- Skill 4.1: Configure security for storage
- Skill 4.2: Configure security for databases
- Skill 4.3: Configure and manage Key Vault

Skill 4.1: Configure security for storage

Unsecured data storage containers are the source of many data breaches in the cloud. These breaches occur because storage containers that administrators believe are only accessible to a select group of authorized people are, in fact, configured so that they are accessible to everyone in the world who knows the storage container's address. This objective deals with how to secure storage in Azure, from how to configure access control for storage accounts through how to manage storage account keys. You'll learn about shared access signatures, storage service encryption shared access policies, and how to use Azure AD to authenticate user access to storage resources in Azure.

Configure access control for storage accounts

Storage accounts are containers for Azure Storage data objects, such as blobs, files, queues, tables, and disks. Azure supports the following types of storage accounts:

- **General-Purpose V2 accounts**   Stores blobs, files, queues, and tables. They are recommended for the majority of storage scenarios. General-Purpose V2 accounts replace General-Purpose V1 accounts, which you should not use for new deployments and should be migrated away from if they are used in existing deployments.

- **BlockBlobStorage accounts**   Storage accounts are recommended for scenarios in which there are high transaction rates for block blobs and append blobs. Also, they are recommended for scenarios that require smaller objects or consistently low storage latency.

- **FileStorage accounts**   High-performance, files-only storage accounts. Recommended for high-performance applications.

- **BlobStorage accounts**   Legacy storage account type that you should not use for new deployments and should be migrated away from if they are used in existing deployments.

The recommended method of managing access control for storage accounts in the management plane is to use RBAC roles. RBAC roles for storage can be assigned at the following levels:

- **Individual container**   Role assignments at this scope apply to all blobs in the container. Role assignments also apply to container properties and metadata when the container is accessed at the management plane.

- **Individual queue**   Role assignments at this scope apply to all messages in the queue. Role assignments also apply to queue properties and metadata when the queue is accessed at the management plane.

- **Storage account**   Role assignments at this scope apply to all containers, all blobs within those containers, all queues, and all messages.

- **Resource group**   Role assignments at this scope apply to all storage accounts in the resource group as well as all items within those storage accounts.

- **Subscription**   Role assignments at this scope apply to all storage account in the subscription as well as all items within those storage accounts.

- **Management group**   Role assignments at this scope apply to all storage accounts as well as all items within those storage accounts within all subscriptions in the management group.

When assigning an RBAC role, remember the rule of least privilege and assign the role with the narrowest possible scope. This means that if an individual user or application only requires access to a specific storage account and there are multiple storage accounts in a resource group, you should only assign the role at the storage account level. In addition to the rule of least privilege, remember to assign roles to groups rather than individual users. This way, role assignment becomes a matter of adding and removing user accounts from a specific group. Rather than assigning roles to individual users or applications, you should assign the role to a group and then add the user and application accounts to that group as a way of managing the role assignments. Table 4-1 lists the RBAC roles that are appropriate for storage accounts:

TABLE 4-1 Storage account RBAC roles

Storage related RBAC role	RBAC role description
Storage account Contributor	Allows management of storage accounts. Has access to the account key and can access data using Shared Key authorization.
Storage account Key Operator Service Role	Can list and regenerate storage account access keys.
Storage Blob Data Contributor	Can read, write, and delete Azure Storage containers and blobs.
Storage Blob Data Owner	Allows full access to Azure software blob containers and data.
Storage Blob Data Reader	Can view and list Azure Storage containers and blobs.
Storage Blob Delegator	Can generate a user delegation key. This key can be used to create a shared access signature for containers or blobs that are signed with Azure AD credentials.
Storage File SMB Share Contributor	This role allows read, write, and delete access to files and directories on Azure Files file shares.
Storage File Data SMB Share Elevated Contributor	In addition to read, write, and delete access to files and directories on Azure Files file shares, this role can also modify the Access Control Lists on files and directories.
Storage File Data SMB Share Reader	Has read only access to files and directories in Azure Files file shares.
Storage Queue Data Contributor	Read, write, and delete Azure Storage queues, as well as queue messages.
Storage Queue Data Message Processor	Perform peek, retrieve, and delete messages from Azure Storage queues.
Storage Queue Data Message Sender	Can add messages to an Azure Storage queue.
Storage Queue Data Reader	Can read and list the contents of an Azure Storage queue and queue messages.

To assign a role to a storage account in the Azure portal, perform the following steps:

1. In the Azure portal, open the Storage account for which you want to assign an RBAC role.

2. On the Storage account's page, select **Access Control (IAM)** from the menu, as shown in Figure 4-1.

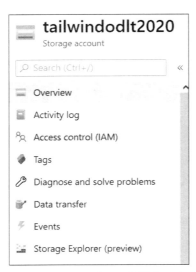

FIGURE 4-1 Access Control (IAM) node of a storage account

3. On the **Access Control (IAM)** blade, select **Role Assignments** and then click **Add**> **Role Assignment**, as shown in Figure 4-2. This will bring up the **Add Role Assignment** page.

FIGURE 4-2 Role Assignments page

4. On the **Add Role Assignment** page shown in Figure 4-3, select the security principal— preferably an Azure AD group—to which you want to assign the role, and click **Save**.

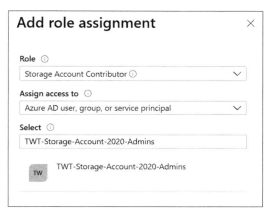

FIGURE 4-3 Storage account Contributor role assignment

MORE INFO **RBAC ROLES FOR BLOB AND QUEUE DATA**

You can learn more about RBAC role access for blob and queue data at *https://docs.microsoft.com/en-us/azure/storage/common/storage-auth-aad-rbac-portal*.

Configure Storage Service Encryption

Azure Storage encryption is enabled by default for all storage accounts regardless of performance or access tiers. This means you don't have to modify code or applications for Azure Storage Encryption to be enabled. Data stored in Azure is transparently encrypted and decrypted using 256-bit AES encryption. You cannot disable Azure Storage encryption, and it isn't necessary to alter code or applications to take advantage of Azure Storage encryption.

Any block blobs, append blobs, or page blobs written to Azure Storage since October 20, 2017, is subject to Azure Storage encryption. Microsoft has undertaken a process where all blobs created prior to this date are being retroactively encrypted. If you are concerned that a blob is not encrypted, you can view that blob's encryption status using the following technique:

1. In the Azure portal, navigate to the storage account you want to check.

2. In the **Containers** section of the Storage account's page, select **Containers** under **Blob Storage** and then locate the container that hosts the blob you are interested in checking. Open that container.

3. In the container you opened, select the blob you want to check.

4. On the **Overview** page, verify that the **Server Encrypted** setting is set to `true`, as shown in Figure 4-4.

FIGURE 4-4 Verify blob encryption status

You can check the encryption status of a blob using the following PowerShell code, substituting the values in the example code for the values of the blob that you want to check:

```
$account = Get-AzStorageAccount -ResourceGroupName <resource-group> '
    -Name <storage-account>
$blob = Get-AzStorageBlob -Context $account.Context '
    -Container <container> '
    -Blob <blob>
$blob.ICloudBlob.Properties.IsServerEncrypted
```

To check the encryption status of the blob using Azure CLI, use the following command substituting the values in the example code for the values of the blob that you want to check:

```
az storage blob show \
    --account-name <storage-account> \
    --container-name <container> \
    --name <blob> \
    --query "properties.serverEncrypted"
```

If you have a blob in Azure that was created prior to October 20, 2017, and which is not encrypted, you can simply rewrite the blob, which will force encryption to occur. One method of doing this is to download the blob to your local file system using AzCopy and then copying the blob back to Azure Storage.

> **MORE INFO** **STORAGE SERVICE ENCRYPTION**
>
> You can learn more about Storage Service Encryption at *https://docs.microsoft.com/en-us/ azure/storage/common/storage-service-encryption*.

Encryption Key Management

By default, Azure Storage accounts encrypt data stored using an encryption key managed by Microsoft. If having Microsoft managing Azure Storage account encryption keys is considered undesirable, you can manage encryption using your own keys, as shown in Figure 4-5.

FIGURE 4-5 Configure encryption type

When you choose the option of managing encryption with keys that you provide, you have the following options:

- **Use a customer-managed key with Azure Key Vault** In this scenario, you upload your encryption key to an Azure Key Vault or use Azure Key Vault APIs to generate keys. The storage account and the Key Vault need to be in the same Azure region and associated with the same Azure AD tenancy. The storage account and Key Vault do not need to be in the same subscription.
- **Use a customer-provided key on Blob Storage operations** In this scenario, encryption keys are provided on a per-request basis. Customer-provided keys can be stored in Azure Key Vault or in an alternate key store.

Infrastructure encryption

As you learned earlier in the chapter, Azure Storage automatically encrypts all data in an Azure Storage account using 265-bit AES encryption. When you enable infrastructure encryption, the data in the storage account will be encrypted twice. Data is first encrypted using one encryption algorithm and one key at the service level and then is encrypted at the infrastructure level using a separate encryption algorithm and encryption key. This double encryption protects data if one of the encryption algorithms or keys becomes compromised. While service-level encryption allows you to use either Microsoft-managed or customer-managed keys, infrastructure-level encryption only uses a Microsoft-managed key. Infrastructure encryption must be enabled during storage account creation. It is not possible to convert an existing storage account to support infrastructure encryption if it was not created with that option enabled.

> **MORE INFO**   **STORAGE ACCOUNT WITH INFRASTRUCTURE ENCRYPTION**
>
> You can learn more about infrastructure encryption for storage accounts at *https://docs.microsoft.com/en-us/azure/storage/common/infrastructure-encryption-enable*.

Encryption Scopes

Azure Storage accounts use a single encryption key for all encryption operations across the storage account. Encryption scopes allow you to configure separate encryption keys at the container and blob levels. This allows for scenarios such as storing customer data from different customers in the same storage account while having each customer's data protected by a different encryption key.

To create a new encryption scope, perform the following steps:

1. In the Azure portal, open the storage account for which you want to configure encryption scopes.

2. On the storage account's page, select **Encryption**, as shown in Figure 4-6, and then select **Encryption Scopes**.

FIGURE 4-6 Encryption scopes

3. On the **Encryption Scope** page, click **Add**.

4. On the **Create Encryption Scope** page, provide an encryption scope name and then specify whether the encryption scope will use **Microsoft-Managed Keys** or **Customer-Managed Keys**, as shown in Figure 4-7.

FIGURE 4-7 Create Encryption Scope

Once you have encryption scopes present for a storage account, you can specify which encryption scope will be used for individual blobs when you create the blob or specify a default encryption scope when you create a container, as shown in Figure 4-8.

FIGURE 4-8 New Container Encryption Scope

You can modify the encryption key for an encryption scope by performing the following steps:

1. In the Azure portal, open the storage account for which you want to configure encryption scopes.
2. On the storage account's page, select **Encryption** > **Encryption Scopes**.
3. Select the **More** button next to the encryption scope for which you want to update the encryption key.
4. On the **Edit Encryption Scope** page shown in Figure 4-9, change the **Encryption Type** and click **Save**.

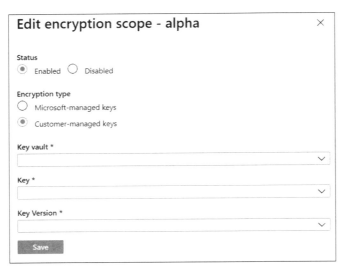

FIGURE 4-9 Edit Encryption Scope

> **MORE INFO** **STORAGE ACCOUNT ENCRYPTION SCOPES**
>
> You can learn more about storage account encryption scopes at *https://docs.microsoft.com/en-us/azure/storage/blobs/encryption-scope-manage*.

Microsoft Defender for Storage

Microsoft Defender for Storage (previously known as Advanced Threat Protection (ATP) for Azure Storage) allows you to detect unusual and malicious attempts to interact with Azure Storage accounts. When you enable Microsoft Defender for Storage, security alerts will trigger when Azure detects anomalous storage account activity. These detections are based on existing recognized patterns of malicious activity identified by Microsoft security researchers. These alerts are integrated with Microsoft Defender for Cloud and can also be forwarded by email to administrators of the subscription. The alert information will detail the nature of the suspicious activity as well as provide recommendations on how to further investigate and remediate these issues. Specifically, a Microsoft Defender for Storage alert will inform you of

- The nature of the anomaly
- Storage account name
- Event time
- Storage type
- Probable causes
- Investigation steps
- Remediation steps

Microsoft Defender for Storage is available for Blob Storage, Azure Files, and Azure Data Lake Storage Gen2. General-Purpose V2, block blob, and Blob Storage accounts support this service.

> **MORE INFO** **AZURE STORAGE ADVANCED THREAT PROTECTION**
>
> You can learn more about Azure Storage Advanced Threat Protection at *https://docs.microsoft. com/en-us/azure/defender-for-cloud/defender-for-storage-introduction*.

Configure storage account access keys

Storage account access keys allow you to authorize access to storage account data. Each Azure Storage account has an associated pair of 512-bit storage account access keys. If someone has access to an Azure Storage account key, they have access to the storage account associated with that key. The best practice is to only use the first key and to keep the second key in reserve. You then switch to using the second key when you perform key rotation. This allows you to then generate a new primary key, which you will switch to when you perform key rotation in the future. The recommended location for storing storage account access keys is Azure Key Vault. You will learn more about Azure Key Vault later in this chapter.

Because there is only a single pair of access keys associated with a storage account, you should rotate and regenerate access keys periodically. Rotating storage account access keys ensures that if a storage account key leaks, the leak will be automatically remediated when existing storage account keys reach their end of life. For example, if you rotate keys every six weeks, the maximum amount of time a leaked key remains valid is six weeks. Even if you don't have reason to believe that a storage account key has leaked, the best practice is to rotate them periodically. Just because you don't have reason to believe that a storage account key hasn't leaked doesn't mean that it isn't accessible to someone who shouldn't have access to it.

View storage account access keys

Viewing a storage account access key requires Service Administrator, Owner, Contributor, or Storage account Key Operator Service roles on the storage account the key is associated with. You can also access the key if you have been assigned an RBAC role that includes the Microsoft.Storage/storageAccounts/listkeys/action permission on a scope that includes the Storage account.

To view a storage account's storage account keys in the Azure portal, perform the following steps:

1. In the Azure portal, navigate to the storage account for which you are interested in learning the storage account access key details.

2. On the Storage account page, select **Access Keys** under **Settings**, as shown in Figure 4-10.

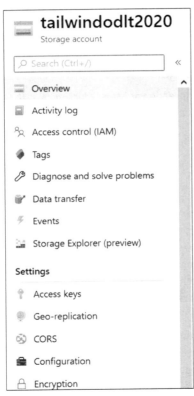

FIGURE 4-10 Access Keys in the Storage Account keys menu

3. On the **Access Keys** page shown in Figure 4-11, you can view and copy the first and second keys.

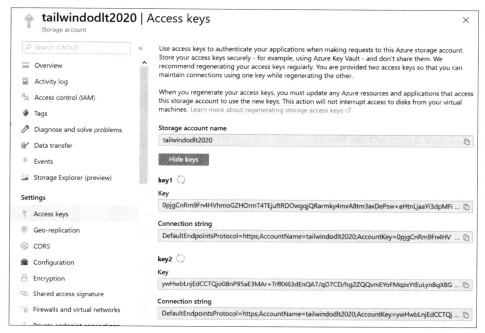

FIGURE 4-11 Storage account Access Keys

To view the storage account access keys using PowerShell, use the following PowerShell command:

```
$storageAccountKey = '
    (Get-AzStorageAccountKey '
    -ResourceGroupName <resource-group> '
    -Name <storage-account>).Value[0]
```

To view the storage account access keys via Azure CLI, use the following command:

```
az storage account keys list \
  --resource-group <resource-group> \
  --account-name <storage-account>
```

> **MORE INFO MANAGE STORAGE ACCOUNT ACCESS KEYS**
>
> You can learn more about managing storage account access keys at *https://docs.microsoft. com/en-us/azure/storage/common/storage-account-keys-manage*.

Manually rotating storage account access keys

The best practice is to rotate storage account access keys periodically. You should only use one storage account key at a time. Using only one key at a time will allow you to switch any application to the second storage account key of the pair before rotating the first. As discussed earlier, after some time has passed, you repeat the process, switching the application to the newly rotated storage account key before then regenerating the second key in the pair. To manually rotate your storage account access keys using the Azure portal, perform the following steps:

1. Ensure that you have updated the connection strings in any application code that reference the storage account access key you will be replacing.

2. Navigate to the **Access Keys** page for the storage account.

3. To regenerate the key, select the regenerate icon shown in Figure 4-12. This will generate a new storage account access key and connection string. (The regenerate icon appears as a pair of curved arrows.)

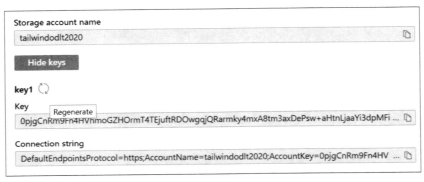

FIGURE 4-12 The regenerate icon

To regenerate the storage account key using PowerShell, use the following command, substituting resource group name and storage account name and either key1 or key2, as appropriate.

```
New-AzStorageAccountKey -ResourceGroupName <resource-group> '
  -Name <storage-account> '
  -KeyName key1
```

To regenerate the storage account key using Azure CLI, use the following command, substituting resource group name and storage account name and specifying whether the key you want to regenerate is either the primary or secondary key.

```
az storage account keys renew \
  --resource-group <resource-group> \
  --account-name <storage-account>
  --key primary
```

There are mechanisms that allow you to automate the rotation of storage account access keys. You will learn about these mechanisms later in this chapter.

Configure Azure AD authentication for Azure Storage and Azure Files

Azure AD authenticates a security principal's identity and then returns an OAuth 2.0 token. The client includes this token in the request to the Blob or Queue Storage being accessed by the security principal. You need to register an application with an Azure AD tenant before tokens can be issued in this manner. You can use Azure AD to authorize access to Blob and Queue Storage.

The method that you use to assign specific rights to blob or queue storage is to configure RBAC permissions against the appropriate container, queue, or storage account. You determine what access is required by the user or application, create an Azure AD group, assign the group the appropriate RBAC permission, and then add the user account or service principal to the Azure AD group.

Azure includes the following built-in roles for authorizing access to blob and queue data:

- **Storage Blob Data Owner**   Allows the security principal to set ownership and manage POSIX access control for Azure Data Lake Storage Gen2.
- **Storage Blob Data Contributor**   Grants the security principal read/write/delete permissions to Blob Storage resources.
- **Storage Blob Data Reader**   Allows the security principal to view items in Blob Storage.
- **Storage Blob Delegator**   Allows the security principal to acquire the user delegation key, which in turn, can be used to create a shared access signature for a container or blob. This shared access signature is signed with the security principal's Azure AD credentials.
- **Storage Queue Data Contributor**   Grants the security principal read/write and delete permissions to Azure Storage queues.
- **Storage Queue Data Reader**   Allows the security principal to view the messages in Azure Storage queues.
- **Storage Queue Data Message Processor**   Allows the security principal to peek, retrieve, and delete messages in Azure Storage queues.
- **Storage Queue Data Message Sender**   Allows the security principal to add messages in Azure Storage queues.

> **MORE INFO**   **AZURE AD FOR BLOBS AND QUEUES**
>
> You can learn more about Azure AD authorization for blobs and queues at *https://docs. microsoft.com/en-us/azure/storage/common/storage-auth-aad*.

Configure Azure AD Domain Services authentication for Azure Files

When you enable AD DS authentication for Azure Files, your Active Directory Domain Services (AD DS) domain-joined computers can mount Azure File shares using AD DS user credentials.

Access occurs over an encrypted Server Message Block (SMB) protocol connection. You can secure Azure Files using identity-based authentication over Server Message Block (SMB) where either Azure AD DS or an on-premises Active Directory Domain Services Domain (AD DS) functions as the identity provider. Azure AD Domain Services authentication for Azure Files currently supports the following scenarios:

- If you are using AD DS as your identity provider, you must use Azure AD Connect to synchronize identities to Azure AD.
- If you are using AD DS as your identity provider, you can access the file share using a computer that is a member of an AD DS domain. You cannot access the file share using a computer that is joined to the Azure AD DS domain.
- If you are using Azure AD DS as an identity provider, you will need to access the file share using a computer that is a member of the Azure AD DS domain.
- When enabled, this form of authentication supports Azure file shares that are integrated with Azure File Sync.
- This form of authentication supports single sign-on.
- This form of authentication only supports access from accounts in the AD DS forest in which the storage account is registered unless a specially configured forest trust is present.

Your first step when enabling AD authentication for Azure file shares is to create a storage account that is in a proximate region to the users who will access the files stored in the file share on that storage account. You should do this simply because accessing a storage account that is closer to you will provide a much better user experience than trying to open and save files to a file share located on the other side of the world. At the start of the process, you won't need to create any file shares from the storage account. Before creating the file shares, you'll need to enable Active Directory authentication at the storage account level rather than at the individual file shares level.

Enabling AD DS authentication

When enabling AD DS authentication, the first step is to create an identity to represent the storage account in your on-premises Active Directory instance. To do this, first create a new Kerberos key for the storage account using the following Azure PowerShell commands from Cloud Shell:

```
$ResourceGroupName = "<resource-group-name-here>"
$StorageAccountName = "<storage-account-name-here>"
New-AzStorageAccountKey -ResourceGroupName $ResourceGroupName -Name $StorageAccountName
-KeyName kerb1
Get-AzStorageAccountKey -ResourceGroupName $ResourceGroupName -Name $StorageAccountName
-ListKerbKey | where-object{$_.Keyname -contains "kerb1"}
```

Once the key has been generated, create a service account in your on-premises domain and configure the account with the following service principal name (SPN): `"cifs/your-storage-account-name-here.file.core.windows.net"` using the setspn.exe command. Set the account password to the Kerberos key, configure the account's password to never expire, and note the account security identifier (SID). You can use the `Get-AdUser` PowerShell cmdlet to determine the SID of a user account.

The next step is to use Azure PowerShell to enable Active Directory authentication. You can do this with the following command, substituting the appropriate values:

```
Set-AzStorageAccount '
        -ResourceGroupName "<your-resource-group-name-here>" '
        -Name "<your-storage-account-name-here>" '
        -EnableActiveDirectoryDomainServicesForFile $true '
        -ActiveDirectoryDomainName "<your-domain-name-here>" '
        -ActiveDirectoryNetBiosDomainName "<your-netbios-domain-name-here>" '
        -ActiveDirectoryForestName "<your-forest-name-here>" '
        -ActiveDirectoryDomainGuid "<your-guid-here>" '
        -ActiveDirectoryDomainsid "<your-domain-sid-here>" '
        -ActiveDirectoryAzureStorageSid "<your-storage-account-sid>"
```

You also have the option of using the `AzFilesHybrid` PowerShell module to perform steps similar to these. Using the `AzFilesHybrid` PowerShell module involves downloading the most recent version of the module from Microsoft's website, installing it on a domain-joined computer, and performing the following steps:

1. First, change the execution policy to allow the `AzFilesHybrid` PowerShell module to be imported:

    ```
    Set-ExecutionPolicy -ExecutionPolicy Unrestricted -Scope CurrentUser
    ```

2. Switch to the directory where `AzFilesHybrid` has been decompressed and copy the files into your path so that the files can be called directly:

    ```
    .\CopyToPSPath.ps1
    ```

3. Import the module into the current PowerShell session:

    ```
    Import-Module -Name AzFilesHybrid
    ```

4. Initiate a session to your Azure subscription using an Azure AD credential that has either storage account–owner or contributor access to the storage account you created to host the Azure file share instance:

    ```
    Connect-AzAccount
    ```

5. Populate the PowerShell session with the appropriate parameter values and then select the appropriate subscription if your account is associated with multiple subscriptions:

    ```
    $SubscriptionId = "<your-subscription-id-here>"
    $ResourceGroupName = "<resource-group-name-here>"
    $StorageAccountName = "<storage-account-name-here>"
    Select-AzSubscription -SubscriptionId $SubscriptionId
    ```

6. The next step involves registering the target storage account with your on-premises AD environment. You should choose an appropriate OU. Use the `Get-ADOrganizationalUnit`

cmdlet to determine the name and `DistinguishedName` of the OU that you want to host the registered account:

```
Join-AzStorageAccountForAuth '
        -ResourceGroupName $ResourceGroupName '
        -StorageAccountName $StorageAccountName '
        -DomainAccountType "<ComputerAccount|ServiceLogonAccount>" '
        -OrganizationalUnitDistinguishedName "<ou-distinguishedname-here>" # If
            you don't provide the OU name as an input parameter, the AD identity that
            represents the storage account is created under the root directory.
```

The `Debug-AzStorageAccountAuth` cmdlet allows you to conduct a set of basic checks on your AD configuration with the logged-in AD user once you have performed account registration:

```
Debug-AzStorageAccountAuth -StorageAccountName $StorageAccountName -ResourceGroupName
$ResourceGroupName -Verbose
```

If you are unable to configure the on-premises service account so that its password does not expire, you'll need to use the `Update-AzStorageAccountADObjectPassword` cmdlet to update the Azure Storage account each time your on-premises service account password changes. This cmdlet is a part of the `AzFilesHybrid` module and must be run on a computer in the on-premises AD DS-joined environment with an account that has permissions within AD DS and owner permissions to the storage account. The following command—with appropriate variable substitutions—acquires the second storage account key and updates the password of the service account registered in AD DS:

```
# Update the password of the AD DS account registered for the storage account
# You may use either kerb1 or kerb2
Update-AzStorageAccountADObjectPassword '
        -RotateToKerbKey kerb2 '
        -ResourceGroupName "<your-resource-group-name-here>" '
        -StorageAccountName "<your-storage-account-name-here>"
```

Configuring share-level permissions

You configure share-level permission by assigning RBAC roles at the Azure file share. The following three roles are available for assigning file share permissions:

- **Storage File Data SMB Share Reader**   This role provides read access to Azure file shares over SMB to users who have this role.
- **Storage File Data SMB Share Contributor**   This role allows users who hold it read, write, and delete access to the Azure Storage file shares over SMB.
- **Storage File Data SMB Share Elevated Contributor**   This role allows read, write, and delete access, as well as the ability to modify Windows Access Control Lists (ACLs) of Azure Storage File shares over SMB.

When multiple roles are assigned, permissions are cumulative. The exception to this rule is when a deny permission applies; in this case, the deny permission overrides any `allow` permissions. While it is possible to assign RBAC roles and therefore, configure share-level permissions at the storage account level, you should instead assign RBAC roles at the individual file share-level. Full administrative control of file shares, which includes the ability to take ownership of files, currently requires the storage account key. You cannot take ownership of a file using Azure AD credentials.

Configuring file and folder permissions

Once you have assigned share-level permissions to an Azure File share using RBAC, you should then configure file and folder permissions on the contents of the share. When reading the Azure documentation, most Windows Server administrators will recognize that NTFS permissions are referred to as Windows ACLs.

You can configure file and folder permissions using the Set-ACL PowerShell cmdlet, using the icacls.exe command, or using Windows File Explorer if you have mounted the shared folder on a computer running a Windows Client or Windows Server operating system.

> **MORE INFO   AD AUTHENTICATION FOR AZURE FILES**
>
> You can learn more about AD Authentication for Azure Files at *https://docs.microsoft.com/ en-us/azure/storage/files/storage-files-identity-auth-active-directory-domain-service-enable*.

Azure AD DS authentication

Earlier in the chapter, you learned about using on-premises AD DS authentication to secure Azure File shares. Also, you can use Azure AD Domain Services to configure authentication for SMB connections to Azure File shares. Azure AD Domain Services is an Azure service that works with Azure AD to provide the functionality of domain controllers on an Azure subnet. When you enable Azure AD DS, you can domain join a Windows client or server VM that is hosted on an Azure subnet without having to deploy VMs that function as domain controllers. You can't use on-premises Active Directory authentication and Azure AD DS authentication on the same storage account or file shares.

Once you have enabled Azure AD DS on a subscription, you can enable identity-based access through AD DS when creating the storage account by selecting the **Azure Active Directory Domain Services (Azure AD DS)** identity option. You can also enable this option on the **Configuration** page of the storage account, as shown in Figure 4-13.

FIGURE 4-13 Enable Azure AD DS authentication

You can also use the `Set-AzStorageAccount` PowerShell cmdlet with the `EnableAzureAc-`
`tiveDirectoryDomainServicesForFile` parameter to enable Azure AD DS authentication for
an Azure file share. For example, to enable Azure AD DS authentication for the Azure file share
named `tailwind-files` stored in the resource group `FilesRG`, run this PowerShell command:

```
Set-AzStorageAccount -ResourceGroupName "FilesRG" '
   -Name "tailwind-files" '
   -EnableAzureActiveDirectoryDomainServicesForFile $true
```

You can use the `az storage account update` Azure CLI command with the `--enable-`
`files-adds` option to enable Azure AD DS authentication for an Azure file share. For example,
to enable Azure AD DS authentication for the Azure file share named `tailwind-files` stored
in the resource group `FilesRG`, run the Azure CLI command:

```
az storage account update -n tailwind-files -g FilesRG --enable-files-adds $true
```

Once Azure AD DS authentication has been enabled on the storage account, you can use
the **Access Control (IAM)** page of the storage account's properties to assign one of the
Storage File Share RBAC roles discussed earlier in this chapter as a share-level permission.
Figure 4-14 shows that the Tailwind-Engineers Azure AD group has assigned the Storage File
Data SMB Share Contributor role to the `tailwind-share` Azure File share.

FIGURE 4-14 File share Role Assignments

The process for configuring NTFS permissions on files and folders is the same as it is when
you enable authentication for on-premises AD DS accounts. You first mount the file share on
a Windows client or server computer, and then you use tools such as Windows File Explorer,
PowerShell, or the `icacls.exe` utility to configure the permissions.

> **MORE INFO   AZURE AD DS AUTHENTICATION**
>
> You can learn more about Azure AD DS authentication for Azure Files at *https://docs.microsoft.*
> *com/en-us/azure/storage/files/storage-files-identity-auth-active-directory-domain-service-*
> *enable*.

Configure delegated access

Shared Access Signatures (SAS) allow you to provide secure, granular, and delegated access to storage accounts. Using an SAS, you can control what resources a client can access, the permissions the client has to those resources, and the length of time that access will persist. An SAS is a signed Uniform Resource Identifier (URI) that provides the address of one or more storage resources and includes a token that determines how the resource may be accessed by the client.

Azure Storage supports the following types of SAS:

- **User delegation SAS**   User delegation SAS can only be used with Blob Storage. User delegation SAS are secured by Azure AD and the permissions configured for the SAS.
- **Service SAS**   Service SAS is secured with storage account keys. This SAS delegates access to one type of storage resource. Service SAS can be configured for Azure Files, Blob Storage, Queue Storage, or Table storage.
- **Account SAS**   Account SAS is secured with the storage account keys. These keys can be used to delegate access. In addition to all the operations that can be made available using User delegation SAS or Service SAS, Account SAS allows you to delegate access to operations that apply at the service level, such as Get/Set Service Properties. Account SAS also allows you to delegate access to read, write, and delete operations on blob containers, file shares, tables, and queues that are not possible with a Service SAS.

SAS comes in the following two forms:

- **Ad hoc SAS**   An ad hoc SAS includes the start time, expiry time, and resource permissions within the SAS URI. All SAS types can be ad hoc SAS.
- **Service SAS with stored access policy**   Stored access policies are configured on resource containers, which include blob containers, tables, queues, or file shares. A service SAS with stored access policies inherit the start time, expiry time, and permissions that have been configured for the stored access policy.

As is the case with storage account access keys, if an SAS is leaked, anyone who has access to the SAS has access to the storage resources to which the SAS mediates access. Application developers should also remember that SAS periodically expire, and if the application is not configured to automatically obtain a new SAS, the application will lose access to the storage resources to which the SAS mediates.

Microsoft has a list of best practices for the use of SAS, which includes:

- **Use user delegation SAS when possible**   This type of SAS has the best security because it is secured through a user's Azure AD credentials. This means that account keys will not be stored with application code.
- **Be ready to revoke an SAS when necessary**   If you determine that an SAS has been compromised, ensure that you can quickly revoke the SAS and replace it with one that is not compromised.

- **Configure stored access policies for service SAS** An advantage of stored access policies is that you can revoke permissions for a service SAS without having to regenerate storage account access keys.
- **Configure short expiration times for ad-hoc SAS** If an ad hoc SAS is compromised, the short expiration time will ensure that the compromised SAS isn't valid for a long time.
- **If necessary, ensure clients renew SAS** If clients regularly make requests to storage using SAS, configure the application so that the client can request SAS renewal before the SAS expires.

> ***MORE INFO*** **SHARED ACCESS SIGNATURES**
>
> You can learn more about Shared Access Signatures at *https://docs.microsoft.com/en-us/ azure/storage/common/storage-sas-overview*.

Create user delegation SAS

To create a user delegation SAS for a storage container using PowerShell, first create a storage context object by substituting the appropriate values into the following PowerShell code:

```
$ctx = New-AzStorageContext -StorageAccountName <storage-account> -UseConnectedAccount
```

Create a user delegation SAS token by substituting the appropriate values in the following PowerShell code:

```
New-AzStorageContainerSASToken -Context $ctx '
    -Name <container> '
    -Permission racwdl '
    -ExpiryTime <date-time>
```

To create a user delegation SAS for a blob, substitute the appropriate values in the following PowerShell code:

```
New-AzStorageBlobSASToken -Context $ctx '
    -Container <container> '
    -Blob <blob> '
    -Permission racwd '
    -ExpiryTime <date-time>
    -FullUri
```

You can revoke a user delegation SAS using the `Revoke-AzStorageAccountUser DelegationKeys` command. For example, use the following PowerShell code, substituting the appropriate values where necessary:

```
Revoke-AzStorageAccountUserDelegationKeys -ResourceGroupName <resource-group> '
    -StorageAccountName <storage-account>
```

To create a user delegation SAS for a storage container using Azure CLI, run the following Azure CLI command, substituting the appropriate values where necessary:

```
az storage container generate-sas \
    --account-name <storage-account> \
    --name <container> \
    --permissions acdlrw \
    --expiry <date-time> \
    --auth-mode login \
    --as-user
```

To create a user delegation SAS for a blob using Azure CLI, run the following Azure CLI command, substituting the appropriate values where necessary:

```
az storage blob generate-sas \
    --account-name <storage-account> \
    --container-name <container> \
    --name <blob> \
    --permissions acdrw \
    --expiry <date-time> \
    --auth-mode login \
    --as-user
    --full-uri
```

To revoke a user delegation SAS using Azure CLI, run the following command, substituting the appropriate values where necessary:

```
az storage account revoke-delegation-keys \
    --name <storage-account> \
    --resource-group <resource-group>
```

It is important to note is that because Azure Storage caches user delegation keys and Azure role assignments, the revocation process might not occur immediately.

> **MORE INFO   CREATE A USER DELEGATION SAS**
>
> You can learn more about creating a user delegation SAS at *https://docs.microsoft.com/en-us/ rest/api/storageservices/create-user-delegation-sas*.

Create an account SAS

The first step when creating an account SAS is creating an Account SAS URI. The Account SAS URI includes the URI of the storage resource to which the SAS provides access and the SAS token. SAS tokens are special query strings that include the data used to authorize resource requests and determine the service, resource, and access permissions. SAS tokens also include the period for which the signature will be valid.

Table 4-2 lists the required and optional parameters for the SAS token:

TABLE 4-2 SAS token parameters

SAS Query Parameter	Description
Api-version	**Optional** Allows you to specify the storage service version to use when executing the request.
SignedVersion (sv)	**Required** Specifies the signed storage service version to authorize requests. Must be configured to 2015-04-05 or later.
SignedServices (ss)	**Required** Allows you to specify the services accessible with the account SAS. Options include ■ Blob ■ Queue ■ Table ■ File
SignedResourceTypes (srt)	**Required** Allows you to specify which resource types the SAS provides access to ■ **Service** Access to service-level APIs. ■ **Container** Access to container-level APIs. ■ **Object** Access to object-level APIs.
SignedPermission (sp)	**Required** Permissions for the account SAS. Permissions include ■ **Read** Valid for all resource types. ■ **Write** Valid for all resource types. ■ **Delete** Valid for container and object resource types, not including queue messages. ■ **List** Valid for service and container resource types. ■ **Add** Valid for queue messages, table entities, and append blobs. ■ **Create** Valid for blobs and files. ■ **Update** Valid for queue messages and table entities. ■ **Process** Only valid for queue messages.
SignedStart (st)	**Optional** The time the SAS becomes valid.
SignedExpiry (se)	**Required** The time the SAS becomes invalid.
SignedIP (sip)	**Optional** Allows you to specify an allowed range of IP addresses.
SignedProtocol (spr)	**Optional** Determines which protocols can be used for requests made with the account SAS. Options are both HTTPS and HTTP or HTTPS only.
Signature (sig)	**Required** Used to authorize the request made with the SAS. Signatures are hash-based message authentication codes calculated over the signed string and the storage account access key using the SHA256 algorithm. This signature is then encoded using Base64 encoding.

To construct the signature string, you need to encode the string as UTF-8 that you want to sign from the fields included in the request and compute the signature using the HMAC-SHA256 algorithm.

Stored Access Policies

Stored access policies allow you to specifically control service-level shared access signatures. You can configure stored access policies for blob containers, file shares, queues, and tables. Stored access policies consist of the start time, expiry time, and permissions for an SAS. Each of these parameters can be specified on the signature URI rather than in a stored access policy. You can also specify all these parameters on the stored access policy or use a combination of the two. It is important to note that it is not possible to specify the same parameter on both the SAS token and the stored access policy without problems occurring.

Azure allows you to set a maximum of five concurrent access policies on individual containers, tables, queues, or shares. To create or modify a stored access policy, you need to call the Set ACL operation for the resource you want to protect with the request body of the call that lists the terms of the access policy. The following is a template that you can use for the request body where you substitute your own start time, expiry time, abbreviated permission list, and a unique signed identifier of your choosing:

```
<?xml version="1.0" encoding="utf-8"?>
<SignedIdentifiers>
  <SignedIdentifier>
    <Id>unique-64-char-value</Id>
    <AccessPolicy>
      <Start>start-time</Start>
      <Expiry>expiry-time</Expiry>
      <Permission>abbreviated-permission-list</Permission>
    </AccessPolicy>
  </SignedIdentifier>
</SignedIdentifiers>
```

To change the existing stored access policy parameters, call the access control list operation for the resource type and specify new parameters while ensuring that the unique ID field remains the same. To remove all access policies from a storage resource, call the Set ACL operation with an empty request policy.

Skill 4.2: Configure security for databases

This objective deals with the steps that you can take to secure Azure SQL database instances. To master this objective, you'll need to understand how to configure database authentication, the options for database auditing, the benefits of Azure SQL Database Advanced Threat Protection, how to configure database encryption, and how to enable Azure SQL Database Always Encrypted on specific database table columns.

Enable database authentication by using Azure AD

When you create an Azure SQL database server instance, you create an administrator login and a password associated with that login. This administrative account granted full administrative permissions on all databases hosted off the Azure SQL instance as a server-level principal. This login has all the possible permissions on the Azure SQL instance and cannot be limited.

A separate user account called dbo is created for the administrator login for each user database. The dbo user has all database permissions and is mapped to the db_owner database role. You can determine the identity of the administrator account for an Azure SQL database on the **Properties** page of the database in the Azure portal, as shown in Figure 4-15.

FIGURE 4-15 Server Admin Login

The admin log-in identifier cannot be changed once the database is created. You can reset the password of this account by selecting the Azure SQL server in the Azure portal and selecting **Reset Password** from the **Overview** page, as shown in Figure 4-16.

FIGURE 4-16 Reset Password

When adding administrative users, the following options are available:

- You can create an Azure Active Directory Administrator account. If you enable Azure Active Directory authentication, you can configure a user or group account in Azure AD with administrative permissions. You can do this by selecting the **Active Directory Admin** section under the **Azure SQL Instances** setting and then configuring an admin account by clicking the **Set Admin** button (see Figure 4-17).

FIGURE 4-17 Configuring Active Directory Admin for Azure SQL Server

- Create an additional SQL login in the master database, create a user account associated with this login in the master database, and then add this user account to the dbmanager role, the loginmanager role, or both roles in the master database using the ALTER ROLE statement.

To create additional accounts for non-administrative users, create SQL logins in the master database and then create user accounts in each database to which the user requires access and associate that user account with the SQL login.

> **MORE INFO**   **LOGINS, USER ACCOUNTS, ROLES, AND PERMISSIONS**
>
> You can learn more about logins, user accounts, roles, and permissions at *https:// docs.microsoft.com/en-us/azure/azure-sql/database/logins-create-manage*.

Enable database auditing

Auditing allows you to track database events, such as adding or dropping tables. Audit logs for Azure SQL databases can be stored in an Azure Storage account, in a Log Analytics workspace, or in Event Hubs. Auditing for Azure SQL can be defined at both the server and database levels. The differences are as follows:

- If you configure a server policy, it will apply to all existing and any newly created databases on the Azure SQL server instance.

- When server auditing is enabled at the instance level, it will always apply to the database.

- Enabling auditing on individual Azure SQL databases will not override any server auditing settings, with both audits existing in parallel.

- Microsoft recommends against enabling both server auditing and database blob auditing unless you want to use a different storage account, retention period, or Log Analytics Workspace for a specific database or if you want to audit a separate set of event types of categories for a specific database.

To enable auditing for an SQL instance, perform the following steps:

1. In the Azure portal, open the Azure SQL instance on which you want to configure auditing.

2. Under the **Security** node, select **Auditing**, as shown in Figure 4-18.

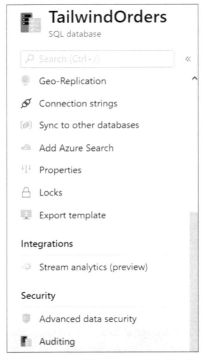

FIGURE 4-18 Auditing in an Azure SQL Server's properties page

3. Set the **Auditing** slider to **On**, as shown in Figure 4-19. Specify the audit log destination. You can choose between **Storage**, **Log Analytics**, or **Event Hub** and click **Save**.

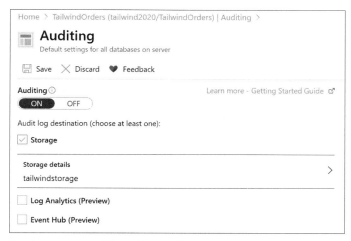

FIGURE 4-19 Azure SQL auditing settings

You can configure audit logs to be written to Azure Storage accounts, Event Hubs, and to Log Analytics workspaces, which Azure Monitor logs can consume. You can choose to have data written to multiple locations should you so choose. When auditing to a storage destination, the retention period is unlimited. You can modify retention settings to keep audit logs for a shorter amount of time. Figure 4-20 shows the **Retention (Days)** setting configured to 14 days.

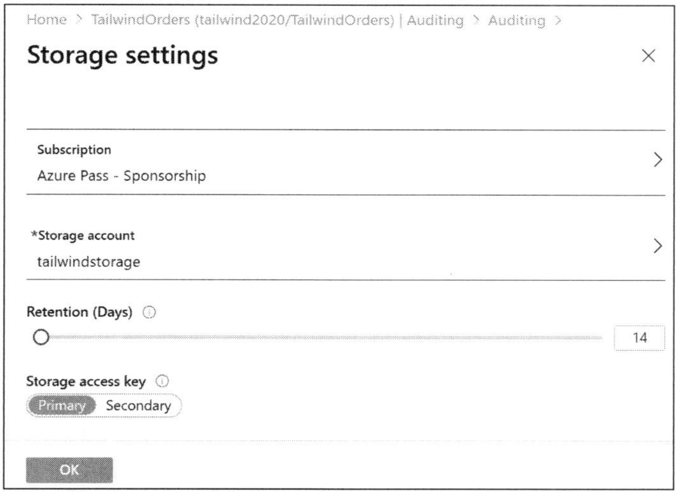

FIGURE 4-20 Auditing storage retention

You can view audit logs by clicking on the **View Audit Logs** item from the **Auditing** page of the Azure SQL server's instance. You can view audit information from the server or database level from this page, as shown in Figure 4-21.

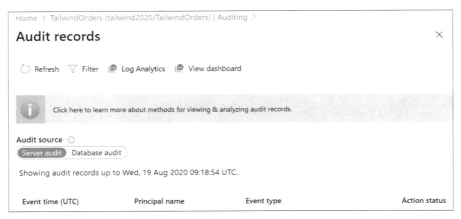

FIGURE 4-21 Audit records

You also can click **Log Analytics** to view the logs in the Log Analytics workspace. If you click **View Dashboard**, you'll be able to view an auditing dashboard that will include access to sensitive data and security insight information, as shown in Figure 4-22.

FIGURE 4-22 Auditing dashboard

> **MORE INFO   AUDITING FOR AZURE SQL DATABASE**
>
> You can learn more about auditing for Azure SQL Database at *https://docs.microsoft.com/en-us/azure/azure-sql/database/auditing-overview*.

Configure dynamic masking on SQL workloads

Dynamic masking allows you to configure SQL Server to hide sensitive data stored in the database from users who don't have the appropriate privileges. For example, a query run against a table in a database that stores credit card information by an unprivileged user might only reveal the final four digits of the credit card with the rest of the credit card number hidden through dynamic masking.

Dynamic data masking can be configured through dynamic data masking policies available under Security in the SQL Database configuration pane. Dynamic data masking cannot currently be configured in the Azure Portal for an SQL Managed Instance. Dynamic data masking policies have the following elements:

- **SQL users excluded from masking**   This is the set of SQL users or Azure AD identities who can retrieve unmasked data when performing SQL queries. Users that have administrative privileges on the database will always be able to view complete data without masks being applied.

- **Masking rules**   These are the rules that determine which fields will be masked and how the masks will be applied. You can identify fields using database schema name, table name, and column name.

- **Masking functions**   These are a set of functions that manage the display of data for different scenarios.

The masking functions available for Azure SQL are listed in Table 4-3.

TABLE 4-3 Masking functions

Masking function	Masking logic
Default	▪ Use XXX or fewer Xs if the size of the field is less than four characters for string data types (nchar, ntext, nvarchar). ▪ Use zero value for numeric data types (bigint, bit, decimal, int, money, numeric, smallint, smallmoney, tinyint, float, and real). ▪ Use 01-01-1990 for date/time data types (date, datetime2, datetime, datetimeoffset, smalldate, time). ▪ For an SQL variant, the default value of the current type is used. ▪ For XML, the <masked/> document is used. ▪ Use an empty value for special data types (timestamp table, hierarchyid, <DS>GUID</DS>, binary, image, varbinary special types)
Credit card	Masking method that exposes only the final four digits of a credit card and substitutes a constant string (such as XXXX-XXXX-XXXX-1234) for the masked parts of the result.
Email	This masking method displays only the first letter of an email address and replaces the email domain with XXX.com.
Random number	Masks data using random numbers.
Custom text	Exposes the first and last characters of the data and substitutes a custom string in the middle in the form prefix[padding]suffix.

MORE INFO   **DYNAMIC DATA MASKING**

You can learn more about dynamic data masking at *https://docs.microsoft.com/en-us/azure/ azure-sql/database/dynamic-data-masking-overview.*

Implement database encryption for Azure SQL Database

Transparent data encryption (TDE) allows you to protect Azure SQL databases by encrypting data at rest. When you enable TDE, the databases, associated backups, and transaction log files are automatically encrypted and decrypted, as necessary. TDE is enabled by default for all new Azure SQL Databases. TDE is configured at the server level and is inherited by all databases hosted on the Azure SQL Server instance.

Azure SQL TDE has a database encryption key (DEK) protected by a built-in server certificate that is unique to each Azure SQL instance and leverages the AES 256 encryption algorithm. Microsoft automatically rotates these security certificates.

Customer-managed TDE, also known as "Bring Your Own Key" (BYOK), is supported in Azure SQL. When you configure BYOK, the TDE protection key is stored within Azure Key Vault. When you configure BYOK, you configure an Azure Key Vault with permissions so that the Azure SQL instance can interact with the Key Vault to retrieve the key. The database will be inaccessible if the Key Vault is removed or the Azure SQL instance loses permissions to the Key Vault in a BYOK scenario.

You can verify that TDE is enabled for an Azure SQL instance by selecting the **Transparent Data Encryption** section of a database server instance's properties page in the Azure portal, as shown in Figure 4-23.

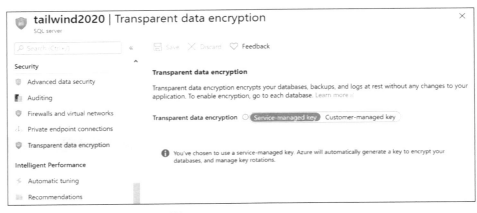

FIGURE 4-23 TDE Service-Managed Key

If you want to switch to a customer managed key for an Azure SQL instance, you should first create and configure an Azure Key Vault in the same region as the Azure SQL instance. You can then use the portal to create a key in the Key Vault and configure the Azure SQL instance with the appropriate permissions. To switch a database to a customer-managed key, perform the following steps:

1. On the **Transparent Data Encryption** page of the Azure SQL database instance, select **Customer Managed Key**.

2. The **Key Selection Method** offers two choices: You can choose **Enter A Key Identifier**, or you can choose **Select A Key** and then click the **Change Key** link, as shown in Figure 4-24.

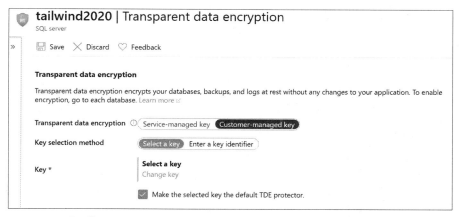

FIGURE 4-24 Configure Customer-Managed Key

3. On the **Select Key From Azure Key Vault** page, select the subscription and the **Key Vault** that will host the key.

4. If no suitable key is present in the Key Vault, you can click **Create New**. This will allow you to create a key, as shown in Figure 4-25.

FIGURE 4-25 Create a key for BYOK

5. On the **Select Key From Azure Key Vault** page, select the version of the key, as shown in Figure 4-26. If you've just created the key, only the most recent version available will be available.

FIGURE 4-26 Selecting a key for BYOK

6. Click **Save** to configure Azure SQL to use your customer key.

> **MORE INFO** **AZURE SQL DATABASE ENCRYPTION**
> You can learn more about Azure SQL Database encryption at *https://docs.microsoft.com/en-us/ sql/relational-databases/security/encryption/sql-server-encryption?view=azuresqldb-current*.

Implement Azure SQL Database Always Encrypted

Always Encrypted is a technology available for Azure SQL that allows you to protect specific types of sensitive data that has a known recognizable pattern, such as passport numbers, tax file identification numbers, and credit card numbers. When Always Encrypted is enabled, clients interacting with the database server will encrypt the sensitive data inside the client applications and will not forward the encryption keys used to decrypt that data to the database server that will store that data. This ensures that administrators who manage Azure SQL servers cannot view sensitive data protected by Always Encrypted.

Deterministic or Randomized Encryption

Always Encrypted supports two forms of encryption: deterministic encryption and randomized encryption:

- **Deterministic encryption**   When you use deterministic encryption, the same encrypted value will always be generated for the same plain text value, though this value will be unique to each database. Implementing deterministic encryption will allow you to perform point lookups, equality joins, grouping, and indexing on encrypted columns. It may, however, allow unauthorized users to guess information about encrypted values by looking for patterns in encrypted columns. This is especially true if there are a small set of possible values. Deterministic encryption requires that the column collation is configured with a binary2 sort order for character columns.

- **Randomized encryption** When you configure randomized encryption, data is encrypted less predictably. While randomized encryption is more secure than deterministic encryption, enabling randomized encryption prevents searching, grouping, indexing, and performing joins on encrypted columns.

In general, you should plan to use deterministic encryption if columns will be used for searchers or where you will be grouping parameters. An example of this is where you need to search for a specific passport number. The client will be able to perform the hash of the query value and then locate values within the database that match that encrypted hash. You should use randomized encryption if your database has information that isn't grouped with other records and isn't used to join tables, such as medical notes.

Configuring Always Encrypted

Configuring Always Encrypted is an activity that requires the use of client-side tools. You can't use Transact SQL statements to configure Always Encrypted; instead, you must configure Always Encrypted using SQL Server Management Studio or PowerShell. Configuring Always Encrypted requires performing the following tasks:

- Provisioning column master keys, column encryption keys, and encrypted column encryption keys with corresponding column master keys
- Creating key metadata in the database
- Creating new tables with encrypted columns
- Encrypting existing data in selected database columns

Always Encrypted is not supported for columns that have the following characteristics:

- Columns with xml, timestamp/rowversion, image, ntext, text, sql_variant, hierarchyid, geography, geometry, alias, and types or user-defined types
- FILESTREAM columns
- Columns with the IDENTITY property
- Columns with ROWGUIDCOL property
- String columns with non-bin2 collections
- Columns that are keys for clustered and non-clustered indexes (if you are using randomized encryption)
- Columns that are keys for full-text indexes (if you are using randomized encryption)
- Computed columns
- Columns referenced by computed columns
- Sparse column set

- Columns referenced by statistics (if you are using randomized encryption)
- Columns using alias types
- Partitioning columns
- Columns with default constraints
- Columns referenced by unique constraints (if you are using randomized encryption)
- Primary key columns (if you are using randomized encryption)
- Referencing columns in foreign key constraints
- Columns referenced by check constraints
- Columns tracked using change data capture
- Primary key columns on tables that have change tracking enabled
- Columns masked using Dynamic Data Masking
- Columns in Stretch Database Tables

To configure Always Encrypted on an Azure SQL database using SQL Server Management Studio, perform the following steps:

1. Connect to the database that hosts the tables with columns you want to encrypt using Object Explorer in SQL Server Management Studio. If the database does not already exist, you can create the database and then create the tables that you will configure to use Always Encrypted.

2. Right-click the database and select **Tasks** > **Encrypt Columns**. This will open the **Always Encrypted Wizard**. Click **Next**.

3. On the **Column Selection** page, expand the database tables, and then select the columns that you want to encrypt.

4. For each column selected, you will need to set the **Encryption Type** attribute to **Deterministic** or **Randomized**.

5. For each column selected, you will need to choose an **Encryption Key**. If you do not already have an encryption key, you can have one automatically generated.

6. On the **Master Key Configuration** page, choose a location to store the key. You will then need to select a master key source.

7. On the **Validation** page, select whether you want to run the script immediately or use a PowerShell script later.

8. On the **Summary** page, review the selected option and click **Finish**.

MORE INFO **AZURE SQL DATABASE ALWAYS ENCRYPTED**

You can learn more about Azure SQL Database Always Encrypted at *https://docs.microsoft. com/en-us/sql/relational-databases/security/encryption/always-encrypted-database-engine?view=sql-server-ver15*.

Implement network isolation for data solutions, including Azure Synapse Analytics and Azure Cosmos DB

You can isolate data solutions, including Azure Synapse Analytics and Azure Cosmos DB, using IP firewall rules, private endpoints, and managed virtual networks. These network isolation technologies work in the following ways:

- Service endpoints
- IP firewall rules
- Azure Private Link

Service endpoints

Virtual network service endpoints provide access to Azure services over the Azure backbone networks. You can use virtual network service endpoints to allow private IP addresses on a specific virtual network to reach a specific service without requiring the hosts on the virtual network to have a public IP address. Virtual network service endpoints are supported for the following Azure services:

- Azure Storage
- Azure SQL Database
- Azure Synapse Analytics
- Azure Database for PostgreSQL server
- Azure Database for MySQL server
- Azure Database for MariaDB
- Azure Cosmos DB
- Azure Key Vault
- Azure Service Bus
- Azure Event Hubs
- Azure Data Lake Store Gen 1
- Azure App Service
- Azure Cognitive Services
- Azure Container Registry

Azure Service Endpoints allow access to the service but don't limit access to a specific instance of that service. For example, if you configure a service endpoint to Azure SQL Database, a host on the configured virtual network will be able to connect to all SQL database instances rather than a specific instance.

> **MORE INFO** **AZURE SERVICE ENDPOINTS**
>
> You can learn more about Azure Virtual Network Service Endpoints at *https://docs.microsoft. com/en-us/azure/virtual-network/virtual-network-service-endpoints-overview*.

IP Firewall rules

Most Azure services allow access to authenticated connections from any host on the Internet, with unauthenticated connections automatically dropped. Using IP firewall rules, organizations that want to go further can limit access to a specific known range of IP addresses used by the organization. IP firewall rules can be used in conjunction with other technologies such as Azure Service Endpoints or Azure Private Link. IP firewall rules limit traffic based on IP address. When configuring IP firewall rules for an Azure data source, you don't configure rules to include a port or protocol. Firewall rules can be configured on the Networking section of the Azure service's properties.

> **MORE INFO   IP FIREWALL**
>
> You can learn more about configuring IP Firewall for Cosmos DB at *https://docs.microsoft.com/en-us/azure/cosmos-db/how-to-configure-firewall*.

Azure Private Link

Azure Private link allows you to connect a data solution such as Azure Synapse Analytics or Azure Cosmos DB to a private endpoint. Private endpoints are collections of private IP addresses in a subnet in a virtual network. When you use Private Link you can limit access to the data solution so that it can only be accessed by hosts that use those specific private IP addresses. You can combine Private Link with network security group rules. Private link can be used to limit access so that it can only occur from a specific virtual network or any peered virtual network as long as the IP addresses on that virtual network or peered virtual network are specified when configuring the private endpoint.

Azure Private Link provides the following benefits:

- Private access to Azure services. Allows you to connect virtual networks to services without requiring a public IP address at the source or destination. Communication occurs over the Azure backbone network.

- Access to on-premises and peered networks. Private Link can be configured to allow access from on-premises networks connected to a configured virtual network through ExpressRoute private peering, VPN tunnels, and peered virtual networks.

- Data leakage protection. You map private endpoints to a specific Azure Cosmos DB, Azure Synapse Analytics, or Azure PaaS instance. This means that connections using the Private Link can only access that specific instance of the data service, not all data services such as the case that occurs when you use a service endpoint.

> **MORE INFO   AZURE PRIVATE LINK**
>
> You can learn more about Azure Private Link at *https://docs.microsoft.com/en-us/azure/private-link/private-link-overview*.

Configure Microsoft Defender for SQL

Microsoft Defender for SQL (previously Azure SQL Database Advanced Threat Protection) allows you to detect unusual activity that indicates that a third party might be trying to attack your organization's Azure SQL databases. When you enable Microsoft Defender for SQL, you will be notified when unusual database activity occurs, when there are potential database vulnerabilities given the current configuration, and when SQL injection attacks occur. Microsoft Defender for SQL integrates with Microsoft Defender for Cloud, so you will also be provided with recommendations on how to further investigate and remediate suspicious activity and threats.

To configure Microsoft Defender for SQL, perform the following steps:

1. In the Azure portal, open the Azure SQL Server instance for which you want to configure Microsoft Defender for SQL.

2. Under the **Security** node, click **Microsoft Defender for Cloud**, as shown in Figure 4-27.

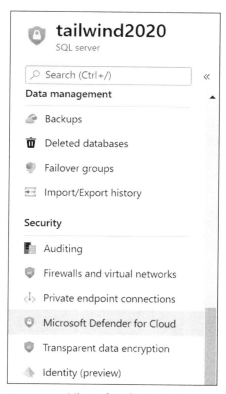

FIGURE 4-27 Microsoft Defender for Cloud item

3. Click **Configure** next to Microsoft Defender for SQL as shown in Figure 4-28.

FIGURE 4-28 Configure Microsoft Defender for SQL

4. On the **Microsoft Defender for SQL** page shown in Figure 4-29, configure the following settings:

- **Microsoft Defender for SQL** This functionality has a per-month cost, which includes Data Discovery, Classification, Vulnerability Assessment, and Advanced Threat Protection. These services allow you to detect data that might be at risk, such as personal data stored within the database, as well as vulnerabilities that might not be detected by other means but which become apparent through analysis of database activity. Can be set to On or Off.

- **Subscription** This setting determines which subscription the vulnerability assessment settings will be billed against.

- **Storage account** This is where data from assessments will be logged.

- **Periodic recurring scans** This setting determines whether periodic vulnerability assessment scans are run against the Azure SQL instance. You can specify the email address to which scan reports will be sent.

- **Advanced Threat Protection Settings** You can configure where advanced threat protection information will be forwarded in Defender for Cloud.

Advanced Threat Protection for SQL allows you to detect and be notified about the following threats:

- **SQL Injection** SQL injection has occurred against a monitored SQL instance.
- **SQL Injection Vulnerability** An application vulnerability to SQL injection was detected.
- **Data Exfiltration** Activity resembling data exfiltration was detected.
- **Unsafe Action** A potentially unsafe action was detected.
- **Brute Force** A brute force attack was detected.
- **Anomalous Client Login** A login with suspicious characteristics was detected.

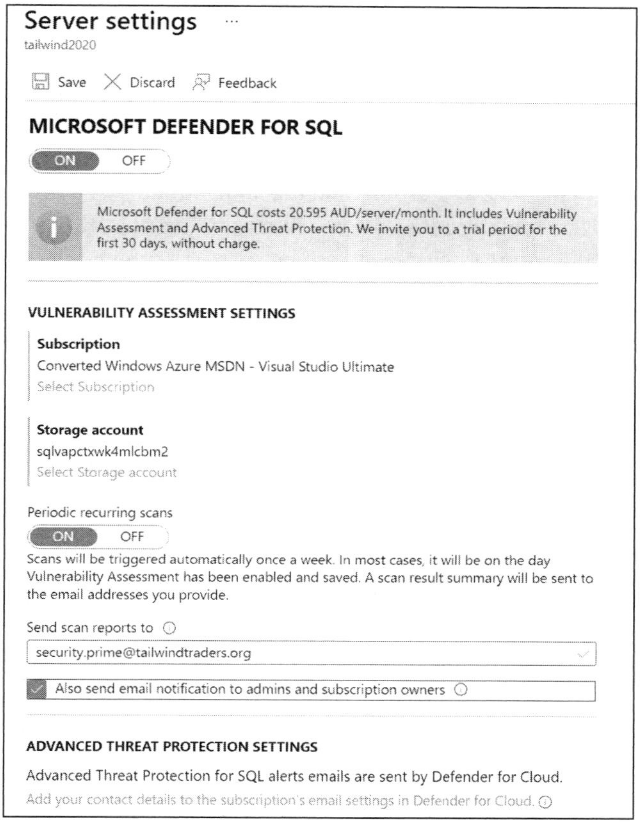

Server settings

tailwind2020

🖫 Save ✕ Discard ⤵ Feedback

MICROSOFT DEFENDER FOR SQL

⬤ ON OFF

> ℹ️ Microsoft Defender for SQL costs 20.595 AUD/server/month. It includes Vulnerability
> Assessment and Advanced Threat Protection. We invite you to a trial period for the
> first 30 days, without charge.

VULNERABILITY ASSESSMENT SETTINGS

Subscription

Converted Windows Azure MSDN - Visual Studio Ultimate

Select Subscription

Storage account

sqlvapctxwk4mlcbm2

Select Storage account

Periodic recurring scans

⬤ ON OFF

Scans will be triggered automatically once a week. In most cases, it will be on the day
Vulnerability Assessment has been enabled and saved. A scan result summary will be sent to
the email addresses you provide.

Send scan reports to ○

| security.prime@tailwindtraders.org | ∨ |

| ☑ Also send email notification to admins and subscription owners ○ |

ADVANCED THREAT PROTECTION SETTINGS

Advanced Threat Protection for SQL alerts emails are sent by Defender for Cloud.

Add your contact details to the subscription's email settings in Defender for Cloud. ○

FIGURE 4-29 Microsoft Defender for SQL options

> **MORE INFO** **MICROSOFT DEFENDER FOR SQL**
>
> You can learn more about Azure SQL Database Advanced Threat Protection at *https://docs.*
> *microsoft.com/en-us/azure/defender-for-cloud/defender-for-sql-introduction*.

EXAM TIP

Remember the difference between deterministic and randomized encryption.

Skill 4.3: Configure and manage Key Vault

This objective deals with configuring and managing Azure Key Vault, which can be thought of as a cloud hardware security module (HSM). You can use Azure Key Vault to securely store encryption keys and secrets, including certificates, database connection strings, and virtual machine passwords. In this section, you'll learn how to ensure that the items stored in Azure Key Vault are only accessible to authorized applications and users. To master this objective, you'll need to understand how to manage access to Key Vault, including how to configure permissions to secrets, certificates, and keys. You'll also need to understand how to configure RBAC for managing Key Vault. You'll also need to understand how to manage the items within Key Vault, including how to rotate keys and how to perform backup and recovery on secure Key Vault items.

Create and configure Key Vault

Azure Key Vault allows you to store information that should not be made public, such as secrets, certificates, and keys. To create an Azure Key Vault using the Azure Portal, perform the following steps:

1. In the Azure portal menu, select **Create A Resource**.

2. In the **Search** box, type **Key Vault** and then select **Key Vault** from the list of results. Click **Create**.

3. On the **Create Key Vault** page, provide the following information:

    - **Name**   Provide the Key Vault with a name unique within the subscription you are creating the Key Vault in.

    - **Subscription**   Select which subscription the Key Vault will be associated with.

    - **Resource Group**   Select which resource group will host the Key Vault. You have the option of creating a new resource group.

    - **Location**   Select which Azure location will host the Key Vault.

    - **Pricing Tier**   Allows you to choose between **Standard** and **Premium**. Premium tier provides a dedicated Hardware Security Module (HSM) for the vault.

To create a Key Vault using Azure CLI, use the following command, specifying a unique Key Vault name, existing appropriate resource group, and location:

```
az keyvault create --name "<your-unique-keyvault-name>" --resource-group
"myResourceGroup" --location "EastUS"
```

To create a Key Vault using Azure PowerShell, use the following command, specifying a unique Key Vault name, existing appropriate resource group, and location:

```
New-AzKeyVault -Name "<your-unique-keyvault-name>" -ResourceGroupName "myResourceGroup"
-Location "East US"
```

Configure access to Key Vault

Because Key Vaults can store sensitive information, you naturally want to limit who has access to it rather than allowing access to the entire world. You manage Key Vault access at the management plane and at the data plane. The management plane contains the tools you use to manage Key Vault, such as the Azure portal, Azure CLI, and Cloud Shell. When you control access at the management plane, you can configure who can access the contents of the Key Vault at the data plane. From the Key Vault perspective, the data plane involves the items stored within Key Vault, and access permissions allow the ability to add, delete, and modify certificates, secrets, and keys. Access to the Key Vault at both the management and data planes should be as restricted as possible. If a user or application doesn't need access to the Key Vault, they shouldn't have access to the Key Vault. Microsoft recommends that you use separate Key Vaults for Development, pre-production, and production environments.

Each Key Vault you create is associated with the Azure AD tenancy linked to the subscription that hosts the Key Vault. All attempts to manage or retrieve Key Vault content require Azure AD authentication. An advantage of requiring Azure AD authentication is that it allows you to determine which security principal is attempting access. Access to Key Vault cannot be granted based on having access to a secret or key and requires some form of Azure AD identity.

> **MORE INFO   KEY VAULT SECURITY**
>
> You can learn more about Key Vault Security at *https://docs.microsoft.com/en-us/azure/key-vault/general/overview-security*.

Manage permissions to secrets, certificates, and keys

You use Key Vault access control policies to manage permissions to secrets, certificates, and keys at the data plane level. Each Key Vault access control policy includes entries specifying what access the designated security principal has to keys, secrets, and certificates. Each Key Vault supports a maximum of 1,024 access policy entries.

An access policy entry grants a distinct set of permissions to a security principal. A security principal can be a user, service principal, managed identity, or group. Microsoft recommends assigning permissions to groups and then adding and removing users, service principals, and managed identities to and from those groups as a way of granting or revoking permissions.

You can configure the permissions for the keys, secrets, and certificates outlined in Table 4-3.

TABLE 4-3 Key Vault permissions

Certificate Permissions	Key Permissions	Secrets Permissions
■ **Get** View the current certificate version in the Key Vault. ■ **List** List current certificates and certificate versions in the Key Vault. ■ **Delete** Delete a certificate from the Key Vault. ■ **Create** Create a Key Vault certificate. ■ **Import** Import certificate material into a Key Vault certificate. ■ **Update** Update a certificate in Key Vault. ■ **Managecontacts** Manage Key Vault certificate contacts. ■ **Getissuers** View the certificate's issuing authority. ■ **Listissuers** List a certificate's issuing authority information. ■ **Setissuers** Update a Key Vault certificate authority or issuers. ■ **Deleteissuers** Remove information about a Key Vault's certificate authorities or issuers. ■ **Manageissuers** Manage a Key Vault's list of certificate authorities/issuers. ■ **Recover** Recover a certificate that has been deleted from a Key Vault. ■ **Backup** Back up a certificate stored in Key Vault. ■ **Restore** Restore a backed up Key Vault certificate. ■ **Purge** Permanently delete a deleted certificate.	■ **Decrypt** Perform a decryption operation with the key. ■ **Encrypt** Perform an encryption operation with the key. ■ **UnwrapKey** Use the key for key decryption. ■ **WrapKey** Use the key for key encryption. ■ **Verify** Use the key to verify a signature. ■ **Sign** Use the key for signing operation. ■ **Get** Read the public parts of a key. ■ **List** List all keys in the vault. ■ **Update** Modify the key's attributes/metadata. ■ **Create** Create a key in a Key Vault. ■ **Import** Import an existing key into a Key Vault. ■ **Delete** Remove a key from a Key Vault. ■ **Backup** Export a key in protected form. ■ **Restore** Import a previously backed up key. ■ **Recover** Recover a deleted key. ■ **Purge** Permanently delete a deleted key.	■ **Get** Read a secret. ■ **List** List secrets or secret versions. ■ **Set** Create a secret. ■ **Delete** Delete a secret. ■ **Backup** Back up secret in a Key Vault. ■ **Restore** Restore a backed-up secret to a Key Vault. ■ **Recover** Recover a deleted secret. ■ **Purge** Permanently delete a deleted secret.

Key Vault access policies don't allow you to configure granular access to specific keys, secrets, or certificates. You can only assign a set of permissions at the keys, secrets, or certificates levels if you need to allow a specific security principal access to only some and not all keys, secrets, or certificates. Instead, you should store those keys, secrets, or certificates in separate Key Vaults. For example, if there are three secrets that you need to protect using Key Vault, and one user should only have access to two of those secrets, you'll need to store the third of those secrets in a separate Key Vault from the first two.

You use the `Set-AzKeyVaultAccessPolicy` Azure PowerShell to configure a Key Vault policy using Azure PowerShell. When using this cmdlet, the important parameters are the vault name, the resource group name, the security principal identifier, which can be `UserPrincipal-Name`, `ObjectID`, `ServicePrincipalName`, and then the parameters that define permissions to Keys, Secrets, and Certificates. The `Set-AzKeyVaultACcessPolicy` cmdlet has the following format:

```
Set-AzKeyVaultAccessPolicy -VaultName <your-key-vault-name> -PermissionsToKeys
<permissions-to-keys> -PermissionsToSecrets <permissions-to-secrets>
-PermissionsToCertificates <permissions-to-certificates> -ObjectId <Id>
```

If you prefer Azure CLI, you can use the `az keyvault set-policy` command to configure access policies to Key Vault Items. The `az keyvault set-policy` command has the following format:

```
az keyvault set-policy -n <your-unique-keyvault-name> --spn <ApplicationID-of-your-
service-principal> --secret-permissions <secret-permissions> --key-permissions <key-
permissions> --certificate-permissions <certificate-permissions>
```

> **MORE INFO** **MANAGE PERMISSIONS TO KEY VAULT ITEMS**
>
> You can learn more about managing permissions to Key Vault items at *https://docs.microsoft.com/en-us/azure/key-vault/general/group-permissions-for-apps*.

Configure RBAC usage in Azure Key Vault

RBAC allows you to secure Azure Key Vault at the management plane. In mid-2020, Microsoft introduced a new set of RBAC roles that provide a simplified way of assigning permissions to the contents of Key Vaults. Going forward, you should only configure access policies when you need to configure complex permissions that are not covered by the new RBAC roles. You assign Key Vault RBAC roles on the Access Control (IAM) page of a Key Vault's properties, as shown in Figure 4-30. While you can also assign Key Vault RBAC roles at the resource group, subscription, and management group level, security best practice is to assign roles with the narrowest-possible scope.

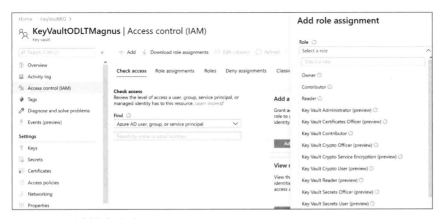

FIGURE 4-30 Add Role Assignment

The RBAC roles for Azure Key Vault are as follows:

- **Key Vault Administrator**   Can perform any action on secrets, certificates, and keys in a Key Vault, except managing permissions
- **Key Vault Certificates Officer**   Can perform any actions on Key Vault certificates, except managing permissions
- **Key Vault Contributor**   Allows for the management of Key Vault but does not allow access to the items within a Key Vault
- **Key Vault Crypto Officer**   Can perform any actions on Key Vault keys, except managing permissions
- **Key Vault Crypto Service Encryption**   Has read access to key metadata and can perform wrap and unwrap operations
- **Key Vault Crypto User**   Can perform cryptographic operations on keys and certificates
- **Key Vault Reader**   Can read Key Vault item metadata but not Key Vault item contents
- **Key Vault Secrets Officer**   Can perform all actions on Key Vault secrets except managing permissions
- **Key Vault Secrets User**   Can read the contents of secrets

> *MORE INFO*   **CONFIGURE RBAC IN KEY VAULT**
>
> You can learn more about configuring RBAC in Key Vault at *http://docs.microsoft.com/en-us/azure/key-vault/general/secure-your-key-vault*.

Key Vault Firewalls and Virtual Networks

The Networking page of a Key Vault's properties page, shown in Figure 4-31, allows you to configure the network locations from which a specific Key Vault can be accessed. You can configure the Key Vault to be accessible from all networks or specific virtual networks and sets of IPv4 address ranges.

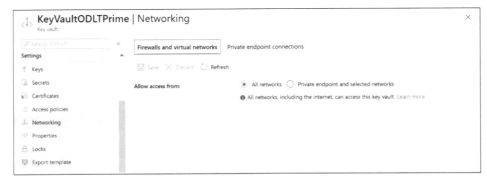

FIGURE 4-31 Firewalls And Virtual Networks

When configuring network access rules for Azure Key Vault, keep the following in mind:

- Each Key Vault can be configured with a maximum of 127 virtual network rules and 127 IPv4 rules.

- /31 and /32 CIDR subnet masks are not supported. Instead of individual IP addresses, rules should be allowed when allowing access from these subnets.

- IP network rules can only be configured for public IP address ranges. You should use virtual network rules for private IP address ranges.

- IPv6 addresses are not presently supported by Azure Key Vault firewall rules.

You can configure Key Vault firewalls and virtual networks in the Azure portal by performing the following steps:

1. In the Azure portal, open the Key Vault that you want to configure.

2. Under **Settings**, select **Networking**. On the **Networking** page, select **Firewalls And Virtual Networks**.

3. By default, the Key Vault will be accessible from all networks. Select the **Private Endpoint And Selected Networks** option. When you enable this option, trusted Microsoft services can bypass the firewall. You can disable access from trusted Microsoft services if you choose.

4. To add an existing virtual network or a new virtual network, click the **Add Existing Virtual Networks** or **Add New Virtual Networks** items, as shown in Figure 4-32.

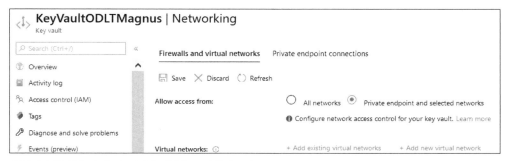

FIGURE 4-32 Private Endpoint And Selected Networks

5. When you add a virtual network, you must select the subscription, virtual network, and subnets that you want to grant access to the Key Vault, as shown in Figure 4-33. If a service endpoint isn't present on the virtual network subnet, you can enable one.

FIGURE 4-33 Add Networks

6. To add an IPv4 address range, enter the IPv4 address or CIDR range, as shown in Figure 4-34.

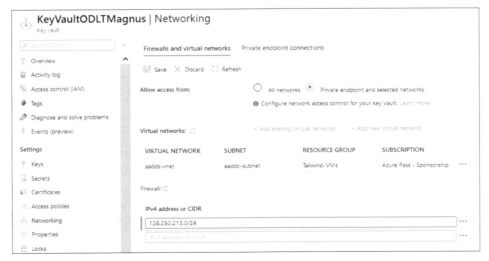

FIGURE 4-34 Key Vault Firewall

7. Click **Save** to save the **Firewall And Virtual Networks** configuration.

You can use the **Private Endpoint Connections** tab to add private endpoint access to a specific Key Vault. An Azure Private Endpoint is a network interface that allows a private and secure connection to a service using an Azure Private Link. Azure Private Link allows access to Azure PaaS Services, such as an Azure Key Vault over a private connection on the Microsoft network backbone. No traffic that traverses a private link passes across the public Internet.

> **MORE INFO**   **KEY VAULT FIREWALLS AND VIRTUAL NETWORKS**
>
> You can learn more about Key Vault firewalls and virtual networks at *https://docs.microsoft. com/en-us/azure/key-vault/general/network-security*.

Manage certificates, secrets, and keys

Azure Key Vault supports the following management actions for x509 certificates:

- Allows for the creation of an x509 certificate or for importing an x509 certificate
- Supports Certificate Authority-generated certificates and self-signed certificates
- Allows a Key Vault certificate owner to store that certificate securely without requiring access to the private key
- Allows a certificate owner to configure policies that allow Key Vaults to manage certificate lifecycles
- Allows certificate owners to provide contact information so that they can be notified about lifecycle events, including certificate expiration and renewal
- Can be configured to support automatic certificate renewal with specific Key Vault partner x509 certificate authorities

Certificate policies provide information to the Key Vault on how to create and manage the lifecycle of a certificate stored within the Key Vault. This includes information on whether the certificate's private key is exportable. When you create a certificate in a Key Vault for the first time, a policy must be supplied. Once this policy is established, you won't need the policy for subsequent certificate creation operations. Certificate policies contain the following elements:

- **X509 certificate properties**   Includes subject name, subject alternate names, and other properties used during the creation of an x509 certificate.
- **Key properties**   Specifies the key type, key length, whether the key is exportable, and how the key should be treated in renewal fields. These properties provide instruction on how a Key Vault generates a certificate key.
- **Secret properties**   Specifies secret properties, including the type of content used to generate the secret value when retrieving a certificate as a Key Vault secret.
- **Lifetime actions**   Specifies lifetime settings for the Azure Key Vault certificate. This includes the number of days before expiry and an action option, which either emails specified contacts or triggers autorenewal of the certificate.
- **Issuer**   Includes information about the x509 certificate issuer.
- **Policy attributes**   Lists attributes associated with the policy.

Azure Key Vault presently can work with two certificate-issuance providers for TLS/SSL certificates: DigiCert and GlobalSign. When you onboard a certificate authority provider, you gain the ability to create TLS/SSL certificates that include the certificate authority provider as the apex of the certificate trust list. This ensures that certificates created through the Azure Key Vault will be trusted by third parties who trust the certificate authority provider.

Certificate contacts information includes the addresses where notifications are sent when specific certificate lifecycle events occur. Certificate contacts information is shared across all certificates generated by a Key Vault. If you have configured a certificate's policy so that auto-renewal occurs, notifications will be sent

- Prior to certificate renewal
- After successful certificate auto-renewal
- If an error occurs during auto-renewal
- If manual renewal is configured, you are provided with a warning that you should renew the certificate

> **MORE INFO STORING X509 CERTIFICATES IN KEY VAULT**
>
> You can learn more about storing x509 certificates in Key Vault at *https://docs.microsoft.com/en-us/azure/key-vault/certificates/about-certificates*.

Creating and importing certificates

You can add certificates to Key Vault by importing them or generating them using the Key Vault. When generating certificates, you can have the certificate self-signed or have it be generated as part of a trust chain from a trusted CA provider.

To create a self-signed certificate using the Azure portal, perform the following steps:

1. In the Azure portal, open the **Key Vault** properties page and click **Certificates**, as shown in Figure 4-35.

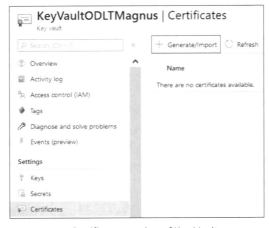

FIGURE 4-35 Certificates section of Key Vault

2. Select **Generate/Import**. On the **Create A Certificate** page shown in Figure 4-36, set the **Method Of Certificate Creation** as **Generate**. You can also set this to **Import An Existing Certificate**, which you will learn about later in this chapter. Ensure that **Type Of Certificate Authority (CA)** is set to **Self-Signed Certificate**. Provide a **Certificate Name**, a **Subject**, and any **DNS Names**, and then click **Create**.

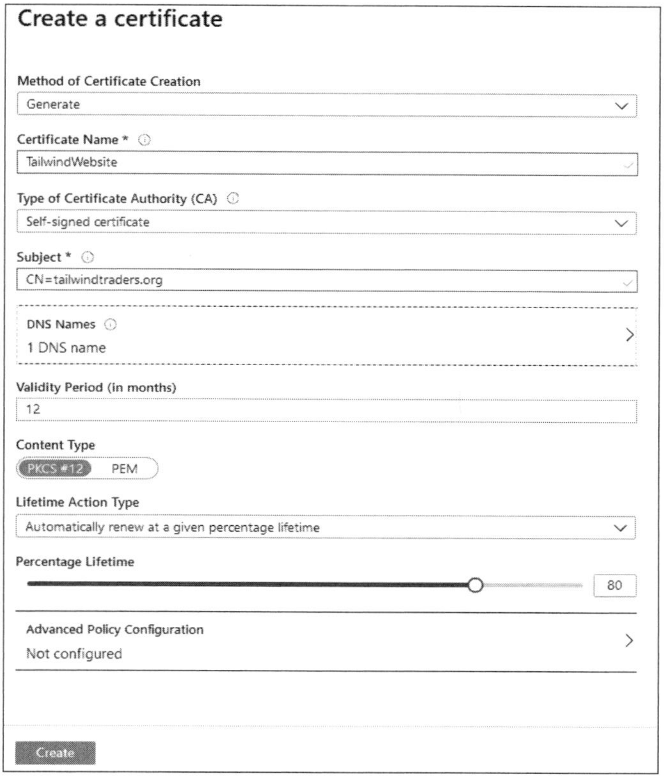

FIGURE 4-36 Create A Certificate

You can use Azure Key Vault to create TLS/SSL certificates that leverage a trust chain from a trusted CA provider after you have performed the following steps to create an issuer object:

1. Performed the onboarding process with your chosen Certificate Authority (CA) provider. At present, DigiCert and GlobalSign are partnered with Microsoft to support TLS/SSL certificate generation. Certificates generated in this manner will be trusted by third-party clients.

2. The chosen CA provider will provide credentials that can be used by Key Vault to enroll, renew, and implement TLS/SSL certificates. You can enter these credentials on the **Create A Certificate Authority** page in the Azure portal, as shown in Figure 4-37. You get to this page by selecting **Certificate Authorities** on the **Certificates** page of Key Vault and then clicking **Add**.

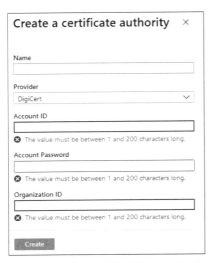

FIGURE 4-37 Create A Certificate Authority

3. Add the certificate issuer resource to the Key Vault.

4. Configure **Certificate Contacts** for notifications. This step isn't required, but it is recommended. You can do this on the **Certificate Contacts** page, available through the **Certificates** page, as shown in Figure 4-38.

FIGURE 4-38 Certificate Contacts

Once you have configured the relationship with the issuing CA, you will be able to create TLS/SSL certificates using the portal or by creating a request using JSON code similar to the following. (This requires the `CertificateIssuer` resource created earlier, and this example assumes a partnership with DigiCert.)

```
{
  "policy": {
    "x509_props": {
      "subject": "CN=TailwindCertSubject1"
    },
    "issuer": {
```

```
        "name": "mydigicert",
        "cty": "OV-SSL",
      }
    }
}
```

The POST method to send this request URI is similar to the following, with your Key Vault's address substituted where appropriate: *https://mykeyvault.vault.azure.net/certificates/mycert1/create?api-version={api-version}*.

To create a Key Vault certificate manually instead of relying on the partner certificate authority provider, use the same method as outlined above, but don't include the issuer field. As an alternative, you can create a self-signed certificate by setting the issuer name to "Self" in the certificate policy, as shown here:

```
"issuer": {
      "name": "Self"
    }
```

You can import an x509 certificate into Key Vault that has been issued by another provider, as long as you have the certificate in PEM or PFX format and you have the certificate's private key. You can perform an import through the Azure portal, as shown in Figure 4-39, by using the az certificate import Azure CLI command or by using the Import-AzKeyVaultCertificate PowerShell cmdlet.

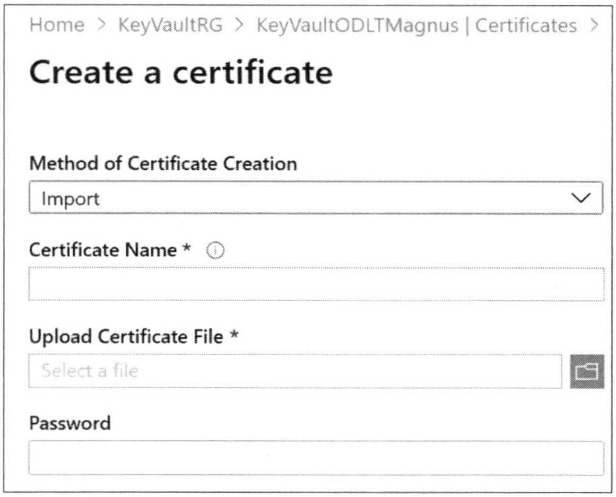

FIGURE 4-39 Import a certificate

You can use the PowerShell cmdlets in Table 4-4 to manage Azure Key Vault certificates:

TABLE 4-4 PowerShell cmdlets for managing Azure Key Vault certifications

PowerShell cmdlet	Description
■ Add-AzKeyVaultCertificate	Adds a certificate to Azure Key Vault
■ Add-AzKeyVaultCertificateContact	Adds a contact for certificate notifications
■ Backup-AzKeyVaultCertificate	Backs up a certificate already present in an Azure Key Vault
■ Get-AzKeyVaultCertificate	Views a Key Vault certificate
■ Get-AzKeyVaultCertificateContact	Views the contacts registered with the Key Vault for notifications
■ Get-AzKeyVaultCertificateIssuer	Views the certificate issuers configured for a Key Vault
■ Get-AzKeyVaultCertificateOperation	Views the status of any operations in the Key Vault
■ Get-AzKeyVaultCertificatePolicy	Views the policy for certificates in a Key Vault
■ New-AzVaultCertificateAdministratorDetail	Creates an in-memory certificate administrator details object
■ New-AzKeyVaultCertificateOrganizationDetail	Creates an in-memory organization details object
■ New-AzKeyVaultCertificatePolicy	Creates an in-memory certificate policy object
■ Remove-AzKeyVaultCertificate	Removes a certificate from a Key Vault
■ Remove-AzKeyVaultCertificateContact	Removes a contact registered for Key Vault notifications
■ Remove-AzKeyVaultCertificateIssuer	Removes a configured issuer certificate authority from a Key Vault
■ Remove-AzKeyVaultCertificateOperation	Removes an operation that is running in a Key Vault
■ Restore-AzKeyVaultCertificate	Restores a certificate from backup
■ Set-AzKeyVaultCertificateIssuer	Configures an issuer certificate authority for a Key Vault
■ Set-AzKeyVaultCertificatePolicy	Creates or modifies a certificate policy in a Key Vault
■ Stop-AzKeyVaultCertificateOperation	Cancels a pending operation in a Key Vault
■ Undo-AzKeyVaultCertificateRemoval	Recovers a deleted certificate and places it in an active state
■ Update-AzKeyVaultCertificate	Modifies editable attributes of a certificate

If you prefer to use Azure CLI to manage certificates in Azure Key Vault, you can use the commands shown in Table 4-5:

TABLE 4-5 Azure CLI commands for managing Azure Key Vault certifications

Command	Description
■ `Az keyvault certificate backup`	Backs up an x509 certificate in an Azure Key Vault
■ `Az keyvault certificate contact`	Manages informational contacts for certificates in an Azure Key Vault
■ `Az keyvault certificate contact add`	Adds informational contacts for certificates in an Azure Key Vault
■ `Az keyvault certificate contact delete`	Deletes informational contacts for certificates in an Azure Key Vault
■ `Az keyvault certificate contact list`	Lists informational contacts for certificates in an Azure Key Vault
■ `Az keyvault certificate create`	Creates a certificate in an Azure Key Vault
■ `Az keyvault certificate delete`	Deletes a certificate from an Azure Key Vault
■ `Az keyvault certificate download`	Downloads the public part of a certificate from an Azure Key Vault
■ `Az keyvault certificate get-default-policy`	Views the properties of the default Key Vault certificate policy
■ `Az keyvault certificate import`	Imports a certificate into a Key Vault
■ `Az keyvault certificate issuer`	Manages issuer certificate authorities
■ `Az keyvault certificate issuer admin`	Manages administrators for issuer certificate authorities
■ `Az keyvault certificate issuer admin add`	Adds an administrator for an issuer certificate authority
■ `Az keyvault certificate issuer admin delete`	Removes a configured administrator for a specific issuer certificate authority
■ `Az keyvault certificate issuer admin list`	Lists the administrators configured for a specific issuer certificate authority
■ `Az keyvault certificate issuer create`	Configures an issuer certificate authority for an Azure Key Vault
■ `Az keyvault certificate issuer delete`	Deletes an issuer certificate authority from an Azure Key Vault
■ `Az keyvault certificate issuer list`	Lists the issuer certificate authorities for a specific Azure Key Vault
■ `Az keyvault certificate issuer show`	Views information about a specific issuer certificate authority

Command	Description
■ Az keyvault certificate issuer update	Updates information about issuer certificate authority
■ Az keyvault certificate list	Lists certificates in an Azure Key Vault
■ Az keyvault certificate list-deleted	Views a list of deleted certificates that can be recovered
■ Az keyvault certificate list-versions	Views the versions of a certificate
■ Az keyvault certificate pending	Manages certificate-creation operations
■ Az keyvault certificate pending delete	Terminates the pending creation of a certificate
■ Az keyvault certificate pending merge	Merges a certificate or a certificate chain with a key pair that is present in the Key Vault
■ Az keyvault certificate pending show	Views the status of a certificate's creation operation
■ Az keyvault certificate purge	Permanently deletes a deleted certificate
■ Az keyvault certificate recover	Recovers a deleted certificate
■ Az keyvault certificate restore	Restores a backed-up certificate to a Key Vault
■ Az keyvault certificate set attributes	Updates a certificate's attributes
■ Az keyvault certificate show	Views certificate information
■ Az keyvault certificate show-deleted	Views information on a deleted certificate

MORE INFO **GETTING STARTED WITH KEY VAULT CERTIFICATES**

You can learn more about getting started with Key Vault certificates at *https://docs.microsoft. com/en-us/azure/key-vault/certificates/certificate-scenarios*.

Manage secrets

Secrets, in the context of Azure Key Vault, allow you to securely store items such as passwords and database connection strings. Key Vault automatically encrypts all stored secrets. This encryption is transparent. The Key Vault will encrypt a secret when you add it, and it decrypts the secret when an authorized user accesses the secret from the vault. Each Key Vault encryption key is unique to an Azure Key Vault.

Key Vault secrets are stored with an identifier and the secret itself. When you want to retrieve the secret, you specify the identifier in the request to the Key Vault. You can add a secret to a Key Vault using the az keyvault secret set command. For example, to add a secret to the Key Vault named `TailwindKV` where the secret identifier name is `Alpha` and the value of the secret is `Omega`, you would run this command:

```
az keyvault secret set \
    --name Alpha \
    --value Omega \
    --vault-name TailwindKV
```

You can view a secret using the `azure keyvault secret show` Azure CLI command, and you can delete a secret using the `azure keyvault secret delete` Azure CLI command. To add the same secret to the same Azure Key Vault used in the example above using PowerShell, run the command:

```
$secretvalue = ConvertTo-SecureString 'Omega' -AsPlainText -Force
$secret = Set-AzKeyVaultSecret -VaultName 'TailwindKV' -Name 'Omega' -SecretValue $secretvalue
```

You can view an Azure Key Vault Secret with the `Get-AzureKeyVaultSecret` cmdlet. You can modify an existing Azure Key Vault secret with the `Update-AzureKeyVaultSecret` Azure PowerShell cmdlet, and you can delete an Azure Key Vault secret with the `Remove-AzureKeyVaultSecret` cmdlet.

You can manage secrets using the Azure portal from the **Secrets** section of a Key Vault's properties page, as shown in Figure 4-40.

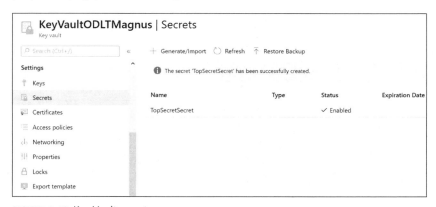

FIGURE 4-40 Key Vault secrets

Beyond the secret ID and the secret itself, you can configure the following attributes for Azure Key Vault secrets.

- **Expiration time (exp)**   Allows you to specify a specific time after which the secret should not be retrieved from the Key Vault. Using this attribute does not block the use of the secret, just as the expiration date on food doesn't stop you from eating it after that date has passed. The expiration time attribute simply provides the secret keeper with a method of recommending that a secret is beyond its use-by date.
- **Not before (nbf)**   Similar to the expiration time attribute, the `not before` attribute allows the secret keeper to specify the time at which a secret becomes valid. For

example, you could store a secret in a Key Vault and set the not before attribute to 2030, which would inform anyone retrieving the secret that the secret information itself won't be useful until 2030.

- **Enabled** Allows you to specify whether secret data is retrievable. This attribute is used in conjunction with the exp and nbf attributes. Any operation that involves the Enabled attribute that doesn't include the exp or nbf attributes will be disallowed.

You can use the Azure PowerShell cmdlets in Table 4-6 to manage secrets in Azure Key Vault.

TABLE 4-6 PowerShell cmdlets for managing Key Vault secrets

PowerShell cmdlet	Description
■ Backup-AzKeyVaultSecret	Securely backs up a Key Vault secret
■ Get-AzKeyVaultSecret	Views the secrets in a Key Vault
■ Remove-AzKeyVaultSecret	Deletes a Key Vault secret
■ Restore-AzKeyVaultSecret	Restores a Key Vault secret from a backup
■ Set-AzKeyVaultSecret	Creates or modifies a secret in a Key Vault
■ Undo-AzKeyVaultSecretRemoval	Recovers a deleted secret that has not been permanently removed
■ Update-AzKeyVaultSecret	Updates the attributes of a secret in a Key Vault

You can use the Azure CLI commands in Table 4-7 to manage Key Vault Secrets.

TABLE 4-7 Azure CLI commands for managing Key Vault secrets

Azure CLI command	Description
■ Az keyvault secret backup	Backs up a specific secret in a secure manner
■ Az keyvault secret delete	Deletes a specific secret from the Key Vault
■ Az keyvault secret download	Downloads a secret from the Key Vault
■ Az keyvault secret list	Lists secrets in a specific Key Vault
■ Az keyvault secret list-deleted	Lists secrets that have been deleted but not purged from the Key Vault
■ Az keyvault secret list-versions	Lists all versions of secrets stored in the Key Vault
■ Az keyvault secret purge	Permanently removes a specific secret so that it cannot be recovered from the Key Vault
■ Az keyvault secret recover	Recovers a deleted secret to the latest version
■ Az keyvault secret restore	Restores a backed-up secret
■ Az keyvault secret set	Creates or updates a secret in Key Vault

Azure CLI command	Description
■ Az keyvault secret set-attributes	Modifies the attributes associated with a specific Key Vault secret
■ Az keyvault secret show	Retrieves a specific secret from an Azure Key Vault
■ Az keyvault secret show-deleted	Views a specific deleted, but not purged, secret

---

MORE INFO **KEY VAULT SECRETS**

You can learn more about Key Vault secrets at *https://docs.microsoft.com/en-us/azure/ key-vault/secrets*.

Manage Keys

Cryptographic keys stored in an Azure Key Vault are stored as JSON Web Key (JWK) objects. Azure Key Vault supports RSA and Elliptic Curve (EC) keys only. Azure Key Vault supports two types of protection for keys, software protection, and hardware secure module (HSM) protection. These differences manifest in the following manner:

- **Software-protected keys** The key is processed in software by Azure Key Vault. The key is protected using encryption at rest, with the system key stored in an Azure HSM. RSA or EC keys can be imported into an Azure Key Vault configured for software protection. You can also configure Azure Key Vault to create a key that uses these algorithms.

- **HSM-protected keys** The key is stored in a specially allocated HSM. Clients can import RSA or EC keys from a software protected source or from a compatible HSM device. You can also use the Azure management plane to request that Key Vault generate a key using these algorithms. When you use HSM-protected keys, the key_hsm attribute is appended to the JWK.

Azure Key Vault allows the following operations to be performed on key objects:

- **Create** This operation allows a security principal to create a key. The key value will be generated by Key Vault and stored in the vault. Key Vault supports the creation of asymmetric keys.

- **Import** Allows the security principal to import an existing key into Key Vault. Key Vault supports the importation of asymmetric keys.

- **Update** Allows a security principal to modify key attributes (metadata) associated with a key that is stored within Key Vault.

- **Delete** Allows a security principal to remove a key from Key Vault.

- **List** Allows a security principal to list all keys in a Key Vault.

- **List versions** Allows a security principal to view all versions of a specific key in a Key Vault.
- **Get** Allows a security principal to view the public elements of a specific key stored in a Key Vault.
- **Backup** Exports a key from the Key Vault in a protected form.
- **Restore** Imports a previously exported Key Vault key.

You can use keys that are stored within an Azure Key Vault to perform the following cryptographic operations:

- Sign and Verify
- Key Encryption / Wrapping
- Encrypt and Decrypt

You can manage Key Vault keys using Azure portal by navigating to the Key Vault and selecting **Keys** under **Settings**, as shown in Figure 4-41.

FIGURE 4-41 Keys page

To create a key using Azure Key Vault in the Azure portal, perform the following steps:

1. In the Azure portal, open the Key Vault that you want to create the key in and navigate to **Keys** in the **Settings** section.
2. On the **Keys** page, click **Generate/Import**. This will open the **Create A Key** page.
3. On the **Create A Key** page, make sure that the **Options** drop-down menu is set to **Generate**. Provide a name for the key, specify the key properties, specify whether the key has an activation or expiration date, and specify whether the key is enabled. Azure Key Vault will generate the key when you click **Create**.

You can use the Azure PowerShell cmdlets in Table 4-8 to manage Azure Key Vault keys:

TABLE 4-8 PowerShell cmdlets for managing Azure Key Vault keys

PowerShell cmdlet	Description
■ `Add-AzKeyVaultKey`	■ Creates or imports a key in an Azure Key Vault
■ `Backup-AzKeyVaultKey`	■ Backs up a key stored in an Azure Key Vault
■ `Get-AzKeyVaultKey`	■ Views keys stored in an Azure Key Vault
■ `Remove-AzKeyVaultKey`	■ Deletes a key stored in an Azure Key Vault
■ `Restore-AzKeyVaultKey`	■ Recovers a key to Azure Key vault from a backup
■ `Undo-AzKeyVaultKeyRemoval`	■ Undeletes a deleted Azure Key Vault key
■ `Update-AzKeyVaultKey`	■ Allows you to update the attributes of a key stored in an Azure Key vault

You can use the Azure CLI commands in Table 4-9 to manage Azure Key Vault keys.

TABLE 4-9 Azure CLI commands to manage Azure Key Vault keys

Command	Description
■ `Az keyvault key backup`	Backs up an Azure Key Vault key
■ `Az keyvault key create`	Creates a new Azure Key Vault key
■ `Az keyvault key decrypt`	Uses an Azure Key Vault key to decrypt data
■ `Az keyvault key delete`	Deletes an Azure Key Vault key
■ `Az keyvault key download`	Downloads the public part of a stored key
■ `Az keyvault key encrypt`	Encrypts data using a key stored in Azure Key Vault
■ `Az keyvault key import`	Imports a private key
■ `Az keyvault key list`	Lists the Azure Key Vault keys in a specific vault
■ `Az keyvault key list-deleted`	Lists Azure Key Vault keys that have been deleted but can be recovered
■ `Az keyvault key list-versions`	Lists Azure Key Vault key versions
■ `Az keyvault key purge`	Permanently deletes an Azure Key Vault key from the Key Vault
■ `Az keyvault key recover`	Recovers a deleted key
■ `Az keyvault key restore`	Restores a key from a backup
■ `Az keyvault key set-attributes`	Allows you to configure the attributes of an Azure Key Vault key

Command	Description
■ `Az keyvault key show`	Views the public portion of an Azure Key Vault key
■ `Az keyvault key show-deleted`	Views the public portion of a deleted Azure Key Vault key

> ***MORE INFO*** **KEY VAULT KEYS**
>
> You can learn more about Key Vault keys at *https://docs.microsoft.com/en-us/azure/key-vault/keys*.

Configure key rotation

Key rotation is the process of updating an existing key or secret with a new key or secret. You should do this on a regular basis in case the existing key or secret has accidentally or deliberately become compromised. How often you do this depends on your organization's needs, with some organizations rotating keys every 28 days and others rotating them every six months.

Earlier in this chapter, you learned about the concept of key rotation that followed this process:

1. The access keys to a storage account were rotated through a process by which the applications that used the first key were switched to the second key.

2. The first key was retired and replaced.

3. Eventually, the applications were migrated back to use the first key.

4. Once the applications were migrated back to the first key, the second key was replaced, and the process could start again.

While Microsoft recommends the use of identity rather than secrets for authentication, there are workloads that run in Azure that cannot leverage identity-based authentication and which must instead rely upon keys and secrets for authentication.

When you publish a secret into an Azure Key Vault, you can specify an expiration date for that secret, as shown in Figure 4-42. You can use the publication of a "near expiry" event to Azure Event Grid as the trigger for a functions app that would generate a new version of the secret and that then updates the relevant workload to use the newly generated secret, allowing the existing secret to be discarded.

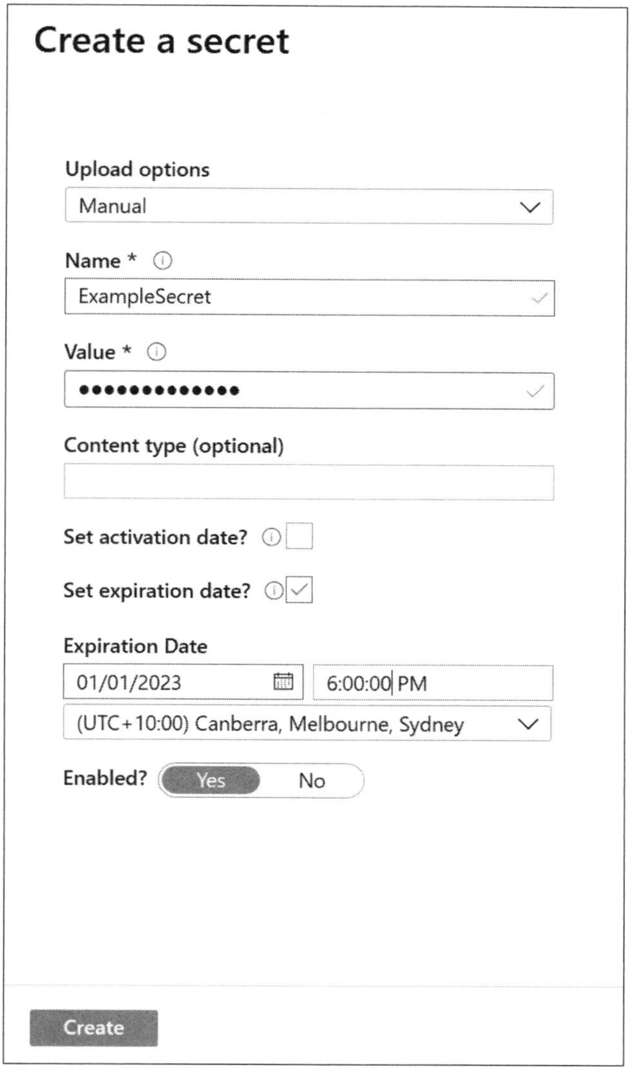

FIGURE 4-42 Creating a secret

MORE INFO **ROTATE SECRETS**

You can learn more about automating secret rotation at *https://docs.microsoft.com/en-us/azure/key-vault/secrets/tutorial-rotation*.

Configure backup and recovery of certificates, secrets, and keys

The items stored in Key Vault are, by their nature, valuable and something to which you don't want to lose access. As Key Vault items are valuable, you should ensure that these items are backed up and can be recovered if something goes wrong. "Something goes wrong" can include items being accidentally deleted or corrupted, or it can mean an administrative error that causes you to lose access to the Key Vault itself. For example, you could lose access to the Key Vault if a malicious actor gains control of your subscription or if a distracted administrator incorrectly reconfigures RBAC permissions or the Key Vault's Access policy. Unlike on-premises hardware security modules that store secrets, Azure Key Vaults will failover to a paired Azure region without requiring intervention should something disastrous happen to the datacenter that hosts the primary instance of the Key Vault.

When you back up a Key Vault Item, the item will be available for download as an encrypted blob. Recovery involves recovering this encrypted blob to the same or another Key Vault within the same subscription. It is important to note that this encrypted blob can only be decrypted inside a Key Vault within the same Azure subscription and Azure geography as the Key Vault the item was first backed up from. For example, if you backed up a secret stored in a Key Vault that was hosted in Australia in subscription A, you wouldn't be able to restore that secret to a Key Vault in an Azure geography outside Australia or in a Key Vault associated with any subscription other than subscription A.

At the time of writing, Azure Key Vault does not allow for the entirety of a Key Vault in a single back-up operation. Microsoft cautions that you should perform Key Vault back up operations manually rather than automatically. This is because automatic operations using the currently available tools are likely to result in errors. It's also possible, using automatic operations, to exceed the Key Vault's service limits in terms of requests per second. If this occurs, the Key Vault will be throttled causing any back-up operation to fail. Using scripts or automated actions to back up Key Vault items is not supported by Microsoft or the Azure Key Vault development team.

To back up objects in an Azure Key Vault, the following conditions must be met:

- Contributor-level or higher permissions on the Key Vault
- A primary Key Vault that contains items that you want to back up
- A secondary Key Vault where the secrets will be restored

To back up an item in the Azure portal, perform the following steps:

1. In the Azure portal, open the Key Vault. On the **Settings** page, select the item type that you want to back up and then select the item you want to back up. In Figure 4-43, the **Secrets** section is selected.

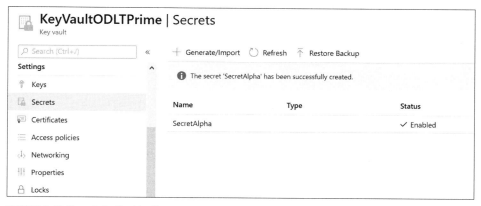

FIGURE 4-43 Secrets in Key Vault

2. Select the item that you want to back up and on the item's page, shown in Figure 4-44, and select **Download Backup**.

FIGURE 4-44 Download backup

3. Select **Download** to download the encrypted blob.

To restore an item using the Azure portal, perform the following steps:

1. In the Azure portal, open the Key Vault to which you want to restore the item. On the **Settings** page, select the item type that you want to restore.

2. Click **Restore Backup** (see Figure 4-45).

3. On the **File Upload** page, select the encrypted blob that you want to restore to the Key Vault and then select **Open**. The encrypted blob will be uploaded to the Key Vault. An item will be restored as long as the Key Vault is in the same subscription and geographic region as the Key Vault that hosted the originally backed up item.

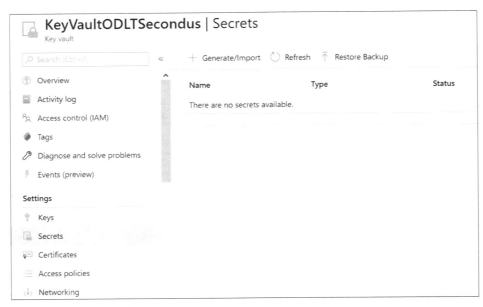

FIGURE 4-45 Restore backup

You can use the Azure CLI commands in Table 4-10 to back up Key Vault Items.

TABLE 4-10 Azure CLI commands for backing up Key Vault items

Azure CLI command	Description
■ Az keyvault certificate backup	Use this command to back up specific certificates stored in an Azure Key Vault.
■ Az keyvault key backup	Use this command to back up specific keys stored in an Azure Key Vault.
■ Az keyvault secret backup	Use this command to back up specific secrets stored in an Azure Key Vault.

You can use the Azure CLI commands shown in Table 4-11 to back up Key Vault Items.

TABLE 4-11 Azure CLI commands for backing up Key Vault items

Azure CLI commands	Description
■ Az keyvault certificate restore	Use this command to restore a specific certificate to an Azure Key Vault.
■ Az keyvault key restore	Use this command to restore a specific key to an Azure Key Vault.
■ Az keyvault secret restore	Use this command to restore a specific secret to an Azure Key Vault.

You can use the Azure PowerShell commands shown in Table 4-12 to back up Key Vault items.

TABLE 4-12 Azure PowerShell commands to back up Key Vault items

Azure PowerShell commands	Description
■ `Backup-AzureKeyVaultCertificate`	Use this cmdlet to back up specific certificates stored in an Azure Key Vault.
■ `Backup-AzureKeyVaultKey`	Use this cmdlet to back up an Azure Key Vault Key.
■ `Backup-AzureKeyVaultSecret`	Use this cmdlet to back up a specific secret that is stored in an Azure Key Vault.

You can use the Azure PowerShell commands in Table 4-13 to restore Key Vault items.

TABLE 4-13 Azure PowerShell commands to restore Key Vault items

Azure Powershell Commands	Description
■ `Restore-AzureKeyVaultCertificate`	Use this cmdlet to restore specific certificates stored in an Azure Key Vault.
■ `Restore-AzureKeyVaultKey`	Use this cmdlet to restore an Azure Key Vault Key.
■ `Restore-AzureKeyVaultSecret`	Use this cmdlet to restore a specific secret that is stored in an Azure Key Vault.

MORE INFO **KEY VAULT ITEM BACKUP AND RECOVERY**

You can learn more about backup and recovery of Key Vault at *https://docs.microsoft.com/en-us/azure/key-vault/general/backup*.

EXAM TIP

Remember that you can only restore Key Vault items if the Key Vault you are using in the restore operation is in the same subscription and geographic region as the Key Vault where the original backup was taken.

Thought experiment

In this thought experiment, demonstrate your skills and knowledge of the topics covered in this chapter. You can find answers to this thought experiment in the next section.

Securing data at Tailwind Traders

Tailwind Traders has migrated some of their operations to Azure and are now attempting to improve the security of the data stored in their Azure subscription. With this information in mind, Tailwind Traders has the following challenges they need to address:

Members of the product research team need to be able to add and remove data in Blob Storage across several storage accounts. They should not be assigned any unnecessary permissions.

To comply with local government regulations, Tailwind Traders needs to manage the keys used for transparent data encryption on their Azure SQL instance. They will be configuring BYOK.

Members of the sales team at Tailwind Traders need to be able to regularly perform cryptographic operations with keys and certificates stored in an Azure Key Vault but should not be assigned any unnecessary permissions.

With this information, answer the following questions:

1. Which RBAC role should you assign to the product research team?
2. Where should Tailwind Traders store its TDE key?
3. Which RBAC role should the sales team be assigned to the Key Vault?

Thought experiment answers

This section contains the solution to the thought experiment. Each answer explains why the answer choice is correct.

1. The product research team should be assigned the Storage Blob Data Contributor role as this provides the minimum necessary permissions to add and remove data from Blob Storage.
2. Tailwind Traders should store the TDE key in an Azure Key Vault as this is the only location in which you can store a key in a BYOK scenario.
3. The sales team should be assigned the Key Vault Crypto User RBAC role because this allows them to perform cryptographic operations on keys and certificates.

Chapter summary

- There are two storage account access keys that can be used to provide access to a storage account. You should only use one at a time so that you can perform key rotation on a regular basis:
  - Shared Access Signatures (SAS) allow you to provide secure granular delegated access to storage accounts.
  - Stored access policies allow you to specifically control service-level shared access signatures.

- Rather than rely upon storage account keys or shared access signatures, you can use Azure AD to authorize access to Blob and Queue Storage. Azure AD authenticates a security principal's identity and then returns an OAuth 2.0 token.

- When you enable AD DS authentication for Azure Files, your Active Directory Domain Services (AD DS) domain-joined computers can mount Azure File shares using AD DS user credentials.

- You configure share-level permission by assigning RBAC roles at the Azure File share-level. Once you have assigned share-level permissions to an Azure File share using RBAC, you should then configure file and folder permissions on the share's contents.

- Azure Storage encryption is enabled by default for all storage accounts regardless of performance tier or access tier. This means you don't have to modify code or applications for Azure Storage Encryption to be enabled.

- Encryption scopes allow you to configure separate encryption keys at the container and blob level.

- Advanced threat protection for Azure Storage allows you to detect unusual and malicious attempts to interact with Azure Storage accounts.

- When you create an Azure SQL database server instance, you create an administrator login and a password associated with that login. This administrative account granted full administrative permissions on all databases hosted off the Azure SQL instance as a server-level principal.

- Auditing allows you to track database events, such as tables being added or dropped. Audit logs for Azure SQL databases can be stored in an Azure Storage account, in a Log Analytics workspace, or in Event Hubs.

- Azure SQL Database Advanced Threat Protection allows you to detect unusual activity that might indicate that a third party might be trying to attack your organization's Azure SQL databases.

- Transparent data encryption (TDE) allows you to protect Azure SQL databases by encrypting data at rest. When you enable TDE, the databases, associated backups, and transaction log files are automatically encrypted and decrypted, as necessary.

- Always Encrypted is a technology available for Azure SQL that allows you to protect specific types of sensitive data that has a known recognizable pattern, such as passport numbers, tax file identification numbers, and credit card numbers.

- Azure Key Vault allows you to store information that should not be made public, such as secrets, certificates, and keys.

- You use Key Vault access control policies to manage permissions to secrets, certificates, and keys at the data plane level. Each Key Vault access control policy includes entries specifying the designated security principal's access to keys, secrets, and certificates.

Index

A

B

C

Q-R

S

Plug into learning at

MicrosoftPressStore.com

The Microsoft Press Store by Pearson offers:

- Free U.S. shipping

- Buy an eBook, get three formats – Includes PDF, EPUB, and MOBI to use with your computer, tablet, and mobile devices

- Print & eBook Best Value Packs

- eBook Deal of the Week – Save up to 50% on featured title

- Newsletter – Be the first to hear about new releases, announcements, special offers, and more

- Register your book – Find companion files, errata, and product updates, plus receive a special coupon* to save on your next purchase

 Pearson